POLICE
IN AMERICA

DOCUMENTS RELATING TO
INTELLIGENCE BUREAU
OR
RED SQUAD OF LOS ANGELES
POLICE DEPARTMENT

U.S. Committee
on Education and Labor

ARNO PRESS & THE NEW YORK TIMES
NEW YORK,   1971

Reprint Edition 1971 by Arno Press Inc.

Reprinted from a copy in
The State Historical Society of Wisconsin Library

LC# 73-154593
ISBN 0-405-03388-5

Police In America
ISBN for complete set: 0-405-03360-5
See last pages of this volume for titles.

Manufactured in the United States of America

VIOLATIONS OF FREE SPEECH AND RIGHTS OF LABOR

HEARINGS

BEFORE A

SUBCOMMITTEE OF THE
COMMITTEE ON EDUCATION AND LABOR
UNITED STATES SENATE

SEVENTY-SIXTH CONGRESS

THIRD SESSION

PURSUANT TO

S. Res. 266
(74th Congress)

A RESOLUTION TO INVESTIGATE VIOLATIONS OF THE
RIGHT OF FREE SPEECH AND ASSEMBLY AND
INTERFERENCE WITH THE RIGHT OF
LABOR TO ORGANIZE AND BAR-
GAIN COLLECTIVELY

DOCUMENTS RELATING TO INTELLIGENCE BUREAU OR RED SQUAD OF LOS ANGELES POLICE DEPARTMENT

UNITED STATES
GOVERNMENT PRINTING OFFICE
89562   WASHINGTON : 1940

II

DOCUMENTS RELATING TO INTELLIGENCE BUREAU OR RED SQUAD OF LOS ANGELES POLICE DEPARTMENT [1] [2]

1. CORRESPONDENCE OF COMMITTEE WITH CITY OF LOS ANGELES RE PRESENT STATUS OF BUREAU

EXHIBIT 10210

[Copy]

FEBRUARY 15, 1939.

The Honorable FLETCHER BOWRON,
    Mayor, City of Los Angeles,
        City Hall, Los Angeles, California.

MY DEAR MR. MAYOR: In connection with our recent studies in Los Angeles and of the material in the files of former Captain William F. Hynes of the Intelligence Bureau of the Los Angeles City Police Department, it is necessary that we have some official record, preferably from you, describing the present status of former Captain Hynes in your Police Department today and of the present status of the Intelligence Bureau former Captain Hynes headed. Would you be good enough to have these papers prepared by the proper official and forwarded to us airmail?

All of us are very grateful for the cooperation and assistance you rendered the Committee during our studies in your city.

With expressions of highest esteem, I am
    Sincerely yours,

ROBERT WOHLFORTH,
Secretary, Subcommittee of the Committee On
Education and Labor under S. R. 266.

EXHIBIT 10211–A

FLETCHER BOWRON, *Mayor*

OFFICE OF THE MAYOR, CITY HALL

LOS ANGELES, CALIFORNIA, *February 27, 1939.*

Mr. ROBERT WOHLFORTH,
    Secretary, Subcommittee of the Committee on Education and Labor,
        United States Senate, Washington, D. C.

MY DEAR MR. WOHLFORTH: This is to acknowledge your letter of February 15th, requesting certain data with regard to former Police Captain William F. Hynes and the Intelligence Bureau of the Los Angeles police department.

---

[1] For testimony relating to further activities of the Intelligence Bureau of the Los Angeles Police Department under the supervision of Acting Captain Wm. F. Hynes, see pt. 52, pp. 19071 and 19098.

[2] All documents, unless otherwise noted, were received from the files of the Los Angeles Police Department under subpena.

A copy of your communication has been forwarded to Chief of Police David A. Davidson, with a request that he give it his immediate attention, replying directly to you.

Thanking you for the kind expressions contained in your letter, and with kind regards, I am

Very truly yours,

FLETCHER BOWRON, *Mayor.*

FB:HD

EXHIBIT 10211–B

DEPARTMENT OF POLICE, CITY OF LOS ANGELES, CALIFORNIA
D. A. DAVIDSON, *Chief*

MARCH 1, 1939.

1.1.1.

Mr. ROBERT WOHLFORTH,
Secretary, Subcommittee of the Committee on Education and Labor,
United States Senate, Washington, D. C.

DEAR MR. WOLHFORTH: Your communication of February 15, 1939 addressed to the Honorable Fletcher Bowron, Mayor of the City of Los Angeles, concerning the present status of Captain Hynes and the Intelligence Bureau, has been referred to this office for reply.

At the present time Policeman William F. Hynes is assigned as an Acting Detective Lieutenant to the West Los Angeles Division, and is performing regular duties in the Detective Bureau of this division. The Intelligence Bureau that he formerly headed has been abolished.

I trust that this satisfactorily answers your query.

Sincerely yours,

D. A. DAVIDSON,
(D. A. Davidson)
Chief of Police.

DAD/WHP/vv

EXHIBIT 10212

DEPARTMENT OF POLICE CITY OF LOS ANGELES, CALIFORNIA
ARTHUR C. HOHMANN, *Chief*

In replying please give Our Reference No. 1. 1. 2.

JUNE 22, 1940.

HENRY H. FOWLER,
Chief Counsel, Subcommittee of the Committee on Education and Labor Under
S. R. 266, United States Senate,
918 F. Street, Northwest, Washington, D. C.

DEAR SIR: Refer to your letter of June 17th, addressed to the Honorable Fletcher Bowron, Mayor of the City of Los Angeles, in which you request information as to the present status of WILLIAM F. HYNES in our Police Department.

William F. Hynes was appointed to serve as "liaison officer" between this Department and the Federal Bureau of Investigation in connection with developing persons most liable to interfere with the neutrality policy of the United States of America as stated by the President in a communication to J. Edgar Hoover, Director of the Federal Bureau of Investigation, on September 15, 1939.

This work functions out of the Homicide Bureau of the Los Angeles Police Department.

The Police Department does not have an Intelligence Bureau and William F. Hynes is in no way connected with industrial relations.

Very truly yours,

ARTHUR C. HOHMANN,
(Arthur C. Hohmann)
Chief of Police.

ACH:AC/jg

2. ORGANIZATION AND FUNCTION OF BUREAU

A. Statement of William F. Hynes, Commanding Officer of Intelligence Bureau, Outlining Scope and Function of Bureau

Exhibit 10213

Los Angeles Police Department

Office of Chief of Police

Duties Statement

To all employees:

This form, showing certain information as of July 1, 1938, is for the use of the Chief of Police in connection with a survey of the Los Angeles Police Department now being made by the Bureau of Budget and Efficiency. Please fill this form and turn over to your immediate superior for his verification.

Divisional Assignment: Metropolitan.

Organization Unit or Detail: Intelligence Bureau.

Name: William F. Hynes.

Rank (as shown on payroll): Patrolman.

Acting Rank (if any): Captain of Detectives.

Are you responsible for directing the work of others? Yes. If so, how many? See below.

Who directs your work? Myself. His title:

Regular working hours: Irregular (approximately 12 hours per day).

Duties (show *all* assignments you perform, with the approximate percentage of your time devoted to each, total must equal 100%): Commanding officer, Intelligence Bureau, Metropolican Division: the scope, functions and operations of the Intelligence Bureau include:

1. Special confidential investigation, under instructions from the Chief of Police and the Chief of Detectives.

2. Conducting such other special investigation as are assigned to this Bureau by the Chief of Police and the Chief of Detectives, which inestigations cover a general line of police work.

3. Investigations, surveillance, arrest and prosecution of illegal activities in connection with ultra-radical organizations and individuals, such as anarchists anarcho-syndicalists, Communists, syndicalists, socialists, I. W. W.'s and "outlaw" radical labor groups and sympathetic organizations and groups directly affiliated, and all forms of seditious and treasonable activities:

(a) Cooperating with and assisting the United States Immigration Bureau in investigations, apprehension and deportation of alien anarchists, Communists, etc., illegally in the United States in violation of immigration laws, and the investigation of alien criminals as to their alienage status.

(b) Investigation, arrest and prosecution of deportation proceedings under the provisions of the Alien Anarchy Section of the Immigration Act, which Act provides for the deportation of aliens who are members of an unlawful organization, even though lawfully admitted to the United States.

(c) Cooperating with and maintaining cordial relations with the consular officials of the various foreign governments—relative to the activities of the anarchists and Communist elements of their nationals in Los Angeles and vicinity.

(d) Collecting information and data covering the activities, past present and projected, of radical and illegal organizations, groups and individuals.

(e) Preparing and rendering intelligence reports covering the activities of the various radical organizations, groups and individuals for the information of the Chief of Police.

(f) Cooperating with the and rendering reports to the Department of Justice, and to the Army and Navy Intelligence officers in matters of radical activities in the military and naval service.

(g) Reading and studying of radical literature, magazines, books, pamphlets and various publications of the anarchists, Communists, syndicalists, Socialists and other groups.

(h) Preparation of Charts showing in graphic form the connections of the various organizations in the Communist movement, for the information of public officials and the enlightening of the American public.

(i) Preparation and keeping up-to-date of the Los Angeles Police Department's COMMUNIST DISPLAY BOARDS, including membership cards, newspapers, magazines, periodicals and books and booklets, assembled in proper display form on Exhibit Boards, to be displayed at various public gatherings for the information and enlightenment of the American public.

(j) Collecting, filing and indexing data, and preparing permanent office records on individual radicals and organizations.

(k) Covering all open and public mass meetings, demonstrations and gatherings of radical groups and organizations.

(1) Supervising and directing the work of under-cover informants operating within the various anarchists, Communists, syndicalists, socialists and other ultraradical groups.

(m) Enforcement of all federal, state and municipal laws, applicable to the illegal activities of ultra-radicals, such as the Sedition Act, Criminal Syndicalism Law, Red Flag Law, Alien Gun Law, Anti-picketing ordinance, Handbill ordinance, and laws against unlawful assembly and riot, and similar federal, state and municipal legislation.

4. Investigation, surveillance, arrest and prosecution of illegal activities in connection with labor organizations involving strike disturbances, illegal picketing and sabotage:

(a) Investigation and protecting of legitimate business against sabotage, racketeering, illegal picketing, and against molestation and assault of employees.

(b) Conferences with employers, employers' groups, and employees' associations.

(c) Investigation and protection of legitimate labor organizations (A. F. of L. Railroad Brotherhoods, etc.) against activities of the I. W. W., Communists and other Red "borers from within" and cooperating with them against this element.

(d) Conferences with legitimate and conservative labor representatives and with the Commissioner of Conciliation of the U. S. Department of Labor relative to strikes and labor disputes.

5. Cooperating with all federal, state, county and city officers in the enforcement of all laws:

(a) Cooperating and assisting district attorneys and police authorities throughout the state in connection with the travel, plans and activities of ultra-radicals, groups and organizations and labor racketeers.

(b) Cooperating and assisting in the prosecution of persons accused of such activities as covered by this Bureau, in other counties, by providing expert testimony, advice and evidence.

6. Cooperating with, advising and assisting special agents of various public service and public utility organizations in matters relating to the activities of radical individuals, groups and organizations and labor racketeering.

7. Protecting and escorting foreign notables and dignataries visiting Los Angeles.

8. Representing the Police Department on speaking engagements before various civic, patriotic, business, educational and fraternal organizations on matters pertaining to the Bureau's activities; and

(a) Maintaining contact with the press and providing them with such news information and data as is deemed advisable and proper in connection with the Bureau's activities.

(b) Maintaining close contact with the various civic, patriotic, business, educational and fraternal organizations and clubs and providing them with such information and educational data as they request covering subversive activities.

9. Covering various other mass meetings and gatherings, NOT RADICAL, as may be assigned to the Bureau by the Chief of Police.

10. Formulating and submitting to the Chief of Police for his study and approval "plans of action" covering the handling of projected strikes—anticipated riots—and projected radical and racial disturbances, and such other emergencies as may come within the scope of the operatings of the Bureau.

11. Directing the activities of approximately 150 officers at present regularly and temporarily assigned to duty with the Bureau in covering the various phases of activity heretofore enumerated.

VERIFIED BY:

WILLIAM F. HYNES,
Capt. of Detectives LAPD,
Commanding Intelligence Bureau.

B. Personal History and Record of Wm. F. Hynes

Exhibit 10214

(Handwritten:) Hynes Personal file.

Personal History and Record of William Francis Hynes

Patrolman, Los Angeles Police Department.
Acting Captain of Detectives, Commanding Intelligence Bureau.
Born at St. Louis, Missouri, July 30th, 1896.
Education: Educated in Public Schools St. Louis, Mo. and private study-business and correspondence courses, night school etc. Education equivalent to High School graduate.
Occupational History: Telephone operator and clerical work, St. Louis Police Department, November 1912 to October 1913, resigned to enter U. S. Army.
United States Army, November 1913 to April 1919.
Private 12th U. S. Cavalry, Corporal Supply Troop 12th U. S. Cavalry.
Quartermaster Sergeant, Q. M. C. U. S. Army.
Regimental Supply Sergeant, 3rd Squadron, 12th U. S. Cavalry.
Commissioned 2nd Lieutenant, Quartermaster Corps, U. S. Army, August 1918, Served in Executive capacity. Commanding Officer; Motor Transport Division, Q. M. C.
Appointed Quartermaster Clerk Q. M. C. (Civilian) Hachita, N. M., 1919, In charge of Property Division.
Chief Clerk, Construction Division, Utilities Department, Q.·M. C. Camp Harry J. Jones, Douglas, Arizona. From Oct. 1919 to October 1920, Supervising work of some 21 clerks, and handling Employment Bureau for construction work of the camp.
Unemployed, period from November 1920, to January 1921. Traveling in State of California.
San Joaquin Light & Power Co., as Laborer & Investigator—February 1921.
Private investigative work at San Diego and Los Angeles. Period from March 1921 to March 1922.
Appointed Patrolman, Los Angeles Police Department. April 1922.

Immediately upon appointment was assigned by Assistant Chief of Police, as undercover investigator, investigating Vice conditions in the City, and later to investigating the activities of Anarchists, Communists, Syndicalists, Socialists, and other radical groups and organizations.

Served in an undercover capacity in the Communist Party, Industrial Workers of the World, and various other radical and subversive groups and organizations until the later part of 1923. At which time he was withdrawn from under-cover work in the radical field and assigned to the Radical Bureau, and upon formation of the Intelligence Bureau, was placed in charge of the Radical section.

In charge of Radical Section of Intelligence Bureau, until the year of 1926— thence transferred to Pickpocket and Bunco Detail, and later to Flying Squadron. Prior to being transferred, served as Acting Commanding Officer of Intelligence Bureau on numerous occasions.

In 1927, re-assigned to Intelligence Bureau, in charge of Radical Section and Special Confidential Investigations.

In the later part of 1927, was made Commanding Officer, Intelligence Bureau, Los Angeles Police Dept., and has served in such capacity since that date.
Promotional history:

Upon two occasions, namely, 1924–1927—took promotional examinations for grade of "Detective Lieutenant." Upon both occasions received passing grades, and was certified on the eligible list, but have never received appointment.

Also took promotional examination for Secretary of the Police Commission, and passed 5th, and certified on eligible list.

Upon Special assignment—devised method and supervised installation of filing system for the Police Commission.
Record of arrests:

Has been arrested upon three occasions—such arrests being incident to, and on account of my duties as under-cover investigator.

Arrested 1921—Charged "Bookmaking." This while working under-cover investigation for Civic organization. Acquitted.

Arrested Nov. 1922, Charged "Criminal Syndicalism." While working in undercover capacity on Radical activities, and while a member of the Police Department. Held 3 days, and released.

Arrested May 1923, Charged "Criminal Syndicalism." While working in undercover capacity L. A. Police Dept. On I. W. W. Harbor strike, held 2½ days—Released.

Marital Status: Married, one child.

Fraternal Affiliations: American Legion.

Habits: Does not drink, or use narcotics.

C. Description of Duties of Luke M. Lane, Assistant in Charge of Intelligence Bureau

Exhibit 10215

Metropolitan—Intelligence Bureau

LUKE M. LANE, SERGEANT, DET. LIEUT.

YES ?

William F. Hynes, Capt. of Detectives

Irregular (8 to 12 hours a day)

Assistant in charge of Intelligence Bureau, Metropolitan Division, said bureau being charged with the handling of all strikes and labor disputes, and investigation of crime and enforcement of city ordinances in connection therewith; investigation of activities of Communists and various subversive groups and organizations; assisting in supervising and directing the activities of some 140 officers, regularly and temporarily assigned to duty with this bureau; directing the work of special under cover investigations involving violations of state laws and city ordinances.

William F. Hynes,
Capt. of Detectives, Intelligence Bureau.

D. Personnel Roster of Intelligence Bureau

Exhibit 10216

Los Angeles Police Department

Office of Intelligence Bureau—Metropolitan Division   (11–25–38)

ROSTER

Members of Intelligence Bureau

Capt. Wm. F. Hynes	FE 0105
*Lt. Luke M. Lane	WH 0566
Lt. R. A. Wellpott	TW 9733
Abbott, Carl R	RE 8186
Brown, E. D	YO 5461
Butts, F. F	OL 3289
Conn, O. N	Sunset 2–8983
Evans, Chas. J	TH 7651
Evans, Sam G	TW 3631 (temp.)
Gilbreath, E. A	TW 3631
Betty, L. H	HI 1455
Payne, Carl M	MA 5950
Ryan, Thos. E	TH 3657

Members of Intelligence Bureau—Continued

Selbo, R. A.	Sunset 25810
Sitts, LaVerne F.	OX 5035
*Slosson, A. E.	OL 63466
Stephens, J. E.	PL 0568
Walter, Louis F.	OL 66688
Folsom, F. H. (steno.) no phone.	

NOTE.—Lt. Luke M. Lane and A. E. Slosson on duty Metro. Vice.
Cars: Ford 15724, Lic E 19154
    " 15804 " 9 C 9 987
    " 15872 " 2 N 8333 (used temp. by Lt. Lane)

Metropolitan Vice

Lt. Luke M. Lane	WH 0566
Soule, Frank Sgt. Prop. Clerk	MO 12423
Boice, W. ("Hogan" Univ.)	MO 10560
Fitzpatrick, J. F., Holly	WY 1797
Flowers, Sam T., Traf	UN 0457
Dougherty, John J., Wilsh	WA 5025
Shurley, Wm. C., Met	FE 5425
Bartram, B. H., Met	PA 1654
Trout, A. R., Traf	CA 4819
Slosson, A. E., In. Bu	OL 63466

Cars: Chev. 15892 Lic. 7 Y 3 236
    Ford 15764 " 2 C 4 780 (Loaned from Det. Bu.)
    Ford 15687 " E 19332 (Loaned from Supply & Main)

NOTE.—These officers are assigned temporarily and borrowed for this special duty from divisions as indicated.

E. LIST OF STRIKES AND LABOR DISPUTES COVERED BY INTELLIGENCE BUREAU
JULY 1937–JUNE 1938

EXHIBIT 10217

INTELLIGENCE BUREAU,
Metropolitan Division, August 24th, 1938.

Miss RODA CROSS,
    Statistician.

DEAR MADAM: In compliance with your request of August 8th 1938, for a report of activities of this Bureau during fiscal year July 1st 1937 to June 30th 1938, I am enclosing a list of strikes and disputes covered by this Bureau for the period mentioned.

It might be stated that these strikes and disputes varied in length of time, number of people affected, and officers assigned. From a very short period of two or three days affecting in some cases only three or four persons, and requiring but one or two officers, up to the strike affecting the trucking service of a large department store which lasted about 8 months, and which affected hundreds of people and required a large detail of officers. Also the Fishermen's strike at Los Angeles Harbor, which affected 3,000 or more people and necessitated assignment of about 85 officers, day and night for a period of three weeks.

Respectfully,

WILLIAM F. HYNES,
Capt. of Detectives, L. A. P. D., Commanding Intelligence Bureau.

RAW–P

[Attached to preceding letter]

Los Angeles, Calif., *Aug. 23, 1938.*

Re Strike and Labor Disputes covered by Intelligence Bureau, Los Angeles Police Dept. *Period July 1, 1937–June 30, 1938.*

Affecting following types of industry:

Athletic Clubs (restaurants)	2	Mattress Cos	2
Auto Parks	1	Meat Cos. (wholesale-retail)	3
Bag Co	1	Milling Co. (Feeds, etc.)	3
Barber Shops	3	Motor Car distributors	1
Battery factories	1	Motor Car Factories	1
Bedding Mfgr	1	Newspapers	2
Brewing Co	1	News distributors	1
Brick mfgr	1	Nut processors	2
Building Cleaners	4	Oil Cos	1
Can mfgr	1	Optical Cos	3
Cigar Cos	1	Paper Bag Cos	1
Circular distributors	1	Parcel Delivery Services	1
Citrus distributing plants	2	Pleating Cos	1
Cleaners & Dyers	5	Produce Cos	3
Clothiers	1	Plumbing Supplies	1
Contractors & Construction Cos	9	Radio mfgrs	1
Department Store:		Restaurants & Lunches:	
(outfit)	1	Chains	2
(trucking strike)	1	Others	16
Distributing Cos	1	Roofing Cos	1
Drug Cos	3	Sash & Door Mfgrs	1
Dry Cleaning Supplies	1	Sausage Cos	1
Employment Offices	1	Screen Cos	2
Film Industries	1	Service Stations (gas-oil)	1
Finance Corps	1	Shades (window)	2
Fishermen's Strike	1	Shirt Shops	3
Furniture Mfgrs	8	Shoe Stores	1
Garment & Dress Mfgrs	6	Shoe Repair Cos	1
Groceries, Wholesale	1	Show Case mfgr	1
Health Foods	1	Tailoring Co	1
Hotel (restaurant depts.)	2	Theatres	6
House Movers	1	Trunk Cos	2
Knitting Mills	4	Trucking & Freight	1
Leather Goods	1	Uniform mfgr	1
Light Cos	1	Upholstering mfgrs	2
Lingerie mfgr	2	Venetian Blind Cos. (see also	
Linoleum Cos	1	Shades)	3
Liquor Cos	1	Wrecking Cos	2
Luggage Mfgrs	1	Miscellaneous Business & In-	
Lumber companies	2	dustries other than above—	
MARKETS, Gen. Food	11	Estimated	20
Manufacturers of Emblems, Chevrons	2	Total	188

F. List of Meetings Allegedly Broken up by Red Squad and Legal Judgment Against Certain Officers of Squad

Exhibit 10218

[Prepared by John C. Packard, attorney at law, Los Angeles, California, on request of subcommittee]

Public Meetings Broken up or Prevented From Being Held by the Los Angeles Police

May 1923.—During the Maritime Strike of 1923 the Unions were informed by the Los Angeles Police Department that they could hold no public meetings in San Pedro during the strike conditions. Upton Sinclair, Hunter Kimbrough,

Prince Hopkins and Hugh Hardyman were arrested by the Los Angeles Police for appearing in San Pedro and attempting to speak. The four were charged with a conspiracy and when the case was finally brought to court a demurrer interposed by me was sustained and the case dismissed. This probably was the most notorious of all the meetings that were broken up.

1931, 1932 and 1933 were years in which the police stopped many meetings in this county. Following are actual instances, with place, date and persons involved:

September 15, 1931.—Canning Hall, 523 Museum Drive, Los Angeles—Robert Whitaker was to have spoken, but the Red Squad prevented anyone entering the hall.

September 29, 1931.—2706 Brooklyn Avenue,· Los Angeles—Attorney Leo Gallagher prevented from speaking on his recent trip to Russia by Red Squad. The same thing happened at 5409 Santa Monica Boulevard, Los Angeles, and Odd Fellows Hall, Pasadena, on the nights of October 1 and October 27 respectively.

October 27, 1931.—Odd Fellows Hall, Pasadena—In this case Leo Gallagher was to address a public meeting and the Los Angeles Red Squad appeared under the direction and orders of Capt. Hynes and stopped all persons entering the Hall. I was present on the occasion and interviewed Capt. Hynes on the subject.

October 30, 1931.—Philharmonic Auditorium, Los Angeles—Mooney-Harlan mass meeting prevented by the police·throwing a cordon across the entrance. Tear gas bombs were thrown, many beaten up and nine arrested. All Pershing Square was filled with the gas. The affair was one of the most brazen ever pulled here.

November 29, 1931.—Music Art Hall, Los Angeles—ACLU OPEN FORUM meeting which was to discuss the Mooney-Harland cases was prevented by police obstructing entrance and allowing no one in the hall.

January 15, 1932.—Newman Hall, 532 Pine Avenue, Long Beach—250 people assembled to hear lecture on "Economic Conditions in the U. S." Just as the meeting was to start a company of police firemen and Legionnaires led by W. F. Hynes entered the hall and placed everyone under arrest. 120 were selected from the number and taken to the jail; the rest were held more than an hour at the hall and then told to go home. Those jailed were treated barbarously. Most of them were charged with C. S. but eventually were dismissed without trial.

April 22, 1933.—Polytechnic High School, Los Angeles—meeting under the auspices of the Friends of the Soviet Union was broken up by lawless Legionnaires who rushed into the place with shouts and cat-calls after turning off the lights. The Red Squad were present but would do nothing to protect the peaceful audience. Evidently they were in league with the Legionnaires and permitted the meeting to be broken up and a thousand people forced to go home.

May 25, 1932.—I. L. D. Headquarters, 120 Winston Street, Los Angeles—two meetings, one a study class, were broken up by Red Squad raiders. Things were turned topsy turvy and six arrested and charged with C. S.—later released. Another meeting in the same place was broken up on the night of June 10, 1932 and everyone chased out of the hall by the Red Squad.

June 14, 1932.—John Reed Club, on New Hampshire Street, near Hollywood Blvd., Los Angeles—executive committee meeting of 12 broken up by police, one man grabbed and some correspondence seized. In February 1933 on the 11th day of that month the Red Squad and some Legionnaires broke up a meeting in the same hall at which a Japanese program was being run off. One man was arrested and many paintings and other property destroyed.

Cooperative Hall, 2706 Brooklyn Avenue, Los Angeles. Many meetings in this hall have been broken up by the police—one on the night of June 17, 1932 when one man was badly beaten up by the cops.

Home of Cornelius Nelson, 1382½ East Vernon Avenue, Los Angeles. An Unemployed Council meeting attended by 25 was broken up by police and five men were arrested. One of the five, Basil Dell, was shot by Phelps of the Red Squad.

June 26, 1932.—Music Art Hall, 233 South Broadway, Los Angeles. ACLU OPEN FORUM meeting to have been addressed by W. Z. Foster Pres. candidate of the Communist Party was prevented by police—same tactics as the previous November—no one allowed to enter the hall.

June 28, 1932.—The Plaza (Los Angeles Free Speech Area)—W. Z. Foster attempted to speak here but was prevented by the Red Squad and many other cops. Foster and 11 others were grabbed and thrown in jail. 9 were released after 3 hours; Foster was held 12 hours; and two others were held 30 hours. None were ever brought to trial.

August 1, 1932.—International Peace Day—Five meetings at various locations in Los Angeles were broken up by the police, and several arrested and held for hours in jail.

August 2, 1932.—Unitarian Church, 9th and Lime Avenue, Long Beach—F. S. U meeting prevented by Policeman Dungan. Large crowd present—no arrests.

September 20, 1932.—Vernon and Central Avenue, hall, Los Angeles—V. Pres. candidate Jas. W. Ford of the C. P. was scheduled to speak, but the Red Squad terrorized the owner of the hall and also threw a cordon across the entrance to keep people out. Ford was grabbed by the police at his hotel, and others were beaten up in the vicinity of the hall. Several were arrested and thrown into jail.

October 2, 1932.—Music Art Hall, 233 South Broadway, Los Angeles. ACLU OPEN FORUM for the 3d time was prevented meeting by the Red Squad—same tactics as before. Herbert Benjamin of N. Y., leader of the Nat'l Hunger march, was to have spoken.

October 2, 1932.—Free Speech Zone, Long Beach—Scottsborough protest meeting was broken up by police and Legionnaires. Two men were arrested when they tried to speak and held for several hours. A large crowd was present—1,000 anyhow.

November 16, 1932.—David Milder home, 2347 East 3rd Street, Long Beach—a meeting was held to hear a report of an ILD convention. KKK members raided the place, with the approval and cooperation of the police of Long Beach it is believed. Both men and women were beaten up and some of the men tied with ropes and put in autos. But in response to repeated calls of neighbors a squad of Long Beach police arrived and stopped the kidnapping. Three were taken to the hospital, and several in the mob held for questioning at the police station.

Spring of 1933.—Los Angeles police prevented a meeting of people in the Boyle Heights section who desired to ratify several radical candidates for public office. W. F. Hynes was later brought into court in a damage suit over this matter and Judge B. Scheinman found him guilty and assessed a fine of six cents as a judgment against him. Attorney John Hart representing the Constitutional Rights Committee of the Los Angeles Bar Association, appeared in the case and offered an argument.

EXHIBIT 10219

[Submitted by John C. Packard, attorney at law, Los Angeles, California, on request of subcommittee]

IN THE SUPERIOR COURT OF THE STATE OF CALIFORNIA

IN AND FOR THE COUNTY OF LOS ANGELES

WILLIAM W. BUSICK, PLAINTIFF, VS. C. T. CHENOWETH, ET AL., DEFENDANTS

NO. 329–330 JUDGMENT

This action came on regularly for trial on the 5th day of October, 1933, before the Honorable Raymond L. Haight, as judge pro tem, the parties hereto having agreed upon his appointment as judge pro tem to hear and determine this matter, a trial by jury having been waived by the parties hereto; plaintiff appearing in person and by his attorneys, A. L. Wirin, Esq., and John C. Packard, Esq., and defendant C. T. Chenoweth appearing in person and by his attorney Bert L. Wicks, Esq., and defendant John D. Fraser appearing in person and by his attorneys A. L. Lawson, Esq., Bernard Brennan, Esq., and Aubrey N. Erwin, Esq., and evidence having been introduced on behalf of the respective parties and said cause having been duly argued and the same having been submitted to the court for its consideration and decision and the court having made and filed its Findings of Fact and Conclusions of Law wherein, judgment is ordered for plaintiff as therein directed.

IT IS NOW, THEREFORE, ORDERED, ADJUDGED AND DECREED That plaintiff do have and recover from the defendants C. T. Chenoweth and John D. Fraser, and each of them, his damages in the sum of $300.

Dated: 30 day of December, 1933.

RAYMOND L HAIGHT,
Judge Pro tempore.

IN THE SUPERIOR COURT OF THE STATE OF CALIFORNIA

IN AND FOR THE COUNTY OF LOS ANGELES

WILLIAM W. BUSICK, PLAINTIFF, VS. C. E. CHENOWETH AND JOHN D. FRASER,

ET AL, DEFENDANTS

NO. 329330   FINDINGS OF FACT AND CONCLUSIONS OF LAW

This action came on regularly for trial on the 5th day of October, 1933, before HONORABLE RAYMOND L. HAIGHT, as judge protem, the parties herein having agreed upon his appointment as judge pro tem to hear and determine this case, a trial by jury having been waived by the parties herein; the plaintiff appearing in person and by his attorneys, A. L. Wirin, Esq., and John C. Packard, Esq.; the defendant, C. E. Chenoweth, appearing in person and by his attorneys, Burt L. Wix, Esq., Allan Daily, Esq., and H. Burton Noble, Esq.; the defendant, John D. Fraser, appearing in person and by his attorneys A. L. Lawson, Esq., and Bernard Brennan, Esq., and evidence having been introduced on behalf of the respective parties herein and said cause having been submitted to the court for decision and the court having considered the same now makes the following

FINDINGS OF FACT

I

That it is true that on or about the 8th day of October, 1931, at Glendale, California, in the County of Los Angeles, a certain group of persons acting together did forcibly and violently lay hold upon plaintiff and forcibly and by means of violence did remove plaintiff from a public platform from which plaintiff was then addressing a public meeting and imprisoned plaintiff for a short period of time without any cause or justification therefor, and that defendant C. E. Chenoweth was with and constituted a part of said group of persons who so laid hold upon, removed and imprisoned plaintiff and during all of said time remained a part of said group of persons which said group of persons acted together for the common purpose of so laying hold upon, removing and imprisoning plaintiff; that defendant C. E. Chenoweth did not personally lay hands upon plaintiff on that occasion; that said action upon the part of said group of persons including defendant C. E. Chenoweth was done by said persons with the approval, aid, assistance and cooperation of defendant John D. Fraser.

II

That it is not true that defendant C. E. Chenoweth and John D. Fraser or either of them was or were actuated by personal ill will or malice toward the plaintiff. That it is not true that by so doing said defendants desired to show and did show their utter disrespect for governmental authority.

III

That plaintiff by reason of the actions of defendants and others as above set forth, was forcibly and violently dragged from the platform of said school building and suffered extreme indignity and humiliation to his damage in the sum of $300.

From the foregoing Findings of Fact, the court now makes the following

CONCLUSIONS OF LAW

I

The rights and liberties of plaintiff were unlawfully interfered with by defendant C. E. Chenoweth and John D. Fraser to the plaintiff's damage in the sum of $300 and plaintiff is therefore entitled to a judgment against the defendants C. E. Chenoweth and John D. Fraser and each of them in the sum of $300.

Let judgment be entered accordingly.

DATED: this 30th day of December, 1933.

RAYMOND L. HAIGHT,
Judge Pro Tem.

3. DOCUMENTS RELATING TO URBAN LABOR ORGANIZATIONS AND STRIKES

A. Oil Workers Union

Exhibit 10220

Plan of Operation

November 8, 1933.

In combating the union movement concerning which Agents 10 and 20 have been reporting, following is the plan of operation proposed by them:

Agents will concentrate their work to keep the organizing of the men to a minimum for the immediate present and as an ultimate end to disrupt the movement entirely. To accomplish these objects Agents will use many methods successful in the past, the principal one of which is to assume leadership and to secure the removal of aggressive, efficient organizers.

The most aggressive among union organizers and usually radicals and Agents who will turn the names of all such over to the Department of Justice and to the Police in such cities and towns as are administered by officials not in sympathy with radicalism.

Workers who are active in organizing will be reported to their several employing companies so that they may be transferred or discharged. Agents will keep the union treasuries to a minimum by getting the officers to spend money foolishly, in order that no strike benefit fund may be accumulated. Agents will keep notices of meetings and literature from reaching the men to a great degree.

The movement will be discouraged by securing men employed by the companies to talk to their fellow-employees against the union. Agents already have several contacts of this sort who do not like unions and who can be depended upon to discourage the movement. Within the union itself, Agents will promote internal dissension among the members and among the officials and organizers.

It will be possible to assume control over the organizing of the Foremen and Inspector's Union so that this organization will not function in the manner expected by the union officials.

All union meetings, organizational conferences and official committee meetings will be covered and reported by Agents in all sections from Long Beach and Ventura to Coalinga, Taft and Bakersfield.

Agents will secure all information on sabotage, prevent a strike and block every move of the union which holds any promise of effectiveness. The numerical strength of the union will be kept within safe bounds and later disrupted, officials and organizers will be encouraged to dissipate their efforts in fruitless channels, internal quarrels among the members and officers will be purposely created, and dangerous members and officials will be removed through definite action, all by using the above described methods and by other methods known to be effective by Agents.

In addition, of course, the clients will be kept informed at frequent intervals of the activities of the union and photostatic copies of important documents sent to them.

Agents are perfectly familiar with this work and stand very high with the American Federation of Labor headquarters in Washington, to which they have wired for credentials as organizers in this particular union. Agents already have credentials which will admit them without question into any union or executive committee meeting of any organization affiliated with the American Federation of Labor or the Brotherhoods. Agents are also delegates to the conventions of the California State Federation of Labor and of the American Federation of Labor.

Agents have devoted their time for years to this sort of investigation work and are fully trusted in all liberal, radical and labor circles on the Pacific Coast and elsewhere. They always have most valid reasons for their presence at any place or meeting so that no suspicion can possibly arise.

Agents are also in a position to assume control of the newly organized Friends of Organized Labor, and will be able to keep this organization from having any effective influence upon the movement in any way.

There is absolutely no danger of the clients being involved in Agents' activities nor of being embarrassed by them to the slightest degree, as Agents' methods of working preclude any possibility of their being uncovered or even suspected. Agents will always be well within the law in all their actions, and their methods have been found to be more successful than so-called "strong arm" methods.

In order to handle the situation and gain the objects noted above, three men will be necessary. The cost of these men will be ten dollars per day each, plus necessary expenses, and will include any investigation wanted in the area under discussion and reports will cover every section. Agents would prefer to report to Captain H. as there is somtimes considerable danger in sending reports to small towns.

Agents do not consider that the present situation is serious, but it could easily and quickly become so. Since the NRA went into effect, organizers are more active throughout the country than ever before in the history of unionism, and now that open attacks on the NRA and the Roosevelt Administration have started by Hearst and others, American Federation of Labor officials have ordered a redoubling of active effort to solidify the ranks of labor quickly in the event of a dissolution of the NRA setup. Organizers are preparing literature designed to convince workers that the safety of their jobs lies in union organization. Unions everywhere are trying to force the closed shop on employers, and the A. F. of L. is trying to get enough members in the United States, according to several leaders, to carry the next presidential election even if it is necessary to use the A. F. of L. Brotherhoods as the nucleus of a new Labor Party.

Agents would not desire to remain on this investigation for the sole purpose of reporting the activities of the union. This can be secured, except for plans made in conferences of organizers and officials, from employees of the companies for a few extra dollars per week. The cost of breaking up the movement is but a small percentage of the cost which would result were there to be a strike, whether such a strike would result in higher wages or be entirely lost by the union. There will be no local strikes in this industry in the future; all workers will be called out in the event the union is strongly organized and the companies do not recognize it and accede to its demands. The cost of Agents' work will be but a small premium for the security which it will give against trouble with the unions.

Captain H. will vouch for the fact that Agents always bend every effort to disrupt the union and close the case as quickly as possible. They do not "string out" the job as there are many concerns in need of their services at the present time.

Exhibit 10221

[Typed transcription of handwritten notes]

Intra-Departmental Correspondence *Oil Workers* Form 236

Los Angeles Police Department

Office of_____

(Handwritten)

Hgwy to Bakersfield—
    on up on Fresno Road to near Town of Wasco.
    Turn there on Lost Hills Road.
    Then take Kettleman Hills or Avenal Rd.—(Little T_____(Illegible))
    Coalinga 25 Miles from there—
    Assn. called KNDA
        Kettleman North Dome Assn.—
    Fox Hotel—Coalinga—
        Mr. J. A. Jackman
          Fox Hotel—Coalinga
          Report by Friday Night—
A. Marshall 10–20 Sat. Night—7:30 P. M. A. L. Marshall—Fox—
  Rellin   Monday " 6:00 P. M.

(NOTE: On opposite side of original document appears: "Al G. Brownew, 2041 Hancock, CApital 9355".)

EXHIBIT 10222

Intra-Departmental Correspondence.   Form 236

LOS ANGELES POLICE DEPARTMENT

Office of_____

(Handwritten)

Town of Avenal
    Organizers in there going in Independent—
and Standa Oil Co Inpents—
    _____There local Hdq. in Coalinga.
    _____(illegible) are at Avenal— _____(illegible) are at this Place
    _____Bakersfield & Taft—
    _____Also call me at hq. _____ Monday Night (illegible)—at
    Monday—6:00 P. M.—
    Saturday

EXHIBIT 10223

NOVEMBER 3, 1933.

[Confidential Report]

OIL WORKERS UNION

Agents 10 and 20 left Los Angeles November first. They visited Maricopa, Taft, Bakersfield, Coalinga and Avenal on the 1st, 2nd and 3rd of November, contacting the organizers and leaders separately. On the night of the 3rd, both Agents 10 and 20 attended a meeting held in the rear hall of *McNeil's Pool Rooms in Avenal*. The following information was secured at the offices, at the meeting and in contacting the organizers and leaders in the field:

H. A. DUDLEY and B. L. SMITH are working among the men at Maricopa and Taft. Agent 20 contacted Dudley at Maricopa but did not meet Smith, as the latter was in the field and Agent 20 had been instructed to proceed as rapidly as possible to Coalinga. Dudley says that the men are anxious to joing the union but as many of them are afraid of being discharged, the organizers all over California have had to combine open organization methods with secret methods under the cell system. They try to get the men to join the union openly, but if any man shows fear they then proceed to get him into a cell of five men. The man then pays his initiation fee of Three Dollars but his name does not go to the secretary until such time as the union will have the majority of workers in any particular section.

Dudley says that several of the oil companies are not doing anything to intimidate the men, but that others are doing so—particularly STANDARD OIL COMPANY. Dudley says they are going to put a crimp into Standard if they don't do anything else.

Agent 10 contacted E. B. DANIELS and W. A. STAR in Bakersfield. Daniels is the head organizer for the union and is also an official of the Department of Industrial Relations of the State of California. Star is secretary of the Bakersfield Central Labor Council. Here Agent 10 learned that two men are coming to Bakersfield about November 15th: P. R. O'Malley, who will be assigned by the International as organizer for this entire section, working in collaboration with all the present organizers; and A. N. WILSON, who will organize the FRIENDS OF ORGANIZED LABOR in the cities and small towns in the oil fields area.

The FRIENDS OF ORGANIZED LABOR is a movement starting with nuclei all over the state, the object of which is to line up merchants, professional men, housewives and all union sympathizers back of any union activity of the American Federation of Labor. Their appeal to the public is briefly this: If labor does not get its fair share of the value of the product, the residents of the community are robbed of that much purchasing power, as the part that labor does not get eventually finds its way into the pockets of eastern bankers. The FOL will bar from membership any union member as well as any company official who does not actively favor the union cause.

The program of the FOL is to assist in removing the fear that many workers have of joining the union; to prosecute complaints to the NRA of any intimidation by companies; to raise funds for striking unions; to furnish non-union picketers on strikes; to cooperate in boycotts of firms listed as unfair to union labor; and to furnish legal service in protecting the civil and NRA rights of labor.

O'Malley and *Wilson* will not work together, but they are due to arrive in Bakersfield at the same time. The FOL cannot, so Star says, use union organizers because the bosses will then say the FOL is the A. F. of L. under another name. Agents 10 and 20 have made arrangements to meet these men separately under most favorable conditions.

R. H. STECKEL is the organizer *in Coalinga and Avenal*, and is living now at the *Sullivan Hotel in Coalinga*. He is being assisted by HOWARD GEIGER, who acts as secretary for the locals. Secretary for the local at AVENAL is LESLIE BLACKWOOD.

The organizers are somewhat disappointed at their results so far, but they all have big hopes for the immediate future. All of the organizers and leaders say that they will have to strike to get what they want. *Howard Geiger* said last night that as soon as they get 51 per cent of the workers they will make demands, submit a code and demand recognition of the union. He also said that they did not expect to get anything by asking for it, that the union would have to strike, and that the strike would have to be a "rough one." Agent asked if he believed in direct action, and he replied: "And how!"

It was learned in Bakersfield that *Daniels* does not consider *Steckel* to be just the right man for the job. He said that Steckel was not making a hit with the men and would have to be removed. He said that the man coming from the North was just the right type—a man that could be termed a "trouble shooter"— one who could step in anywhere and organize. This man O'Malley has had big success with other crafts. Another man may come down from San Francisco who recently organized the trainmen employed by the United Railway Company there. He said that any man who could organize the employees of that "labor-hating company that sent Mooney to prison and is keeping him there" could do a lot in the oil fields.

The union was organized about two months ago around Avenal and Coalinga, and of approximately 1000 workers in that area, they claim that two or three hundred have applied for membership in the union. No dues will be charged for November to those joining this month, or to those who have already joined, so that they will not have to pay more than those joining later.

Most of the meetings are being held privately because of many workers' fear of company reprisals. These meetings, and the open meetings, are purely organizational in character. No business is conducted at meetings; all plans are discussed by and among the leaders and organizers alone. *Meetings are held in Avenal every Thursday night* and in *Bakersfield every Friday night. Friday night meetings have been held in Coalinga*, but Steckel says that the hall has been too small and they are trying to find a larger one.

Most of the organizational work has been done by direct, individual contact by *Geiger, Blackwood, Dudley, Steckel* and *Daniels*—also by the men who agree to form a cell of five men.

All of the organizers are bitter against *Standard* because, so they say, that company has been most active in intimidating the men. Although they say that all the companies have used the NRA to cut down the incomes of their employees, they are more bitter against Standard than they are against *Superior, Associated, Italo, Texas, Union or the others*.

Tonight Agents 10 and 20 are staging a drinking party with *Blackwood, Geiger*, and *Steckel in Coalinga. Blackwood is a radical and lives with a member of the Communist Party in Avenal*. Steckel says that he expects a big "blow-up" in the United States within the next two or three years, and that he hopes it comes.

A conference of leaders and organizers will be held in Taft Sunday, the 5th, and one of the Agents will attend it. This territory is so large that it is about all two men can do to keep it covered. In fact, to cover the situation with complete satisfaction, three men are necessary: one to cover the Coalinga section, one to cover the Bakersfield-Taft section, and another to cover the Ventura-Long Beach section. So far Agents 10 and 20 have only laid the ground work for future operations, as it is not known exactly what is wanted. Agents can either simply report the activities and plans of the leaders and organizers of the union and of the FOL, or they can keep the entire movement from proceeding much further.

It's a waste of time and money simply to get reports of what these men are doing to organize the workers against the companies. The thing to do, in Agents' opinion,—and what they are able to do with the assistance of one other man—is to disrupt the organizing activities in the entire field. This can be done by assuming leadership, by getting the organizers in trouble, and in many other ways familiar to Agents 10 and 20 and used by them before to break up union organizations. This could be done only by allowing Agents to use their own methods, reporting only results attained, so that the companies would not be a party to it, and so that Agents would not be uncovered.

This has to be done on the entire front. If activities are stopped in only one place, they will be redoubled somewhere else. This is the reason why three men—one in addition to Agents 10 and 20—are necessary. Also Agents would have to have the cooperation of the companies in their doing such things and taking such steps as can legally be taken, so that Agents' work would be the more effective.

This other man, whom Agents have used in the past, would have to be employed directly by Agents. Without a doubt, Agents can hold the union within present bounds—perhaps disrupt it—and keep the FOL from assisting in any way the Oil Workers Union.

The union would have to be killed everywhere. Agents could not hope for success in any other way for this simple reason: Agents could be holding the union down in one section,—say Coalinga. But if, in the Taft or Long Beach section, the union were to gain sufficient strength to be a force this example would give the workers and organizers in the Coalinga section so much impetus that Agents would have extreme difficulty in pursuing their program.

JOINT REPORT FROM AGENTS 10 AND 20.

P. S. This report must be kept secret if Agents are expected to do any more work in this field. Leaks to company officials and superintendents in the field may become leaks, through wives or relations, to men connected with the union.

EXHIBIT 10224

[Confidential Report]

NOVEMBER 7, 1933.

OIL WORKERS UNION

Agents 10 and 20 staged a drinking party the night of November 3rd with Geiger, Blackwood, Steckel and Dungan. The latter is a friend of Blackwood's and very radical. He is not yet a member of the union and is inclined to favor the Communist's Trade Union Unity League, But it is probable he will join with Blackwood.

The following information was obtained at this party, at the conference in Taft on Sunday, November 5th, during investigation by Agent 10 in and about Taft and Bakersfield, and during investigation by Agent 20 in and about Coalinga, Avenal and Kettleman Hills:

Only 11 members of the union have been secured from among Superior Oil Company employees, and Steckel instructed these men not to show up at any meetings but to agitate among their fellow-employees and to hold meetings at private homes. Steckel told them that he was not going to solicit members in the fields or plants of the Superior Oil Company but that he would be glad to meet them at their homes in groups. Blackwood told Steckel that the latter should not even do that, that he (Blackwood) would go to these home meetings, as there are so many company spotters about that the men would lose their jobs.

Geiger stated that the oil companies have men hanging around the pool hall in Avenal in which union meetings are held, and sit in cars parked around the hall, to get the names of men going in. Steckel said he would like to have one man fired for belonging to the union as he would immediately wire Roosevelt and get a lot of publicity. Blackwood said that the company could always find plenty of reasons to fire a man without saying they fired him for joining the union. Blackwood expressed dissatisfaction at the few men turning out for union meetings, and Geiger told him not to let that worry him as they were getting members without holding meetings and when the union gets strong enough there will be plenty of hot meetings.

Steckel told Geiger and Blackwood that he wants one man in each plant as a shop steward to line up the other men in each plant, and this shop steward would be responsible for that unit. The shop stewards are also to collect all complaints under NRA codes applying to that plant and turn them over to the union. The names of these shop stewards are to be kept, not by the local secretaries, but by Steckel himself in order to keep them from leaking out to the company.   Several of these prospective shop stewards were mentioned, but only by their given names.

Steckel impressed it upon Geiger and Blackwood that there was nothing in the code to keep union men from organizing on the job.

A man named Provost, whose brother is in the Coalinga Post Office and who is secretary of the local at Coalinga, was expected at the meeting with Agents, but he did not show up and Steckel said that he was probably at a home meeting.

W. A. Star, secretary of the Bakersfield Central Labor Council, stated to Agent 10 that the union was preparing a code and a set of demands.   He stated that the Union Oil Company pays the lowest wages of any company.   One of the demands will be for full compensation for any man injured even though he may be working only four or four and a half days a week.   Recognition of the union, check-off system and closed shop conditions will also be demanded.

Geiger and Blackwood mentioned similar demands to Agent 20, and stated that some of them were not favored by a few of the "weak sister" union officials but that the radical element would push them through.   Both these men are in favor of the one big union plan and said that the I. W. W. had the right idea.   Geiger said, when mention was made of the strikes going on in California, "if we have a strike in the oil industry, we'll show them what a real strike is like."

Steckel has written to A. W. Hoch, president of the State Federation of Labor, asking for information on organizing locals of the Foremen and Inspectors' Union. This union takes in bosses and petty officials who are not allowed to join the union or attend meetings of the oil workers.   It has proved successful in Los Angeles and San Francisco, and would be, in Steckel's opinion, a great help in organizing the Oil Workers Union.   A foreman or similar employee who belongs to the Foremen and Inspectors' Union is able to get the men under him to join their union even easier, usually, than is the outside organizer.

The union plans one code for the entire oil industry, and no strike will be called that does not include every company in every section, and the union will positively not give in, say the officials, without full recognition by the companies.

It was reported that many men are going to be put to work in the Taft fields because the companies are going to open up the old wells.

Special organization methods classes are going to be held in private homes at which Steckel will instruct union members who want to help in the organization work in how to approach the other men.   Steckel is supposed to have had great success in training organizers.   He is a good talker but not well liked by the men.

Twelve men were signed up in the union last week in Button Willows.

In drawing out Steckel, Agents found out that the principle object in his mind is union recognition.   He says that "after recognition, any union can write its own ticket."

At the Sunday conference in Taft, it was reported that the oil tank drivers in Los Angeles were signed up eighty-five per cent and that they are holding rousing meetings at the Labor Temple on Tuesday evenings.

In talking with other union leaders, such as Star and Daniels, Agents are stating that Steckel is all right but that the men don't like him and don't trust him too far, because, in Agents' opinion, this man is efficient and should be gotten rid of.

One of the principal supporters of the Oil Workers Union in Coalinga is an elderly man named Buchanan who is a local merchant, writer for the radical Pismo Times, former engineering professor and a confirmed Socialist.   He has been made an honorary member of the Union.   Steckel approached him about taking leadership in organizing the Friends of Organized Labor in the Coalinga area and getting the other merchants into it.

The FOL is planning to put women into the field to talk to employees' wives, urging them to get their husbands to join the union to save their jobs and increase their income.

Regarding the plan set forth in our last report, it is not wise to reduce it to writing, especially when such writing is to be mailed.   According to instructions received from Captain H. Agent 10 will be in Los Angeles Thursday, November 9th.   Agent 20 will attend the union local meeting tonight in Coalinga.

If there is any specific or particular information clients desire, Agents will be glad to secure the same, and such requests should be made through Captain H. as it would be dangerous to contact company officials in these small towns.

H. A. Dudley has been handling private home meetings around Maricopa and states that the men there are ready for organization.   B. L. Smith is not employed by the oil companies, but came from Ventura as a special organizer.   He states that they are planning two big meetings in Ventura section in about a week.

On telephoned instructions, Agent 20 joined Agent 10 in Bakersfield Tuesday morning for the purpose of making out this joint report in accordance with orders from Captain H.

Quick action on Agents' suggested plan should be taken, as it is much easier and cheaper to counteract this union movement during its inception than when it has gained a big foothold among the workers.

Joint report from Agents 10 and 20.

EXHIBIT 10225

[Confidential Report]

LOS ANGELES, CALIFORNIA.
November 10th, 1933.

The following information has been obtained from conferences and meetings held in Los Angeles and Long Beach during the past two days:—

Frank Morrison, Secretary of the American Federation of Labor at Washington D. C. sent the following letter to all locals.

"American Federation of Labor, Washington D. C. Nov. 4th. '33.

To be read at next meeting.

Attacks against NRA codes and even the National Recovery Administration itself are increasing. Most of these attacks come from sources opposed to organized labor.

It is possible that the provisions in the several codes for union representation of employees' will soon be revises in a way designated to rob the employee of his right to collective bargaining.

It is important, therefore, that every local of every union do its utmost to strengthen itself so that it will be in a position to successfully oppose all efforts designed to counteract the gains we have made during the last few months.

Organizational work must be greatly increased. Each organizer must redouble his efforts. And every union man must consider himself a vital part of our organizational program. Officers must impress their members with the fact that his own interests are served every time he brings a new member into his local.

Fraternally

(Signed) FRANK MORRISON"

At the meeting of the Oil Workers in Long Beach a vote was taken to redouble their efforts. They took in 73 new members in that section in one week.

J. C. Coulter told Agent that two new organizers are to be put in the field beginning the 15th of this month. One of these whose name was not learned, as Coulter could not think of it at the time, is from the Oklahoma Fields and is reported to be a high preasure man who will get right on the job. This man is to be used in the Bakersfield and Coalinga section. The other is a man named John Maltby, who will work in the Ventura section. Coulter is also going to use two local men in the Long Beach, and Santa Fe Springs section. It was also learned that the Oil Tank Drivers are going to use one of the old drivers who is well known to help make this organization as near one hundred per cent as possible. These boys are going to bring preasure to bear on all tank drivers who do not line up and it is intimated that those who refuse to join the union will have plenty of trouble.

Agent asked about the Standard Oil Company, employees, if they were joining the union etc. Coulter stated that fourteen of them were signed up in one day and that they now have about 60 new applications for membership from the Standard Oil on file in the Long Beach office. He said that there were several who have been members on the q t for some time and he did not know how many they have altogether but he is going to check and find out.

To units or divisions of the Friends of Organized Labor have been formed during the past two days. One in Long Beach and the other San Pedro. This organization is growing faster than any organization designed to help the labor movement every grew. If it continues it will become a political power and will be of great aid to the unions.

At a closed meeting of labor leaders Agent learned that there is a plan on foot to defeat J. W. Buzzell the Secretary of the Central Labor Council. They maintain that Buzzell has not been on the job much of late and that the unions would have been much stronger with a more militant secretary on the job.

Conboy who is an international organizer for the Oil workers and the Teamsters is in charge of the Pacific Coast Labor Bureau, located at 406 South Main Street, MU 6073. He stated this morning that the various unions in the oil fields are to work together and that they are going to canvass all of the oil workers later on regarding a strike; to take a sort of secret vote on making demands and striking for them if necessary. Enclosed are two of their application blanks for the Truck drivers.

The Long Beach Union has jurisdiction over the Huntington Beach and Whittier fields but a charter has been sent for for Whittier.

Agents will have full credentials from the American Federation of Labor; to act as organizers in California within the next two or three days; This will make it possible for Agents to get openly active and assume control of the work in case Client should want the things done mentioned in former letter.

Agent is going to Taft today or perhaps in the morning as it would be well to attend the meeting of the Central Labor Council here tonight.

Agent 20 is in Coalinga or Avenol. One of Agents should go to Ventura and make the necessary contacts there but as nothing has been said about this there is no way to know if Clients are interested there or not.

Exhibit 10226

November 11, 1933

[Confidential Report]

Oil Workers Union

Agent 20, since making the last report, has attended union meetings in Coalinga, Avenal and Bakersfield, has contacted the leaders and organizers in the field and at their homes or temporary residences, and has attended conferences in Taft, Bakersfield and Coalinga, during which he has gained the following information:

Organization of the workers is proceeding more rapidly in the Long Beach section than elsewhere. Men are applying for membership at the average rate of about 50 per week. Last week 73 new applications were received.

Bakersfield is slower because, says E. B. Daniels, there are not so many workers at present in that section and they are moved about too frequently. Bakersfield local took in 19 new members last week, however. This local meets on the 2nd and 4th Fridays of each month, with frequent special meetings.

In Taft, an advisory organizational committee has been formed consisting of H. A. Dudley, organizer; W. L. Altmiller of 220 Phillipine Street, President of the Taft Central Labor Union (a Barbers' Union member); Financial Secretary Garner, who is the leader in several unions and a prominent lodge official in Taft; and F. W. Peck of 30 Center Street, secretary of the Taft Central Labor Union. The Taft local now has 90 members out of possibly 300 prospects in the section, and meets every Tuesday evening at 7:30 in the Central Labor Union hall.

In Kettleman Hills, 70 members constitute the Oil Workers Union local.

The Avenal local and the Coalinga local have about three hundred members and took in 11 last week.

Dudley says that organizing is a little harder around Taft, although he expects to get 50 or 60 per cent membership within a few weeks after which they will "force" the others into the union, but that men who don't belong to the union join up when transferred to some other section.

It is rumored that the Standard Oil Company is trying to put over a company association of employees and are being followed in this tactic by several of the other large companies. R. H. Steckel, speaking to the Avenal local Thursday night, attacked this idea, stating that there were about 500 oil companies in California and company associations would mean that the cause of the workers would suffer for lack of coordination among the 500 company unions.

R. H. Steckel, organizer paid by the International and appointed by President Harvey Fremming, states that each local union is going to put on at least one more full-time organizer who will be paid out of local funds. Steckel gets five dollars a day plus expenses and three dollars a day for hotel room. Steckel is becoming more and more unpopular with the men in spite of the fact that he is very intelligent and a good organizer. His connection with the 1921 strike is one cause of his unpopularity, although his personality is not an attractive one. It is possible that this O'Malley who is due shortly will supplant him, although Agent believes that the original plan was merely to place him in general supervision over all organizing in the Bakersfield-Taft-Coalinga sections.

Agent 20 staged a "beer bust" with Howard Geiger, Leslie Blackwood (secretary, Avenal local, and employee of Los Nietos) and two other union members referred to only as "Ed" and "Burt". He learned that oil workers in California believe that the Richfield company has been warned to fix their equipment but refused to do so, and that the fire in Long Beach was the result of criminal refusal to safeguard the workers. It was also stated that most of the companies except Superior had saved money during the depression by allowing their equipment to be used without proper maintenance and that much of it is highly dangerous. According to these men, Standard employs only 13 men at their Plant No. 33J, but that there is work enough there for 20 men, and that the equipment in this plant is badly run down and dangerous to the men's lives. The union, when it gets strong, will attend to all this, they claim.

Provost joined us later and, in speaking of contemplated demands by the union, he stated that most of the men were satisfied with present hour schedules but that the pay would have to be increased. He said that they cut the hours but did not raise the pay sufficient to make the weekly wage the same as before and that the union would demand such a raise if not more. He also said that, in his opinion, a 30-hour week would be put over this winter with a corresponding decrease in weekly earnings, but that if the union became 51 per cent organized, the companies would not be able to get away with it.

Organizational meetings of small groups are getting under way, says Steckel, in fine shape. These meetings are addressed by Steckel, Geiger, Dudley, Blackwood and union members who are good talkers. Those who are afraid to join the union but would like to are allowed to join a cell, pay their initiation fee and no record is kept by the secretary of their names.

Blackwood states that the more militant and radical workers are the first to join the locals and that they are working hard to convince their fellow-workers of what the union can do for them. At every meeting the statement is made several times that "if the oil workers organize, they can have anything they want as the companies would not dare to fight another strike."

It is reported that the Friends of Organized Labor are getting the following men to back the local organizations: In Coalinga, L. A. BUCHANAN; in Bakersfield, MALCOLM BROCK, LAWRENCE WEILL, FRED FISHERING (manager of Redlick's Department Store); and a blind attorney named RAYMOND HENDERSON. Frank Lowe, president of the Bakersfield Central Labor Council; W. A. Star, secretary of the same; Samuel White, editor of the Kern County Union Labor Journal; and E. B. Daniels are taking an active and enthusiastic part in laying plans for the organization in Bakersfield of the FOL.

Agent 20 has been asked to attend a meeting of this group to discuss plans for the FOL in Bakersfield on Monday, November 13th.

Agent has had several opportunities, which he has not failed to take advantage of, to increase the feeling against Steckel both on the part of the men and on the part of officials of the Oil Workers Union and the various Central Labor Councils, with a view to getting this man removed from this area, because in spite of his unpopularity, he is an excellent organizer.

EXHIBIT 10227

NOVEMBER 14, 1933.

[Confidential Report]

Yesterday Agent 20 attended the conference on the Friends of Organized Labor in Bakersfield as stated in the report of November 11th, and last night he met with several union leaders in Taft, with the following results:

The Friends of Organized Labor is being financed by donations from individuals of liberal views and by some former benefactors of the Socialist Party. However, each local "division" of the FOL is to do most of its own financing, and it is expected that their printing will be done by union printers at cost or less and that unions or Central Labor Councils will donate funds to some extent.

Daniels expects the FOL to be of great value in organizing the Oil Workers Union. He hopes that women members of the FOL will engage in a systematic campaign among oil workers' wives to get them lined up with the union.

The FOL at present is only lining up potential supporters and getting the sanction of various union officials. Printed literature, it was stated, would not be available for a week or two. It was stated that the FOL has the tacit endorsement of every official of the Los Angeles and San Francisco Central Labor Councils, but no official endorsement has been requested as yet. Both Agent 10 and Agent 20 are very close to this situation and believe that they will be able to keep its activities at a minimum.

Daniels and others in Bakersfield are very anxious to line up all the oil tank drivers in the state into the Teamsters and Chauffeurs' International. This organization is second in size in the United States to the Railroad Brotherhoods, only. It is divided into subsidiary groups, such as the Oil Tank Drivers, the Bakery Drivers, Laundry Drivers, Ice Drivers, Taxicab Drivers, etc., and are ruled in each section by a Joint Committee. If one group has a strike, the others are expected to strike in sympathy.

They particularly want to line up the drivers for the Lang Transportation Company, with which they have had considerable difficulties, Agent is informed.

Charters have been issued to 52 new locals of the Oil Workers Union within the last three months, according to Dudley who came up from Maricopa to meet Agent. The strength of the union in the East Texas fields is gaining by leaps and bounds, he states. In one Standard plant in Pennsylvania, there are 300 employees. An organizer was requested by a small group of them but he was delayed two weeks in arriving. When he got there he found that every employee had joined an association and he took them into the union in one group.

Wilson, FOL man, and O'Malley, Oil Workers Union organizer, are expected in Bakersfield Wednesday or Thursday of this week.

Daniels showed Agent a letter from James C. Coulter, International Vice-President with headquarters in Long Beach, in which he stated that he would be in Bakersfield for the meeting of the Oil Workers Union on November 24th, and that he would probably visit Taft, Maricopa, Avenal and Coalinga after that date. Jim Coulter has been connected with this union for many years and formerly worked with Yarrow. He is an energetic, capable executive and the men have great confidence in him.

Daniels says that Standard and other companies are planning to open wells in the Bakersfield district soon, and that this will mean an increase in the number of workers there. He plans to put plenty of organizers in the field when that happens.

Daniels expressed himself about the independent operators, when asked if some one of them would not get back of the FOL. He stated that the independent operators are absolutely no good, that the union has helped them in their battles against the big companies but got nothing but kicks in return. He said "I'd like to see every independent wiped out. I'd rather deal with Standard any day, as much as I despise and hate that outfit."

I heard more rumors about company associations in Bakersfield. The union leaders state that they will be able to break them up before they get a real start by using propaganda against company-controlled unions, by increased organizing activities for their own union, and by getting their own men to join the associations and stir up trouble.

Exhibit 10228

November 15, 1933

[Confidential Report]

In accordance with instructions received, Agents 10 and 20 returned to Los Angeles this morning. Agents would have liked to remain in the field a couple more days, especially as Wilson, FOL organizer, and O'Malley are due to arrive in Bakersfield tomorrow.

Agents have made arrangements to secure the names of the union members in the several districts within the last few days. Nothing was reported on this previously because Agents were not certain that these names could be secured.

Agents have also been admitted into the inner organizational activities of the Friends of Organized Labor and will be present, when advisable, at all meetings of the national and state board of directors of the FOL.

Agent 20, during a visit in the Ventura section, learned that 22 had signed applications for union membership, although only 16 have paid their initiation fees as yet. John Maltby, organizer, is already at work in the Ventura section and has arranged for two meetings in private homes for this week.

An organization conference has been called for November 24th, 25th and 26th. The following men have been sent letters asking them to meet with Jim Coulter in Bakersfield on those dates: H. A. DUDLEY, E. B. DANIELS, R. H. STECKEL, LESLIE BLACKWOOD, HOWARD GEIGER, JOHN MALTBY, and B. L. SMITH. O'Malley is expected to attend also. Coulter is also to confer with A. N. Wilson regarding organization of the FOL in the oil towns, and there is a possibility that the Oil Workers Union will contribute some of the organization funds for the FOL.

Agents have prepared plans other than those mentioned in dealing with this situation, but will not mention them at this time as they may not all materialize.

Joint report from Agents 10 and 20.

EXHIBIT 10229

ACCOUNT OF AGENTS 10 AND 20

November 1 to 15 1923, inclusive:

Salary 10 per day per agent	$300. 00
Expenses Nov. 1–7 inclusive, including 1542 miles driven by 2 cars 5¢ per mile	168. 00
Expenses Nov. 8–15, inclusive, including 1523 Miles by 2 cars @ 5¢ per mile	177. 30
Total	$645. 30
Less received on account expenses	308. 00
Balance due	$337. 30

EXHIBIT 10230

DECEMBER 15, 1933.

[Confidential Report]

OIL WORKERS MEETING FOR STANDARD OIL CO. EMPLOYEES

This meeting was held tonight in the American Legion Stadium in El Segundo. About 70 men were present, of whom about 55 were Standard Oil Company employees.

The meeting was presided over by J. C. Coulter, secretary of Oil Workers Local 128, 1231 Locust Avenue, Long Beach. Coulter's address is 4818 Trimble Court, Long Beach—phone 315–426.

Coulter opened the meeting by stating that it was being held for organization purposes, and then introduced Rev. Robert E. Lucey of St. Anthony's Church, 540 Olive Avenue, Long Beach. Main points of Father Lucey's talk: That the NRA was not satisfactory in every particular, as it was designed primarily for the employers; that no success can come from a system run by the government and employers, but only one run by employers and employees; that the present administration in Washington is friendly to organized labor, but that the next administration may not be, so that now is the time to organize and it is necessary to do so if labor is to have its voice in industry and get its share of production, that the NRA codes are all drafted by the employers, and that not much good can come to labor from codes written by employers for employees; that there are about 45 million workers, with 100 million dependent on their labor; that in normal times there were about 5 million workers in legitimate unions, and that just prior to the NRA the organized workers numbers about 2½ million, as compared with some 6 million at the present time; that in order to obtain proper representation in industry, and to protect and raise the standard of living in the United States, organized labor must secure 30 million members; that Standard has a company union and that he has no use for company unions as they are organized solely for the benefit of the company. He then gave illustrations of the difference between representation by a company union, with men employed by the company as representatives of the men, and representation by an outside man employed by the union whom the company cannot fire. Father Lucey urged the men strongly to join the Oil Workers Union, stating that Section 7a of the NIRA made it possible for them to join without fear of losing their jobs. He was given a tremendous ovation at the close of his speech.

Coulter then called on Brother Forrester, employee of the Union Oil Company. Forrester said that he started out with some applications among his fellow-workers, that during the first week he only got three or four men to sign them, but that now the Union Oil Company is 85 per cent organized.

Warren, employee of the Shell Oil Company, spoke next. He said that this company was always pretty well organized, and now that they were about 85 per cent organized in that section.

Carron, employee of Texaco, was the next speaker. He stated that the Los Angeles Case & Packing Company employees at Terminal Island were about 97 per cent organized.

Coulter then called upon a man named Matthews, who said he had been employed by Shell for twelve years. He said that he had been sent to Washington by the union, at the request of Washington officials, to answer questions in regard to the refining of oil.

Joe Reed, business agent of the Boilermakers Union, spoke next. Reed discussed the benefits of organized labor at some length. He spoke of the firing of an employee of a ship building concern in the East for belonging to the union, and said that the entire force went on strike and, when the matter was brought before a board consisting of the present of Standard Oil of New Jersey, William Green and others, that the Standard official voted with the rest to put the man back on the job, paying him for the time out, because the discharge was in violation of the code. Reed further stated that the Standard official said publicly that he believed in the NRA, in the NIRA and Section 7a, and in the codes, so that no Standard employee need fear to make use of his right to join the union.

Thompason, of the Long Beach local of the Oil Workers, then spoke. He told the men that the initiation fee was five dollars, monthly dues two dollars if employed and fifty cents if unemployed, and that $300 insurance was included. The fifty cents, he said, for unemployed just pays the insurance, but that the member was in good standing all the time.

The next speaker was Jimmie Dunn of the Boilermakers Union 82. He said that Dunn and Joe Reed has an interview with Hiram Johnson recently and that Johnson said that all big business was trying to defeat the NRA and that he would have an interview with Roosevelt before Christmas and would see what could be done about it.

All of these speakers urged the men to join the union in order to protect their future and to safeguard their standards of living.

The chairman (Coulter) then read the provisions of the NIRA applying to labor's right to organize and bargain collectively. He read the oil code showing that the minimum wage was 52 cents per hour, then stated that the union officials were getting impatient with the oil companies who, he said, are chiseling by paying $2.00 per day in cash and the balance in stock. He stated that the minimum wage and maximum hour legislation now in effect can all be traced to union agitation and that if it had not been for the unions none of this protective legislation would ever have been enacted. He said that the only reason Standard pays a couple of cents an hour more than other companies is that this may keep the men from organizing.

Coulter asked all who were in favor of organizing to raise their hands. About 25 did so. He then asked those who did not raise their hands to state their objections. Only one man stood up. He asked, if a little group would have a grievance and strike would all the members have to go out on strike. Coulter said that no officer could call a strike, that it would have to be voted on by the members. He then said that his group would be in the minority, and might have to strike only to help the majority. Coulter replied that in 1921 the Standard men were not called out because that company was paying the union scale. The questioner then said: "Well, what's the use of joining the union, then, and have to pay two bucks a month?" This was explained at some length by Coulter, who said that the unions' pressure on other companies was what made the Standard pay higher wages and that no one should take the advantage of that situation without helping to bear the load. Coulter said that President Wilson asked the men to join the army and fight for democracy, but that Roosevelt was only asking them to organize for democracy, and that he was urging and requesting them to do so for their own and the country's interest. Coulter stated that now a man may get a small pension if he stays with a company long enough, but that if the unions get 30 million members, old age pensions will be put in and there will be no doubt about getting the money.

Fred Phillips, organizer, was supposed to be present but could not on account of illness. Fremming, international president, will be in Long Beach during the week and that two meetings will be held during the holidays. These meetings will be open and the men at this meeting were urged to be present. He said that some of those present might fear to join the union at the meeting, but that they could come to him at any time, or he would see them at their homes or send an organizer. He said that he knew that they were interested as so many had written to him and telephone him about organizing. Several men decided to wait until the first of January, as the initiation fee pays the first month's dues.

After the meeting there was considerable discussion. Agent talked to four men who said they would join the union right after the first of January. B. L. Smith has been working in that section for some time, and after the meeting he told Coulter that there need be no worry, that he had definite assurances that there would be a group organized shortly and that it would go over big after the holidays especially.

Smith told Agent that he goes around dressed as an oil worker so that he can talk to the men without arousing the suspicion of any of the bosses and without causing worry to the men themselves.

There was no great demand that the men join the union at this particular time and no application blanks were passed out. Evidently the statement by Coulter to Agent that organizing among oil workers generally was proceeding better by private solicitation combined by a public meeting such as this one at strategic intervals.

Agent was made very welcome, and responded to inquiries by saying that he had been helping the unions in other fields. Smith asked Agent if he could spend some days with him in the field and Agent replied that he would let him know soon.

Salary _____ $10. 00
Expenses _____ 1. 50

Total _____ $11. 50

EXHIBIT 10231

JANUARY 13, 1934.

[Confidential Report]

It does not look well for Agent to attend only the union meetings in El Segundo and not appear elsewhere, so yesterday afternoon Agent drove to Long Beach and hand a conference with Coulter, Smith and others, as an excuse to get invited to the meeting of last night. Coulter told Agent that the union was having no meeting at El Segundo, but that the meeting for last night was a company employee association meeting. Coulter also stated that he had arranged for a man to go to the association meeting, that this man is a liberal and sympathetic to the union cause, and that this man would attempt to counteract any pro-company statements that night be made at the meeting.

Evidently the man succeeded in getting into the meeting, as one speaker (see below) gave a strong union talk. These company association meetings should be guarded more efficiently so that no one but company employees can get in.

About 125 men attended the meeting of the Standard Employees of California at El Segundo last night. The chairman was a man named Wyman, who did all the talking except for remarks from the floor. Headquarters of the association, Wyman stated, are in San Francisco. He said he had been going the rounds for the past week and that he had visited Taft, Kettleman Hills and Richmond. He said they had quite a membership in Taft and that Kettleman Hills was also organized, but that at Richmond the men did not want to have anything to do with a union and did not even want to hear them speak about it.

Wyman stated that the association was not affiliated with the A. F. of L. or any other union, that they did not want a union and therefore had decided to call the organization an association. He said that many of the men were of the opinion that the A. F. of L. had sold out the interests of the men on many occasions. He also stated that Standard had been one of the first companies to sign up with the N. R. A., and that this company was even now paying the men more than the Code calls for. Nevertheless, he stated, the government wanted the employees to organize and that it was their duty to do so. One of the men stood up at this point and asked the chairman what the men were going to get by belonging to the Association. The chairman answered that the Association was formed for the purpose of advancing the social intercourse of all the employees, to form a grievance committee and committees of appeal which would present any grievances or complaints to the heads of the organization in San Francisco, and then, if the heads saw fit, they would present these petitions to the company and see if they could get them met. The question came up regarding what would happen if something very bad for the men should come up. The chairman stated that they would submit the problem first of all to their executive committee which would consist of a president, a first and a second and a third vice-president, and a secretary-treasurer. This committee would consider the matter and, if in their judgment the grievance was important, they would petition the company to adjust the same. The questioner did not seem to be satisfied with the answer but said nothing more.

Then a young fellow, short, blond, might be a Finlander, stood up. He said he could tell them what could be done about a real grievance. He told them about the N. R. A. provisions for organizing labor, and that they could organize or join a real union, instead of a company association, and were invited by the government to do so, that real unions had the backing of the government but company associations did not. He said it was true that the company was paying more than the union scale of wages and more than the Code provided for, but that was possibly because the company does not want the men to join any unions so that, later on, the company could cut wages and do almost anything else they wanted to do without hindrance from a real union of the employees. He said that he did not want a strike any more than anyone else, but that the N. R. A. had made it unlawful to strike anyhow. He then went on to say that the government had provided a way to settle disputes by setting up the Regional Labor Boards, which would arbitrate any disputes between employers and employees. He said that he thought that they should turn their group into a real union and not leave it be one which would have to petition the company officials to do something for them. He said that it was a time in the country's history right now when organized labor is not only protected by the government, but all labor is encouraged by the government to organize and the government would insure labor a square deal. (This is undoubtedly the man Coulter sent to the meeting, but Agent does not know who he is and could not contact him after the meeting.)

The chairman then proceeded to talk again on the company association, but the last speaker had received the biggest applause of the evening, and the men were considerably agitated. They insisted that the organization send to the Regional Labor Board headquarters in Los Angeles for all information on the subject of union organization and rights of labor under the N. R. A.

The Standard Employees' Association of California has units in El Segundo, Huntington Beach, Inglewood, Torrance, Kettleman Hills, Santa Fe Springs, Bakersfield and Taft, and they are trying to get the Richmond men to join them but have had little success so far. The dues are to be $1.25 per year. Officers will hold office for one year each, with terms interlocking every six months; that is, the President and secretary-treasurer's terms will overlap the terms of the three vice-presidents every six months. They are to meet not less than four times a year as units, and twice a year in general meetings.

Agent heard considerable talk among the men after the meeting in which they expressed their favorable opinion of the union speaker and of joining a union instead of the company association.

Agent also learned that the by-laws of the association call for a meeting one week before each semi-annual meeting for the purpose of nominating officers. The meeting ran for about three hours, being adjourned at 10:30 P. M.

While at Coulter's office, Agent say a copy of a letter written to a union member in Oakland in which Coulter stated that the wages for skilled classifications of labor had not been set by the Oil Code, and that the only wage so far in the Code is 52 cents per hour for common labor. He also stated in this letter that a committee has been appointed to formulate the proper classifications and arrange for differing rates of pay.

STATEMENT

Jan. 5th meeting—salary	$10. 00
" " " —expense	1. 50
Jan. 12th meeting—salary	10. 00
" " " —expense*	3. 50
Total	$25. 00

*Includes trip to Long Beach and dinner, as well as to El Segundo.

EXHIBIT 10232

STATEMENT

Account: HARBOR JOB—AGENTS 10 AND 20:

Investigation I. L. A. Strike Acts.		
From April 3rd to april 14th, Total 7 days @ 17.50		$122. 50
Mileage to Harbor Dist from L. A. & Return—250 miles @ 5¢		12. 50
L. A. to San Francisco & Return		35. 00
Room & Meals San Francisco		8. 00
Total		$178. 00

First report dated April 3rd, last one dated April 13th, Reports covered all activities and information received during period of investigation.

AGENTS 10 & 20.

EXHIBIT 10233

STATEMENT

Account Harbor Job.   Agents 10 and 20:

Salary, April 3rd to 14th, 10 days @ $17.50	$175. 00
Expenses:	
Mileage to Harbor District from L. A. and return, 300 mi. @ 5¢	15. 00
L. A. to San Francisco and Return, 900 mi. @ 5¢	45. 00
Lunches with union leaders in Harbor District	2. 50

Handwritten:)   17. 50
$$\times\ 7$$

122. 50

Room in San Francisco	3. 00
Meals on Frisco trip, 2 days	5. 00
	$245. 50

(Handwritten:)   2. 50
$$\times\ 5$$

12. 50

First report dated April 3rd, last one dated April 13th.   Reports covered all activities and information received during full 10 days.
(Handwritten)

STATEMENT

Account—Investigate—ILA Strikebreakers Agents—10 and 20—Period—April 3rd to 14th	178. 00
Total—7 days @ $17.50	$122. 50
Expenses Mileage to Harbor Dist. fr. Return—250—Miles @ 5¢	12. 50
L. A. to San Francisco	35. 00
Room & Meals—San Francisco	8. 00

EXHIBIT 10234

Meals	$5. 15
51 Gallons Gasoline	7. 14
Oil	. 50
Total	$12. 79

To these actual expenses add:

Room in San Diego	$3. 00

Something for my time.
Something for donations.
Something for cultivation.

Exhibit 10235

[Confidential]

November 17, 1930.

Major A. T. Slaten,
   318 West First Street, Los Angeles, California.

My Dear Slaton: Last Friday, my friend Lieutenant Molloy of the San Francisco Detective Bureau, introduced me to a Mr. M. (or W) B. Rillin, of Los Angeles, as a valuable source of information on communist matters for the West Coast. I was given to understand that Rillin, while a member of the Communist Party and holding a high position in it, is actually working against it from patriotic motives and for some time has been working under cover with Lieutenant Hynes of your bureau.

Rillin is apparently well informed on Communist matters and promised to let me read the basis of testimony before the Fish Committee during its recent hearing in Los Angeles. He also engaged to furnish me lists of addresses of Communist headquarters in the west, as well as names of leaders, etc. While I listened to everything Rillin told me, I did not in any way commit myself until I was assured that he was a proper person to deal with—also, I did not want to appear in the light of crossing wires with your department or Hynes.

Will you be kind enough to drop me a note as to Rillin's standing, status and reliability. If he or his connection with Hynes' work is not known to you, it might be well to so make your inquiry with care, even with respect to Hynes, who may have good reasons for keeping Rillin's identity and connection with his department a secret, or may object to Rillin having revealed himself to Lieutenant Molloy or me.

As you probably noted from the press, the basis for the mission on which you so kindly assisted me, finally cleared up. It was a great relief to me, but again, I want to thank you for what you did.

If you should be up this way any time, be sure and give me a ring.

Best of luck.

F. L. Dengler,
Colonel, G. S. C.

Exhibit 10236

Department of Police, City of Los Angeles, California

R. E. Steckel, *Chief*

Nov. 25, 1930.

Colonel F. L. Dengler,
   Headquarters, Ninth Corps Area, Presidio of San Francisco, California.

Dear Colonel: Enclosed is a report from Lieut. Hynes, covering the subject you requested.

Lieut. Hynes was rather reticent to reveal his contact but I explained to him that I had received a request from G-2 of the General Staff, Washington, D. C.

Trusting this information will be what you desire, and if I come to San Francisco, will surely look you up.

Everything here is O. K.

Respectfully,

Alfred T. Slaten,   (Signed)
(Alfred T. Slaten),
Major, M. I. Reserves.

ATS:JL
ENC. 1

EXHIBIT 10237

DEPARTMENT OF POLICE, CITY OF LOS ANGELES, CALIFORNIA

R. E. STECKEL, *Chief*

[Confidential]

NOVEMBER 24, 1930.

Subject: Mr. S. Rellin, Confidential Informant.

ALFRED T. SLATEN,
Inspector of Detectives, Los Angeles Police Dept., Los Angeles, Calif.

SIR: Reference is had to our conversation of recent date relative to the above named subject, Mr. S. Rellin.

The above is an assumed name, adopted along with various other names, for the obvious reason of covering and protecting his identity.

I have known him intimately and favorably for the past eight years or more and I am well acquainted with his capabilities, record and past history.

Mr. Rellin is well educated, extremely intelligent and bears a reputation of high standing in the community.

He is a family man and his wife and children, as well as himself, are very prominent in club and musical circles. Mr. Rellin is moderately wealthy, being worth probably $100,000.

For a number of years he acted in the capacity as a special, confidential, under cover operative for the U. S. Department of Justice. He secured membership in the various treasonable and seditious organizations and groups which the Government had under its surveillance, including the Communist Party of America (underground section), the I. W. W., several anarchist groups, and various liberal and "pink" sympathetic organizations and groups. He secured credentials as delegate to various national conventions of such organizations, which he attended and covered for the Department of Justice, and also was instrumental in placing other under cover informants or operatives in key positions of these various organizations and groups.

Mr. Rellin is well informed as to the various schools and factions of radicalism and in labor circles and as to the activities of various radical political groups and the various labor organizations and has always had the most valuable and reliable contacts in questioned organizations and groups, so that his information has been found to be reliable and of great value to the authorities.

He had worked with and has supplied exceedingly valuable data to federal, state, county and municipal authorities. He has also been very intimately connected with several nationwide business organizations and groups.

His work is very high grade, and while he has been motivated by patriotism and general good, he usually receives a suitable recompense for his time and efforts.

You will understand that for his protection, and the protection of his family, his business, and for the continued maintenance of his contacts and sources of information, it is impossible to reveal his true identity and, therefore, his cover must be preserved inviolate.

Those inquiring may be assured that he is one of the most intelligent, best informed and reliable under cover contacts in the West and has the full confidence of those authorities and businessmen with whom he has come in contact.

In view of the fact that I have heretofore in confidence pledged myself not to reveal the true name and identity of Mr. Rellin, and as such has been my unalterable policy in dealing with under cover operatives and informants, I feel that I would be violating such confidence in revealing his true name. However, I am confident, knowing the source of your inquiry, that Mr. Rellin would not hesitate to furnish the inquirers personally and confidentially with such data.

Yours very truly,

WILLIAM F. HYNES   (Signed)
(William F. Hynes),
Acting Capt. of Dets., L. A. P. D.,
Commanding Intelligence Bureau.

WFH:F

EXHIBIT 10238

Los Angeles Police Department

Office of In. Bu. Metro. Divn.

JULY 20, 1934.

[Memo.]

Chief Hutchings of El Segundo Police Dept. came in and said he wanted all information possible on any Reds or agitators who might be operating in his district, expecially pertaining to any nuclei or fraction within the El Segundo Refinery of the Standard Oil Co. Said this refinery has some what over a thousand people employed, this is merely a precautionary measure of inquiry to offer due warning to the officials of the Standard Oil Co. at El Segundo, they have no trouble brewing that they know of. H. C. Hanna is mgr. Standard Oil El Segundo.

(In pencil:)

R. C. Goodrich, Red agitator formerly active distributing Red Leaflets.
Mark Beales   "   "   "   "   "   "   "

F   Also recently opened in El Segundo is the NORTHROP CORP. subsidiary of Douglas Aircraft Corp. producing planes at El Segundo, mostly for the government, with about a thousand men on the rolls. W. K. Jay, mgr. of Northrop Corp. also complained to Chief Hutchings that he believed there were agitators within his plants and wants advise and data.

EXHIBIT 10239

[Mailed June 9, 1936 from Bakersfield]

H. C. Loftis, Identification Bureau

SHERIFF, OFFICE, BAKERSFIELD, CALIF.

Lieut. LUKE LANE,
  Intell. Bureau. L. A. Police Dept.

DEAR MR. LANE: Following men working in the Oil fields Tom. Paterson, Paul Moore. A. E. Turke, George Vitman, Herbert Leach, Geo. Rush, C. C. Dunway, P. H. Hinson, A. W. Beaty, Geo. Miller, H. C. Rodney, Burr Bateman, L. W. Overbury, Robert E. Jackson.

Sells in the Richfield and Shell Oil Cos.

Sincerely Yours.

H. C. LOFTIS.

B. TEAMSTERS UNION

EXHIBIT 10240

[Confidential Report]

JANUARY 14, 1934.

*Complimentary
by request of
Captain Hynes*

LAUNDRY WAGON DRIVERS' UNION

This organization is a part of the International Brotherhood of Teamsters, Chauffeurs, Stablemen and Helpers of America, and is affiliated with the American Federation of Labor. It is also represented in the local Central Labor Council and in the Joint Council of the International referred to above.

This Joint Council is composed of 15 organizations, subordinate to the International, as follows: Milk Wagon Drivers, Taxi Drivers, Ice Wagon Drivers, Bakery Drivers, Oil Tank Drivers, Retail Delivery Drivers, Laundry Drivers, Beer Drivers, Municipal Drivers, Teamsters and Truck Drivers, Van, Storage & Furniture Drivers and Chauffeurs, Building Material and Dump Truck Drivers, Studio Transportation Drivers, Dairy Workers, and another local in Long Beach for the Milk Wagon Drivers. S. P Hesse of 854 Hilldale Avenue in West Hollywood is President and Joe Beets is Secretary of this Joint Council. Hesse is also business manager of the Laundry Drivers Union 322.   This places Hesse in an excellent position, of which he is well aware, to swing the entire list of organizations behind the Laundry Drivers in any dispute, boycott or strike.   In fact, both Hesse and Beets have told Agent more than once of late that they believed the time was not far distant when they would "tie up the whole town with a Teamsters' strike."

Beets is one of the most trusted and closest of advisers from the entire union organization in California of Allan M. Wilson, secretary of the fast growing Friends of Organized Labor.

A meeting of this union was held Friday evening, January 12th, at Musicians' Hall, 1417 Georgia Street.   Approximately 125 persons were present, representing practically all of the laundries in this area.   P. A. Coupe, President acted as chairman.   Almost the first remark made was by Hesse who, holding a paper in his uplifted hand, cried: "We've got our first contract signed—Pico Johnson Hand Laundry!   This laundry is now 100 percent union.   Negotiations are on with several others and we'll have them soon."

Speakers during the evening were Judge Thomas P. White, Tony Entenza (labor attorney for Packing House Workers and Amalgamated Street Railway Employees) and O. J. Hyans (assistant secretary of the Central Labor Council). Otto J. Emme, former business agent of the Painters' Union, accompanied Judge White.

Judge White spoke on the historical development of neighborly attitudes; stated that of over 2,000 criminals passing through his court; only 11 percent were members of organized labor and the other 89 percent believed in rugged individualism; urged organization both for selfish interests and in the interests of the country.

Hyans said, "The first thing I'm going to talk about is the milk strike.   I'm not going to say anything for or against it, but I'll tell you this: the milk producers had a chance to deal with a legitimate union and they wouldn't do it, and now they're getting just what is coming to them.   Those fellows had to work for from $10 to $30 a month and found—when you could find it, and then it wasn't fit to eat—and for 14 hours a day."   He then urged organization, stating that if the drivers would organize they would get results.

Tony Entenza received the most applause, the audience seeming to go wild about him and his talk.   He said that the government was asking labor to organize and was standing behind the workers; that government was going into business in order to save business; that if any company would not let its men organize, the government would refuse to let them do business very soon.   He also said that the company always overcharged on every statement handed to a driver, and that no one in the hall could deny it.   He urged them all to join the union.

The men have all been assured that those in arrears on dues, can become reinstated in good standing by paying only the January dues.

Considerable activity in a business way was going on before, during and after the meeting.   It seemed to Agent that fully 90 per cent of those present either paid dues or initiation fees.

Some of the evening was taken up by songs, entertainment and music.   It was announced that on the meeting of January 26th the principal speaker would be Allan M. Wilson, national executive secretary of the Friends of Organized Labor.

The following information was obtained at a meeting of the Executive committee of the Joint Council held Saturday, January 13th; Circulars will be distributed to all Laundry Drivers to insure a big attendance at the next meeting; that they intend to lay plans to have a piece of pro-union literature in every home and business house in the city; that when a strike is called, and they want to call one just as soon as they see the time is ripe, they do not want to call just the laundry drivers or just the bakery drivers or just some other union, but that several of the drivers' unions, or all of them, will strike at once and cripple the city so badly that they will win the strike within a few hours or days.

Agent has known Hesse for a number of years, and is intimately acquainted with Beets, so that he is admitted to these executive meetings where the real plans are discussed and adopted.   Little news is given out at meetings, as they know that the companies have men in these meetings to report them.   Therefore, information coming from Agent and secured in private talks with union officials or in conferences must be handled judiciously in order to keep the channel of information from being closed.

Beets is very militant and quite radical in his beliefs.   He wants to pull a strike as soon as possible.   His plan, and the plan of the Joint Council, is to get organized in a plant to some extent, get the Regional Labor Board to force a vote on union representation, then make demands and, if they are not met promptly, call a strike.

One of the principal matters for discussion at the meeting of the Organizing Committee of the Central Labor Council to be held shortly will be the organizing of the laundry workers and securing the cooperative effort of all union men to that end.

EXHIBIT 10241

LOS ANGELES POLICE DEPARTMENT

Office of In. Bu. Metro. Divn.

AUG. 31, 1934   4.15 p. m.

Memo.   Complaint of Williams Transfer Co. 440 Towne Ave. VA 0432 or VA 1564

Secretary above concern phones in one of their ex-employes causing them considerable trouble, trying to get a strike, talking against them with their customers, etc.

Ask officers to call re this, company will be open tonight working on books
Invest by Vag Squad.
F   COPY METRO. DIVN. request cover.

EXHIBIT 10242

LOS ANGELES POLICE DEPARTMENT

Office of Intelligence Bureau, Metropolitan Division

JUNE 25, 1935

JAMES E. DAVIS,
Chief of Police, City of Los Angeles.

SIR: With reference to the present membership and recruiting drive into the Chauffeurs, Truck Drivers & Helpers Union, especially Local #692, San Pedro and vicinity, a branch of the American Federation of Labor, wish to report as follows:

For some months past, it has been the practise in the harbor district, where the business agent, Mr. Ralph Darling, for Chauffeurs, Truck Drivers & Helpers Union Local #692 is located, to observe various trucks coming from Long Beach, Wilmington, Los Angeles or any city outside of San Pedro, and attempt to have the drivers sign up for a union card into their union in San Pedro so long as they were making deliveries in that location.   The extent of recruiting their membership has been very gratifying to the union, and they feel they have made great headway, and are using various ways and methods of having a non-union driver carry their card, and to paste it on the windshield of truck in plain sight, indicating that the driver is a member of their union.

We have had numerous calls and complaints from various trucking concerns regarding the tactics being used in forcing employes to join the truck drivers union. So far there has not been any violence used against non-union drivers, but they have been threatened and told to get out of San Pedro and not to come back, etc. The following are a few cases of those that have been accosted by officials of the union:

On 5/28/35 Mr. C. H. McGuire of American Contract Carriers, 1412 E. 8th St. MAdison 2481, stated unless the drivers carried union card they were subject to being beaten up, etc.

On 6/11/35 Mr. Moorehouse of Moorehouse Mustard Mills, 1138 San Fernando Road, CA 8683, reports has experienced trouble in the harbor district where he hauls to steamship companies; they have been threatened that their truck will be wrecked if they don't join the union.

On 6/12/35 Mr. H. Levin & Coopers, AN 2111 who have truck going to the harbor, contacting steamship lines; reports union interferring with their drivers in harbor district; trying to force them to sign up with their union.

On 6/24/35 Mr. Pasini, manager of Langendorf Baking Co. 62nd & Western, TW 1101, reports that while his employe was making delivery of bread in San

Pedro on Pacific Ave. he was threatened and told to get out of San Pedro because he did not belong to the union.

On 6/25/35 the Globe Bottling Works, 721 Nord St., CA 11151 (Mr. Abe Kanner, proprietor) complains of emery dust being thrown in their trucks while making deliveries. (This concern made prior complaint on Nov 9/34 regarding the union interferring with their drivers, trying to influence and intimidate them to sign up in the truck drivers union.

Yesterday, after talking to you regarding the Langendorf Bakery driver and his experience in San Pedro, I located last night Mr. Ralph Darling, who is the business agent in San Pedro (office 617 S. Beacon St. phone San Pedro 715) of Local 692, Chauffeurs, Truck Drivers & Helpers Union. He was in a Chevrolet sedan Lic. #2 Y 9 894 and registered to him. He was accompanied by Philip Walter, 3837 Bestwick St. Los Angeles. I questioned him as to the method they were using on approaching these various trucking·concerns and attempting to sign the drivers up with the union. I explained to him we had received a number of complaints as to their threatening attitude, ordering the drivers to take their trucks and leave San Pedro and not return. He stated that at no time had he or any of his associated threatened any individual truck driver, but were trying to persuade the truck drivers to sign up, even though the driver may belong to another local and is a union man, they still insist that he must sign up with them to be able to drive his truck and deliver merchandise in San Pedro.

I then approached Mr. Darling on the subject of the Langendorf Bakery Co. driver on Pacific Street that same day. He stated that they were trying to approach all trucks who did not have the sticker on the windshield indicating they are a union driver from his local within his district, and that he recalled talking to the bakery wagon driver and that he did not threaten him, but did state "If you don't want to join our truck drivers union here, better not come back to San Pedro!" He stated that, "We have a right to organize and we are trying to stay within our right and that at any time someone wanted to make a court issue of their right the best place to decide that was in the courts."

Yesterday morning I received a phone call from Mr. Williams of the Anhauser Brewing Co. whose main office is in Long Beach, who stated that he was experiencing difficult in delivering beer in San Pedro and the Wilmington districts and requesting advice and aid as to how to proceed. He stated that on some day of last week his truck driver had been threatened by officials of the Chauffeurs, Truck Drivers & Helpers Union of San Pedro, and that he was afraid to attempt to make delivery of his products. I instructed him to have the truck loaded with products stop on its way from Long Beach at the Wilmington Sub-Police Station and there would be an escort of three police officers in uniform in a police car detailed to follow the truck to San Pedro and see that it was not molested while making deliveries there. When the truck arrived at its first stop, the proprietor of the place told him, "We are sorry, we cannot use your products any longer, for if we do we will be placed on the unfair list of organized labor!" The driver then proceeded to various other locations to make deliveries and was told the same story. Results were that he did not unload any of his products in San Pedro and was escorted back to city limits of Wilmington towards Long Beach with his full load.

This state of affairs not only applies to any particular trucking concern, and I might state that laundry trucks, wholesale delivery trucks, bakery trucks, milk trucks, and in fact all trucks that make delivery within the harbor district are subject to being intimidated by officials of the union.

Recently, the union has become strong enough, they figure, where they go to the various merchants where a truck unloads any kind of merchandise and if the truck driver is not a union man in their union, they intimidate the merchant by threatening him to an expose of being unfair to organized labor and placing him on the union unfair list. Then, if necessary, they proceed and put out handbills, stickers, etc. "Do not patronize _____ (so and so) as they are unfair to organized labor."

From all indications, the union is attempting to organize all truck drivers so that if there is a coastwise strike this October they feel they will be in a position to stop all cargo moving to and from the docks; that is one reason why they are striving so hard so they will be in complete control of transportation within that area. I am informed that the same procedure is being carried out in the northern part of the state, as well as Seattle and Portland.

Respectfully,

LUKE M. LANE,
Detective Lieut. Commanding, Intelligence Bureau.

L:F

Exhibit 10243

JUNE 26, 1935.

Report of Undercover Operatives

Subject: RALPH DARLING, 617 S. Beacon St., San Pedro.

Checked license number 2Y9 894, Chevrolet Sedan, registered to H. A. McDermott, 1147 Broad Street, Wilmington. Phone WIL 1834, Apartment House. Unable to locate car at this location. Contacted manager of the apartment by phone and asked for Mr. McDermott or a Mr. Darling. The manager hesitated in answering and finally stated that he did not know the men.

Unable to locate Mr. Darling or the car at 617 S. Beacon Street, and phone call to the office brought the information that they did not know where Mr. Darling was but thought that he was out of town.

June 27, 1935.—Staked on the address at 1147 Broad Street, Wilmington, in effort to locate above car, from 6:30 AM to 7:30 AM., then contacted the landlady, who stated that some time ago she remembered seeing mail addressed to a Mr. McDermott, but that he did not live there at present, and that she did not know a Mr. Darling.

We then staked on 617 S. Beacon Street and at 8 AM the office was opened by a young woman described as follows: 5'4" about 115 lbs., Dark hair, long, and tied in knot on back of head.

We secured the number of the office from union card on windshield of a truck, San Pedro 715, phone the office, using the number of card on truck, and asked for Mr. Darling. The office girl informed us that Mr. Darling was in San Diego and would not be back until evening or Friday morning, June 28, 1935.

The Chauffeurs, Truck Drivers and Helpers Union meets each Tuesday evening at CARPENTERS HALL, 361 Ninth Street, San Pedro.

Respectfully submitted.

OPERATORS J–7 AND F–5.

Exhibit 10244

Los Angeles Police Department

Office of Intelligence Bureau Metropolitan Division

JUNE 27, 1935.

Memorandum: For Chief DAVIS.

With reference to the present membership and recruiting drive into the Chauffears, Truck Drivers & Helpers Union, especially Local #692, San Pedro and vicinity, a branch of the American Federation of Labor, wish to report as follows:

For some months past, it has been the practice in the harbor district, where the business agent, Mr. Ralph Darling, for the Chauffeurs, Truck Drivers & Helpers Union Local #692 is located, to observe various trucks coming from Long Beach, Wilmington, Los Angeles or any city outside of San Pedro, and attempt to have the drivers sign up for a union card into their union in San Pedro so long as they were making deliveries in that location. The extent of recruiting their membership has been very gratifying to the union, and they feel they have made great headway, and are using various ways and methods of having a non-union driver carry their card, and to paste it on the windshield of truck in plain sight, indicating that the driver is a member of their union.

We have had numerous calls and complaints from various trucking concerns regarding the tactics being used in forcing employees to join the truck drivers union. So far there has been no physical violence used against non-union drivers, but they have been threatened and intimidated and told to get out of San Pedro and not to come back, etc.

Mr. Williams, the superintendent of branch of the Anhauser Brewing Co. in Long Beach, who was experiencing difficulty in delivering beer in San Pedro and Wilmington district recently requested advice and aid as to how to proceed. He stated that on some day of last week his truck driver had been threatened by officials of the Chauffeurs, Truck Drivers & Helpers Union of San Pedro, and that he was afraid to attempt to make delivery of his products. I instructed him to have the truck loaded with products stop on its way from Long Beach at the Wilmington Sub-Police Station and there would be an escort of three police officers in uniform in a police car detailed to follow the truck to San Pedro and see that it was not molested while making deliveries there. When the truck arrived at its first stop, the proprietor of the place told him: "We are sorry, we cannot use your products any longer, for if we do we will be placed on the unfair list of organized labor and will be boycotted." The driver then proceeded to various other locations to make deliveries and was told the same story.

Results were that the driver did not unload any of his products in San Pedro and was escorted back to city limits of Wilmington towards Long Beach with his full load.

The complaint outlined above is similar to several other firms that are making deliveries in the San Pedro district regardless of the nature of the merchandise being delivered. The Union has tried to have the merchants who are handling the Langendorf Bakery Co. products discontinue the use of same; and there are other similar cases.

LUKE LANE, Intelligence Bureau.

L:F

EXHIBIT 10245

[Intra-Departmental Correspondence]

LOS ANGELES POLICE DEPARTMENT
Office of Intelligence Bureau

JULY 3, 1935.

Memo for Lt. WELLPOTT:

See file for truck drivers organization in San Pedro.

Mr. Fysh of the M & M Association is getting data on complaints of trucking companies that have had trouble in the Harbor District and will get firms names and truck license numbers, days of delivery to San Pedro, kind of merchandise delivering and locations of delivery in San Pedro.

Mr. Fysh and myself interviewed Mr. Newton Kendall of the City Prosecutors office and were advised to proceed wherein any union men interfere with the trucks, that is stopping them on the streets or highways while in motion and to arrest and book under section 147 of the State Motor Vehicle Act.

If the driver is already stopped at the curb and is unloading his products and is approached by members of the union or anyone else and threatened and any profane language is used within the presence of women or children to arrest and book under section 415 of the Penal Code (Disturbing the Peace).

It is thought the best method that we can operate is to assign two officers from this bureau in a car and supply them with information that will be supplied by Mr. Fysh and have them the San Pedro District so they may be able to observe the various locations that will be listed and the truck numbers. If any interference is observed by anyone stopping trucks or talking to truck drivers while making deliveries they should ascertain all information possible and if they have a case make the arrest and it is requested that the cases of arrests be handled here in Los Angeles through Mr. Kendall in securing complaints. *Do not book in San Pedro.*

Keep in touch with Mr. Fysh of the M & M Association as he in close touch with members of the Truck Owners Association.

LUKE LANE.

EXHIBIT 10246

JULY 5, 1935

REPORT OF UNDERCOVER OPERATIVES

Subject: RALPH DARLING et al, 617 Beacon Street, San Pedro.

The drivers of the following described cars called at the office at 617 Beacon Street during the day;

3N9 633, Chevrolet 27 Sedan, Sam Wimmer, 663 W. 7th St., San Pedro.
7Y8 748 Ford 1930 Coupe, E. C. Doinry, 347 Seaside, Terminal Island.
PCJ 1–465 Arden Milk Co.
2Y7 787 Harbor Laundry Company.

At 11:10 AM a man left this office and went to 111 7th Street, Room 10, whom we later found to be James T. Shrive, Customs broker and representative of the Mexican Fisheries, of that address.

In addition to the above the drivers of the following two cars also called at the office during the afternoon;

9Y9 371 33 Chevrolet Sedan, Arthur B. Harmon, 55 Pacific Ave, Highland.

1Y1 439 34 Dodge Coupe, Michael Brothers Trucking Co, 1389 Gladys Ave, Long Beach.

Respectfully

OPERATOR J–7 ET AL.

EXHIBIT 10247

JULY 6, 1935.

REPORT OF UNDERCOVER OPERATIVES

Subject: RALPH DARLING et al, 617 Beacon Street, San Pedro.

Darling was not around the office or was not seen in San Pedro July 5th and 6th. His car was left parked in front of his residence 203 W. 2nd St, during that period of time.

A young man described as. American. 32–35 5'9 150# Light Tan jacket, reddish brown pants and grey cap, has been working with Kelly for the past two days. Have been unable to ascertain his name.

Barwell went to the Union Oil Docks, Berth 150 in company with two men who were in a Essex Coach, License 4Y5 940, registered to W. W. Miller, 2433 Cerritos Ave, Long Beach.

Drivers of the following cars and trucks called at the office at 617 Beacon Street during the day;

PCK 2–559	Polly Ann Bakery.
PCJ 4–084	Coca Cola Company
PCK 3–280	Acmer Beer Dist.
PCJ 725	Budweiser Beer, 4842 Long Beach Avenue.
2Y7 787	Harbor Laundry Co, (Called there on 5th also)
4V3 176	29 Chev Cpe, Gil A. Leano, Gen'l Del Terminal Island.
2Y1 88	34 Dodge Express, San Pedro Wholesale Provision Co, 108 1st St., San Pedro.
1Y9 324	33 Ford Sedan, Harvey Holmsley, 2114 South Street, Long Beach.

Respectfully,

OPERATORS J–7 AND F–5.

EXHIBIT 10248

JULY 8, 1935.

REPORT OF UNDERCOVER OPERATIVES

Subject: RALPH DARLING, 617 Beacon St, San Pedro.

Drivers of the following trucks and cars, called at the office at 617 Beacon Street, during the day.

PCK 2532	Union Ice Co.
4V1 742	Perfection Bread
6Y5 080	Seven-Up Pop Co.
PCB 5928	Globe Beer
PCR 4180	Mikes Transfer
PCK 4386	Meir Beer
PCM 7095	Lucky Lager Beer
PCK 2604	Eckerts Beer
PCK 2590	Harbor Supply Co.
PCB 2045	Tidor Wholesale Co
PCK 1289	Standard Ice Co.

Darling did not come to the office this date. Kelly apparently in charge. Barwell hung around the corner of 5th and Beacon, spending most of his time in the various beer parlors near that intersection.

Respectfully,

OPERATORS F–5 AND J–7.

EXHIBIT 10249

DECEMBER 7, 1935.

[Confidential Report]

Subject: RALPH DARLING etal, San Pedro.

December 5, 1935.—Kelly arrived at the office at 11:45AM and at 12:35PM, he and a man named Nelson, 1108 9th Ave., Long Beach, drove in Kelly's car to 225 B E. 1st St., Long Beach, office of the Chauffeurs and Truck Drivers Union Local #692. At 2:50PM, Kelly returned to the office alone, and a few minutes later, Chester L. Morris arrived at the office with Nelson. Morris left the office at 4:10PM.

At 4:18PM, a woman driving a Chevrolet Sedan, 9T4 802, stopped at the office and Nelson got in the car with her and left. This car is registered to Bessie O. Nelson, 1108 9th Avenue Long Beach.

At 4:45PM a man named Albert Getty, 244 N Bandini St. San Pedro came to the office in a Chevrolet Sedan, South Dakota License 71948. He left at 5:40PM.

At 4:50PM Darling arrived at the office. He had not been there before, this date.

December 6, 1935.—Kelly arrived at the office at 10:40AM and at 11:30AM, Albert Getty came to the office and remained until 12:25. At 11:30AM Nelson arrived at the office and remained around the office practically all day in company with Kelly. At 1:18PM Phillip Watler, 3837 Bestwick Avenue came to the office and he remained until 3:20PM.

Darling came to the office at 1:30PM and at 2:20PM, Getty returned to the office and spent the balance of the day in company with Kelly and Darling.

December 7, 1935.—Darling arrived at the office at 10:50AM. At 11:45AM, driver of Willys Sedan, License 1Y 238 entered the office. This car registered to Charles H. Parker 25 Park Avenue Long Beach. At 12Noon Chadeks wife came to the office and left there in company with a grey haired woman an employee of Darling. At 12:12PM Kelly arrive at the office.

At 12:15PM two men arrived in a Willys Sedan, Lic 7T8 274 registered to James O. Glendenning 1435 Beacon, San Pedro, left at 12:55PM.

At 12:40PM three men arrived in a Ford Coupe, License 5Y2 090, registered to Alice McTully, 1427 E. "L" Street, Wilmington, left at 1PM.

At 1PM Getty came to the office. At 2:30PM, Howard C. Williams arrived at the office.

The afternoon was spent in checking the driver of the Car South Dakota License 71948. Found that the mans name is Albert Getty, 244 N/ Bandini, San Pedro.

J–7 ET AL.

EXHIBIT 10250

DECEMBER 10, 1935.

[Confidential Report]

Subject: RALPH DARLING, etal, San Pedro.

December 9, 1935.—Kelly arrived at the office at 10:25AM, driving a new 1936 model Ford Coach, no license plates. He was accompanied by man named Nelson who lives at 1108 9th Avenue, Long Beach. At 11:15AM, Kelly and Nelso drove to the Mirimar Hotel, Kelly's residence, returning to the office at 11:45AM.

At 11:15AM two men arrived at the office in a 28 Ford Sedan, License 9F8 588, registered to John AMARAL, Niles Road, Hayward Calif. The two men talked to Kelly until 12:15PM.

At 2:10PM, the driver of a 28 Chrysler Sedan, License 6X6 791, registered to F. KIALMASKY, 979 W 3rd St., San Pedro, entered the office and remained until 2:30PM.

At 2:10PM Howard C. Williams arrived at the office, and talked to Kelly until 3:05PM.

Kelly remained in and around the office the rest of the day. NELSON remained with him until 3:40PM when he left on foot. Darling did not appear at the office this date and we were unable to find where he was.

December 10, 1935.—Kelly arrived at the office at 11:15AM. At 12:30PM Howard C. Williams arrived at the office and remained until 2PM. At 12:55PM, NELSON came to the office in company with another man, name unknown, dressed in a grey suit and grey hat. This man has been at the office before and generally wears a white pull over sweater, and is always on foot.

At 1:10PM, Mrs. J. J. CHADEK arrived at the office, and left in company with grey haired woman employed by Darling. The woman returned to the office in one half hour, alone.

At 1:15PM, Albert GETTY, 244 Bandini St. called at the office and remained one hour.

At 2:40PM man driving a car License 8M 143, parked in front of the office and Kelly talked to him for fifteen minutes. This car is registered to J.F. Bigley, 157 E. 71st St, Los Angeles.

At 3:15PM, Darling arrived at the office. This is his first appearance there this week. At 3:30PM, Kelly left driving direct to his hotel. Darling remained at the office the rest of the day and Nelson remained with him.

J–7 ET AL.

EXHIBIT 10251

DECEMBER 17, 1935.

[Confidential Report]

Subject: RALPH DARLING etal, San Pedro.

December 11, 1935.—At 12:30 P. M., Howard C. Williams of 3198 Sanborn Street, L. A. entered the office. This man has been picketing at Smiths Market at 6th and Pacific Ave., for several days. Kelly and Darling have visited him while he was picketing at the market.

At 1·15 P. M., Darling entered the office accompanied by two men who came with Darling in his car.

At 3:00 P. M., Harold Ross, 645 W. 11th St., entered the office and remained until 3:15 P. M.

At 3:30 P. M., Darling and the two men left and drive to the E. K. Wood Lumber Co., Darling entered the office and the two men remained in the car. Darling came out at 3:45 P. M. and they then drove to 6th and Pacific and looked around Smiths market. They then drove to the cookery cafe, 325 W. 7th Street. They looked the place over for two minutes. The Cookery Cafe has been picketed recently. Darling entered the cafe and remained only a minute. He came out and the three drove to 1st Street Landing and boarded a ferry for Terminal Island.

At 4:30 P. M., Howard C. Williams left the office. Kelly did not come to the office during the day.

December 12, 1935.—At 8:45 A. M., observed Darling in his car on the highway between San Pedro and Wilmington. He drove to the Brass Rail Club at Broad and C Streets, Wilmington leaving there at 9:50 A. M., and drove to a parking lot south of the Walker Auditorium at 730 S. Grand, arriving at 10:45 A. M. and went to room 32 in the Walker Auditorium Building, where he remained until 11:20 A. M. This office is headquarters for a Teamsters, Truckers and Chauffeurs Union. Darling then drove to 6th and Spring in Los Angeles, where he was lost in traffic. Operators returned to San Pedro. At 2 P. M., Williams came to the office and remained the balance of the afternoon.

December 13, 1935.—Kelly arrived at the office 10:45 A. M. Darling arrived at the office at 11:15 A. M. At 11:30 A. M. driver of Chevrolet Sedan, License 7Y3 200, registered to Homer P. REDFORD, entered the office. At 11:35 A. M., driver of 32 Ford Coupe, License 2M9 758, registered to Santa Fe Trail Stages Inc. entered the office and talked to Kelly and Darling until 11:55 A. M. At 11:40 A. M. 2 men entered the office and talked to Kelly and Darling until 12:05 P. M., when Darling left with the two men and walked to the Light House Buffet, at 5th and Beacon and they returned to the office 12:35 P. M. At 1:30 P. M. the two men left and drove away in the Chevrolet registered to Homer P. Redford.

At 12:30 P. M., the driver of Chevrolet Landua Sedan, License 9N4–086 talked to Kelly and Darling at the office until 12:50 P. M.   At 1:40 P. M., Kelly left and drove to 525 B "E" 1St Street, Long Beach, headquarters Chauffeurs and Truck Drivers Union #692, returning to the office at 4 P. M.   Kelly and Darling remained around the office the balance of the afternoon.

December 14, 1935.—At 11:30 A. M., Howard C. Williams arrived at the office. At 12:05 P. M., Kelly arrived at the office in his car, he has received new license plates for his car, 1936 Ford Coach, 8X6 132.

At 12:10 P. M., driver of car License 4E6 053 (Not listed in Motor Vehicle) entered the office and talked to Kelly until 12:20 P. M.

At 12:12 P. M., two men, names unknown, entered the office and talked to Kelly.   They left at 12:25 P. M. in a Chevrolet Laundau Sedan, registered to Pearl Bateham, 158 Cedar Ave. Long Beach.   License 5M7 139.

At 12:45 P. M., Howard C. Williams left the office.   At 2:15 P. M., Franics L. Morris, entered the office and remained until 3:20 P. M.

At 3:15 P. M. Williams returned to the office and again left at 4:10 P. M.   Kelly remained at the office the balance of the Day.   Darling was not seen in or around the office this date.

December 16, 1935.—At 10:50 A. M., Kelly arrived at the office, 606 Beacon St, in his car a Ford 8X6 132.

At 11:50 A. M., a woman drove to the office in Darlings car and then drove to 945 W. 1st Street, San Pedro, where she entered the rear duplex on the left.

At 12:05 P. M. A woman thought to be the wife of J. J. Chadek, came to the office for a few minutes.

At 1:35 P. M., Nelson arrived at the office.

At 1:50 P. M., Kelly left the office, returning at 3:05 P. M.

At 4:10 P. M., Howard Williams arrived at the office.

At Smiths market, observed a woman picketing, and a man was also picketing at the Goodyear Service Station at 14th and Pacific.   These two places seem to be the only ones where the pickets are visited by Kelly or Darling.   Darling was was not observed around the office all this date.

OPERATORS J–7 ET AL.

EXHIBIT 10252

DECEMBER 17, 1935.

[Confidential Report]

Subject: RALPH DARLING, etal. San Pedro.

Kelly arrived at 606 Beacon Street at 10:30 A. M.   He was in and out of the office several times during the day going across the street to restaurant and beer parlor.

At 4:30 P. M. a man came out who had been around the office during the entire day.   He went to 16th and Centre Street, Belasco Storage Company where he remained.

At 4:50 P. M., Harold Ross, 645 W. 11th Street, driving a Ford Roadster License 9X9 575, came to the office and remained about 10 minutes.

A Truck License 6V7 378, San Pedro City Transfer has been parked in front of the office for several days, the driver staying inside the office.

Darling did not appear at the office during the day.

Business at the office seemed exceptionally light.   No contacts being made and practically no activity.

December 18, 1935.—Kelly arrived at the office at 10:55 A. M.   At 3:05 P. M. Kelly left and drove to his residence the Miramar Hotel.   At 3:50 P. M. Kelly returned to the office.   He had changed his clothes.   At 3:55 P. M. Kelly left and drove to the office of the Chauffeurs and Truck Drivers Union Local 692, 525 B East 1st Street, Long Beach.

Operators were unable to observe any contacts on this date.   A few people entered the office, but from observations they did not contact Kelly.

Darling did not appear at the office and has not been there for several days.

On Monday December 16, a woman was observed driving Darlings car and she stopped at the office and talked to Kelly.   We learned that this woman was Mrs. George T. Pool, and lives at 947 W. 1st St.

Darling now lives at 1681 W. 251st St. Harbor City.   We observed Darlings car parked in front of this residence today and it is believed that he is sick.

OPERATORS J–7 ET AL.

(In pencil:) "Windup report"

EXHIBIT 10253

1.15.2

DECEMBER 27, 1935.

Mr. C. H. ROBINSON,
  Pres. United Battery Mfg. Co.
    414 So. Ave. 19, Los Angeles, Calif.

DEAR SIR: With reference to your letter of Dec. 14th wherein you set forth you were having difficulty with your truck driver being stopped and intimidated by supposedly union men in the harbor area, please be advised as follows:

This department has been constantly checking on officials of the truck drivers union and have recently put into operation within the San Pedro district a constant patrol of police officers to prevent any stopping or disturbance of trucks loaded with cargo going to or from the San Pedro harbor.

If any more of your trucks are stopped enroute or at the docks by any supposedly union men, please have the driver obtain description of individuals and license number of car used and any other information that would assist us in our program of affording protection to your drivers.

Further suggest that you contact Mr. Fysh of the Merchants & Manufacturers Association here in Los Angeles, as he has considerable data as to the Truck Owners Association and their methods of transporting cargo to and from the harbor district. I feel sure he will be able to enlighten you and perhaps assist you in the future.

Yours very truly,

JAMES E. DAVIS, *Chief of Police.*
By: LUKE M. LANE,
Detective Lieut. Commanding, Intelligence Bureau.

L:F

EXHIBIT 10254

LOS ANGELES POLICE DEPARTMENT

Office of Intelligence Bureau, Metropolitan Division

MARCH 28, 1936.

MEMORANDUM: Re Truck Drivers and Agricultural Workers Union

Threats of serious damage to the spring crops of the Japanese market gardeners in Los Angeles County is contained in warnings to 500 members of the Confederation of Mexican Unions that they will strike by April 1st unless their dedemands for higher wages is met (see attached list of representatives of the union).

The Chauffeurs & Truck Drivers Union Local #208, located at 730 S. Grand Ave., Los Angeles has recently been directed by Ralph Darling, who has been re-assigned from the San Pedro local and placed in charge of Los Angeles County operations. It is their plan to assist in the agricultural workers strike by having union truck drivers not haul produce.

Information is secured that the Truck Drivers Union are laying plans to affect the melon season in Imperial County, as they claim most of the truck drivers are union men who are hauling this produce out of the Valley.

Particular attention is called to one of the delegates of the Chauffers & Truck Drivers Union Local #208 working under Ralph Darling, viz, one: Robt. J. Miller, alias Robt. J. Montague, L. A. #27631-m-2, 1928, wherein later he was sentenced to San Quentin for burglery, San Quentin #46174. This Miller has been very active in organizing the non-union drivers.

(Typewritten note attached:) Received from Lt. James E. Foese L. A. Co. Sheriff's Office copied 3-25-36. (He had rec'd this from L. A. Cham. Com. 3-24-35 from Arthur E. Clark, rm. 442 Cham. Com. phone through Dr. Clements' office, PR 3431.)

EXHIBIT 10255

(RECEIVED FROM MERCHANTS & MFGRS. ASSO. OF L. A. APR. 1936)

UNION ACTIVITY AT THE HARBOR

Fri. March 27, 1936.—Coffee Products of America, salesman P. W. Black warned by H. Waterbury general organizer for Truck Drivers' Union, that if he intends to do business in San Pedro he must hold Truck Drivers' Union card.

Sat. March 28, 1936.—Waterbury threatens Mr. Eastland of Eastland Truck Company on telephone that no scab drivers will be allowed to operate Vegetable Oil Products truck in Harbor. Eastland has taken over all V. O. P. trucks and operating them as Eastland Truck Company.

Mond. March 30, 1936.—Eastland Truck Company driver (non-union) surrounded by Union "beef-gang" in Wilmington. He telephoned Eastland and it so happened Ralph Darling was in Eastland's office when this driver phoned in. Darling phoned Waterbury to pull off the beef-gang and escort the Driver into L. A. for protection's sake.

Tue. March 31, 1936.—Williams Brothers at Norwalk, (Feed, Fuel & Fertilizer business): Two drivers on their way for loads of fertilizer sent back home empty by beef-gang from Wilmington.

Wed. April 1, 1936.—Mr. Phelps, President of California Wholesale Grocery Company not permitted to make delivery on Beacon Street, San Pedro, by Waterbury. Police escort arranged so delivery can be made Friday April 3, 1936.

San Fernando Fruit Growers Exchange trucks stopped from making delivery to ship, upon entering Wilmington.

March 23 to 28th, '36.—One day during the week, West Coast Brewing Company truck between Long Beach and Wilmington near the Coca Cola Plant was run off the road by three cars containing eight men. The driver of the truck was yanked off the truck because he did not have a truck drivers' union card. One car, after the fracas, followed him all the way into 15th and San Pedro Street in L. A. to see that he made no further deliveries.

White Star Soda Works (Japanese) experienced trouble with their Jap driver. In pencil: "File in truck driver's file, San Pedro."

EXHIBIT 10256

[Copy]

CITY OF FRESNO, POLICE DEPARTMENT

APRIL 9, 1937.

JAMES E. DAVIS,
    Chief of Police, Los Angeles, Calif.

DEAR SIR: There has been some industrial trouble here between Unions and the Pacific Freight Lines, of Los Angeles, for the past week and they are sending armed guards thru from Los Angeles to Fresno, and did have them working in Fresno for the first two or three days.

Among others were R. Trousdale, 1343 Wright St., Los Angeles, Calif., Special Police 1074, issued by James E. Davis, Los Angeles, Calif., and Walter Krug, retired Lieutenant of Police, Los Angeles Police Department, Identification card signed by R. C. Combs, Chief of Police.

Are these men in your Department at this time and did you contemplate such activity as their being guards in the employ of the Bodell Industrial Detective Agency of Los Angeles and acting as strike breakers during this strike trouble in this vicinity? As there is liable to be serious trouble, will this jeopardize your bond?

Please let me hear from you.

    Yours truly,

FT–LR

    FRANK TRUAX, *Chief of Police.*

EXHIBIT 10257

[Intra-Departmental Correspondence]

LOS ANGELES POLICE DEPARTMENT

Office of Intelligence Bureau, Metropolitan Division

MAY 11, 1937

1.15.2 (Red #6271–58).

JAMES E. DAVIS,
    Chief of Police, City of Los Angeles.

SIR: With reference to the attached copy of letter from Frank Truax, Chief of Police, Fresno, Cal. dated April 9, 1937, inquiring as to use of armed guards by the Pacific Freight Lines in inter-city service from Los Angeles to Fresno, and mentioning names of two guards as carrying identifications from this department, please be advised:

All guards on such service are *private guards*, employed by the Bodell Detective Agency, which agency is a bona fide licensed detective agency licensed by the Board of Prison Directors, State of California.

The two men mentioned ("R. Trousdale, 1343 Wright St. Los Angeles, Calif. Special Police 1074, issued by James E. Davis, Los Angeles, Calif., and Walter Krug, retired Lieutenant of Police, Los Angeles Police Dept. Identification card signed by R. C. Combs, Chief of Police.") are both *private guards* employed by the Bodell Detective agency, and were assigned to duty on common carriers of the Pacific Freight Lines operating between Los Angeles and Fresno to protect the company's property. It should be emphasized that for a time the company found it necessary to assign private armed guards to their trucks as the unions were sending out carloads of men to interfere with or stop the operation of their carriers.

In connection with retired police officers, I respectfully call your attention to the provision of Section 6 of the Deadly Weapon Act, which specifically provides exceptions for such retired officers.

Men employed as guards on these carriers certainly and definitely do not come within the definition of "strike breakers," but are primarily employed to protect the company's property and employes from injury.

Respectfully,

WILLIAM F. HYNES,
Capt. of Detectives, LAPD,
Commanding Intelligence Bureau.

H:F

EXHIBIT 10258

[Intra-Departmental Correspondence]

LOS ANGELES POLICE DEPARTMENT

Office of Intelligence Bureau, Metropolitan Division

Memorandum: CAPT. HYNES

Re: Expected Strike Call on Arden Farms Co. Distributing Plants, 8 p. m. Wed. May 12-37.

Chief Davis called and sent over to this office Mr. Fred W. Whitaker, executive secy. Dairy Industries, Inc. PR 0129, 417 Chamber of Commerce Bldg. residence phone CR 7631. The Chief is extremely anxious to assist this party in his difficulties; he stated that he had received so much help and cooperation from this party during the recent election and for us not overlook returning full cooperation.

Mr. Whitaker stated that Mr. Dail of the Chauffeurs & Truck Drivers Union Local #208 has served notice it is going to call a strike against the Arden Farms Co. on May 12, Wednesday night, 8 p. m. The two distributing plants that he is concerned with are located at 1918 W. Slauson Ave.; the Arden Dairy Farms Co. Mr. Garrett, night manager; the other is at 103 S. Hamel Dr. or Road; Mr. Ferguson, night manager. These plants are in operation 24 hours per day and will necessitate a 24 hour police detail.

Mr. Whitaker stated that he had been in touch with the M & M Assn. and is arranging for a number of guards from the Bodell Detective Agency and if necessary, they will place a guard on each delivery truck that delivers the milk to the homes.

(103 S. Hamel Drive or Road may possibly be in Beverly Hills; Mr. Whitaker is to call me back re this.)

At each plant there are two gates to cover—the entrance and exit gates.

He does not know at this time whether he wants officers assigned at 8 p. m. tomorrow night, or to have them here on reserve so they may be called by phone in case of picket line starting. However, he will gather more information and will call me tomorrow and discuss the situation further.

LUKE M. LANE.

LL:F

EXHIBIT 10259

[From: 16-Detail sheets general file]

[Intra-Departmental Correspondence]

LOS ANGELES POLICE DEPARTMENT

Office of Intelligence Bureau, Metropolitan Division

APR. 27–38.

Specl. Detail Neutral Thousands, 706 S. Hill St. Room 903, 8 p. m. Wed. Apr. 27, 1938.

Received phone call from Mr. Rittenhouse of The Neutral Thousands that they are holding a meeting of dairy employes tonight and have information A. F. of L. members are coming up to raise trouble; asks police detail to prevent trouble.

Assigned: Officers P. L. Phelps & L. E. Rogers.

By Direction Capt. HYNES.

F

EXHIBIT 10260

MONDAY, JANUARY 16, 1938.

To: Glen E. Bodell Detective Agency.
From: A. B. Reddell, #342.
Subject: Violation.

On Friday, January 7th, 1938, I was assigned as Guard to Truck #56; Route #15, in North Hollywood; Driver, ——— Buckley.

Two men in a Ford Sedan, 1937 license #1–p–4328, yellow wire wheels; with name on steering post, Matthew Shannon, 2314 W. Pico Blvd. Driver said his name is Harrington,—both men are former employes of the May Co., according to my driver Buckley.

They followed us for about 2 hours, taking the addresses of all the places where we stopped. However, they said they were not following us. Harrington said that he is working for the Lyon Van & Storage Co., and taking these addresses for his company. But they did have in their car a supply of Teamsters Union circulars or hand-bills which have been widely distributed through-out the City during the past six weeks, and they gave me one of them.

(Signed)   A. B. REDDELL
A. B. Reddell, #342.

(In pencil:) "Helper on truck was Barnaham. Heard conversation. This is the car picked up."

C. MARITIME WORKERS—DOCUMENTS RELATING TO 1934 LONGSHOREMEN'S STRIKE

EXHIBIT 10261

LOS ANGELES STEAMSHIP COMPANY

LOS ANGELES HARBOR, WILMINGTON, CALIFORNIA, *March 20, 1934.*

OFFICE OF VICE PRESIDENT & GENERAL MANAGER

MERCHANTS & MANUFACTURERS ASS'N.,
1008 I. N. Van Nuys Bldg., Los Angeles, Calif.

Attn. Mr. F. R. Fysh.

GENTLEMEN: This is to request that you be good enough to serve on a Committee, with Capt. William F. Hynes of the Los Angeles Police Department and Mr. E. Nichols of the Marine Service Bureau, to secure and furnish to the Steamship Operators at Los Angeles Harbor such special police officers as they may require to protect their employees and property in case a Longshoremen's strike is called next Friday, the 23rd.

Please signify your willingness to serve on such Committee to Captain Robert Hill, Chairman, Special Committee, Marine Service Bureau, 258 W. 7th St., San Pedro, Calif.

Yours very truly,

J. B. BANNING, Jr.,
J. B. Banning, Jr.,
for Special Committee, Marine Service Bureau.

JBB:LF
cc: Capt. R. Hill.
Capt. William F. Hynes.
Mr. E. Nichols.

[EXHIBIT 948]

[Previously printed in pt. 8 on p. 3084]

Copies to S. F.   F. H. T

[For interoffice use only]

To: New York Office—Principal W. S. B.
From: Los Angeles Office—Manager T. O. S.
Re: Prospective Business.
    Pacific Coast Dock Strike.
(Handwritten Notation: Copy sent to Chi. 3/29)

Date: MAR. 27th, 1934.

DEAR MR. BURNS: As result of solicitation by Howard Chapman, assisted by the undersigned, we were able to obtain an order for thirty five men to be placed on duty commencing Friday, March 23rd, in the event the longshoremen had struck.

We obtained this contract through the cooperation of Captain Hynes of the Red Squad of the L. A. Police Dept., and Mr. Nichols who is manager of the Marine Service Bureau.

As you know, the strike did not materialize, but we actually hod the contract and all the necessary men tentatively employed by the time the President called upon the longshoremen to hold the strike in abeyance.

In order to meet competition, including a rate of $7.00, and $8.00, for twelve hours, as quoted by Pinkertons, we were obliged to quote a rate of $9.00, per day, plus transportation expenses, and the client, which would be the Marine Service Bureau, was to furnish meals for the operatives while they were on duty.

The Marine Service Bureau had complete charge of the interests of all of the major steamship companies and in this they co-operated with by the Merchants and Manufacturers Association.   A pool of $85,000 was created by a subscription from various steamship companies and was held by the Marine Service Bureau for disbursement in the event of a strike.

It is our positive opinion that in the event the longshoremen do strike either now or at sometime in the immediate future we can be positively assured of receiving the major portion of the guard work in this region.

Although we were in a position to make a small service charge for having lined up deputy sheriff guards in anticipation of the work to have started on March 23rd, yet we waived this in view of the effect it might have upon obtaining future work from the same source.

Yours very truly,

LOS ANGELES OFFICE,
(Signed)   Per T. O. SLACK, *Manager.*

TOS:ST

[EXHIBIT 1019]

[Previously printed in pt. 8 on p. 3134]

(Air Mail)

[For interoffice use only]

COPIES TO N. Y. S. F. R. J. B. F. H. T.

To: New York Office.
From: San Francisco Office.
Re Financial, and Los Angeles Operating #4399.

JUNE 6th, 1934.

Mr. RAYMOND J. BURNS,
　　　New York Office.

DEAR MR. BURNS: I note carbon copy of Mr. Bowe's letter regarding the bill of the Marine Bureau.

They had considerable trouble in Los Angeles regarding men making claims for time when they did not have same shown on the supervisors' reports.

The Los Angeles Office mimeographed a number of operative's time reports and gave them to each supervisor, instructing the supervisors to give them to each man employed, advising that the supervisors' reports must be supported by the operatives' time reports.   A sample is herewith attached.

The men handling the strike work were men who were deputy sheriffs, who had worked on other strike cases for Wheeler, and on prior strikes they had never turned in an operative's time report.   The supervisor merely listed each man's name showing where he was, the date, when he came on duty, when he went off duty.   The employees did not even sign the supervisor's time report.   This, of course, gives the supervisors and the men handling the strike, a wonderful opportunity to pad the payrolls.

When the Los Angeles cashier was insisting they must have the operative's time report, and Mr. Slack, as well, the Marine Bureau advised them it was not necessary, that all they wanted was the supervisor's time report.   The Marine Bureau made out a list each day, which they gave to the supervisors showing how many men they required and where they were to be stationed and as the supervisor checked off his men, a representative of the Marine Bureau also stood by and checked off the men.   The supervisor would then take his men and proceed to the different stations.   The fact that the Marine Bureau had checked them off was all they required.   You can then imagine the trouble that ensued trying to get the men to turn in these time reports.

I have gone through the same thing once or twice but I stood firm and insisted on the reports.

For instance, in the Foster and Kleiser Strike when they advised the finks that they did not need to write a report I simply advised the supervisors that any man who did not hand in his time report would not get his pay, that it was necessary to furnish the cashier with these reports, then when we had any discrepancy in the supervisor's time report, we simply exhibited the operative's time report to the client and he paid.

I had the same trouble in handling the Musicians Strike.   Mr. Pantages insisted on four or five more men for his theatre, than the Allied Amusement Company were allotting him.   The Allied Amusement Company was simply an organization to break the strike, it was irresponsible financially and when the strike was over, the theatre men closed it up but I had Mr. Pantages right where I wanted him, his manager had signed every one of the operative's time reports so all I needed to say to Mr. Pantages was that "if the Association does not pay, you will, you ordered the extra men."   He went to the telephone, called up the Allied Amusement Company and advised the manager that his house required the number of men assigned and that they must pay the bill which they did.

While I was in Los Angeles I had every man who claimed extra time fill out an operative's report and we checked some of these with Captain Heiser and had them okehed and Mr. Slack is getting the rest.

I also accompanied Mr. Slack, personally to the Marine Bureau to see about the check and telephoned them several times.   I am happy to report to you that before I left Los Angeles, the Los Angeles Office had a check for $2,000, and the Marine Bureau assured me that as soon as we render the bill the balance will be paid promptly.

Of course, I have been through many of these strikes and I know just how to handle the clients without offending them.   My handling this matter has made for the Agency, three or four times the cost of my trip to Los Angeles, because at first they were not going to pay any of this time.   As a matter of fact, two or three supervisors' reports were missing and the men were claiming time from us but we had no chance to collect from the Marine Bureau until we got the matter straightened out.

Also, while I am on the matter, Mr. Slack claims that he endeavored to get both Mr. Rule and Mr. Oaks to go down and help handle the matter.   Mr. Rule was out of town and later claimed to have some important ABA work.   They both did not relish the idea of going down to the Waterfront and get beaten up. As a matter of fact, the general investigator is worthless in strike matters.   You have to have a regular fink.

In all the strikes I handled, I always secured men who knew the business and my assistant or myself stood beside and we watched the pay roll and kept things going.

Very truly yours,

SAN FRANCISCO OFFICE,
(Signed)   By F. H. THARP, *Manager*.

FHT:X6.
Encl.

EXHIBIT 10262

(WILMINGTON) APRIL 19, 1935.

Re: Oil Tanker Strike in Harbor District.[1]
To: Homer B. Cross, Deputy Chief of Police, City Hall.

SIR: The following is a list of firms affected by labor disturbances and of which it has been necessary to place Police Officers, for protection of life and property
(*Justin Paid*) (100) (Mr. Nickles, Marine Service Bureau 100 left 4–23–35) Paid April 24.)

(100) Shell Oil Company, Berths 172–173–217 (*Mr. Mainland L. A. Office*); *Mr. Jack Malseed*, Supt., Phone Wilmn–687 (1008–W–6th st.)

(100 PAID) Texaco Oil Company, Berths 173–217; *Mr. W. K. Clayton*, Supt., Phone Wilmn–276 (100 left 4–25).

(100 *Paid*) General Petroleum Company, Berths 238–239–240; *Mr. Lloyd Moore*, Supt., Phone San Pedro 2950.   (100 left. 4–23–35).   (*Paid*)

(100 *Paid*) Union Oil Company, Berths 150–151–149, Mr. Albert Pegg, Supt., Phone Wilmn–943).   (100 left 4–24–25).   (*Paid*).

(100 *Paid*)   Standard Oil Company, Berths 97–98–101–102, Mr. Black, Supt., Phone San Pedro 2700 (100 left 4–24–25).   (PAID PAID).

(100) Associated Oil Company, Berths 118–120 Mr. Murray, Supt., Phone San Pedro 1650.   (100 left 4–24–25).

(50) Hancock Oil Company, Berth 215; *Mr. Irdom, Supt.*, Phone San Pedro 4840.

(100) Bethelehem Shipbuilding Corp., Ltd.; *Thomas B Forster*, Supt., Phone San Pedro 1400.

(100) Los Angeles Ship Building Corp.; *Mr. Herman Haubold*, Supt., Phone San Pedro 800 (Purchased 10 from Robee, S. P. Div.).

DRAWBRIDGE, (this City property under Harbor Commissioners, Belt Line Railway—Property has been necessary to cover with Police Detail).
Mr. Alford Phone San Pedro 3219.

And would suggest that the Federal Laboratories, Inc., be contacted, as they have been lucky in placing orders in recent strike troubles for their protection— equipment, A Mr. George Cake was the Salesman, who placed orders of L. A. Street Car Strike, as well as here in Oil Tankers Strike—1350 East 6th Street, Los Angeles, Phone TR–9861.

(*Justin Paid*) (Los Angeles Cotton Compress Warehouse Co. 25 left. *Paid*)
Respectfully,

LUKE M. LANE.

GB

[1] Material in parentheses written in pencil on original document.

Exhibit 10263

Intra-departmental correspondence Form 236 (5 strike details)

Los Angeles Police Department

Office of Intelligence Department, Metropolitan Division

June 19, 1935.

1.15.2
Memorandum for Chief Davis:
Re: Oil Tankers Strike.

As the oil tankers strike is now drawing to a close, I wish to call briefly to your attention the following facts and recommendations:

That the strike was called on March 9, 1935, ships stood idle until a meeting was held in your office on March 29, 1935. A police detail was sent to the harbor district on April 2nd and during this strike it was the first time, to my knowledge, that all affected by labor trouble within the oil shipping industry united together in a united front and pooled their efforts in combatting all subversive activities and the recruiting of labor to fill their ranks; this being done by a committee of three selected among their groups.

They then established an employment office at 6th and Main Sts. Los Angeles, outside of the strike zone. After recruiting their labor at this office, the men selected were not allowed to roam at large on the streets or mingle with pickets; but were housed and feed at the Ritz Hotel, 813 S. Flower St. Los Angeles, until such time as they were taken to San Pedro and placed on board the boat of their regular assignment from then on.

There was placed at our disposal a sufficient supply of gas, hand grenades gas guns and gas masks; there was placed under our command, day and night, two power boats to patrol and observe the oil docks on the water side, which were constantly kept in patrolling and escorting oil tankers in and out of the harbor channel to a point of safety.

And many other items too trifling to mention, but all had a very important bearing on the strike situation.

Through all of their coordination and splendid cooperation, they made it possible for a small police detail to be maintained in their behalf. The total detail on duty days and nights was 45 officers and two cars.

If it had not been for their cooperation as a unit, and if each company had acted independently of each other, as in most cases of strike trouble, it would have taken at least 150 police officers to maintain peace and protect their property. I therefore, wish you to commend them very highly.

I wish to state that all officers assigned to this detail worked 12 hours a day and no days off. They were all exceedingly and well pleased with the duty they had to perform and with the treatment they received from the officials of the various oil companies.

I feel that we have made some wonderful contacts and boosters for you and our department, and furthermore, recommend that each executive from each oil company in the harbor district should be invited and entertained at our police range for lunch, (perhaps next Wednesday) and there presented with a police badge in recognition of their splendid cooperation and in furtherance of their friendly relationship toward you and our department.

Now, the majority of the officials of these oil companies already have police badges. There are perhaps three or four that have not. I think it would be a fitting occasion for you to present them at our lunch with a badge, and if you deem it proper, I will make all arrangements to carry out above suggestions.

Respectfully,

Luke M. Lane,
Detective Lieut. Commanding, Intelligence Bureau.

L:F

Exhibit 10264

[Intra-departmental correspondence   Form 236 (5 strike details)]

Los Angeles Police Department
Office of Intelligence Bureau, Metropolitan Division

June 21, 1935.

Medorandum: For Chief Davis.

The following is a tentative list of various oil company executives that are to be invited to lunch next Wednesday, June 26th:

Central Committee

x William Groundwater, Director of Transportation, Union Oil Co.
P. L. Lamb, Asst. Marine Superintendent, Richfield Oil Co.   L. B.
A. O. Wall, Director & Mgr. Marine Dept. General Petroleum Co.

Regional Committee

H. W. Hanna, Manager of Refineries, So. Ca. Standard Oil Co.
x J. C. MacQuiddy, Marine Supt. San Pedro, Standard Oil Co.
x Frank Black, Terminal Supt. San Pedro, Standard Oil Co.
Frank Coyle, General Supt. of Pipe Lines, Associated Oil Co.
J. C. Reeve, Asst. to Mr. Coyle   "   "
Jim Murray, Terminal Superintendent   "   "
John Salmond, Mgr. of Wilmington Refinery, Union Oil Co.
x A. O. Pegg, Marine Supt.   "   "
x H. E. Kemp, Supervisor of Marine Operations   "   "
George McClain, Port Engineer   "   "
H. Halibesen, Port Captain   "   "
Jack Malseed, Terminal Supt. San Pedro, Shell Oil Co.
Dan Dobler, Marine Supt.   Texas Company
Floyd Nelson, Asst. Marine Supt.   "   "
B. Hallaran, Terminal Supt.   "   "
Fred Cordes, Agent, Hillcone Oil Co.
L. J. Moore, Asst. Mgr. Marine Dept.   General Petroleum Co.
Fred Maurer, Terminal Supt.   "   "
W. B. MacAdmas, in charge of Marine Personnel   "   "
x Edward Nichols, Manager, Marine Service Bureau, San Pedro
William C. Ball, Recruiting Service, Marine Service Bureau, S. P.
Fred R. Fysh, Merchants & Mfgrs. Asso. Los Angeles.
Note x has honorary police badge.
L:F
                                              Luke Lane,
                                          Intelligence Bureau.

Exhibit 10265

Civic Council of Defense of California, Inc.

June 21, 1935.

BULLETIN

General monthly meetings of the Civic Council have been discontinued during the summer months. They will again be held starting in the early fall.

*   *   *   *   *   *

Ferryboat men's Union.—A new union called the Ferryboat men's Union is in process of formation. This union is to be composed of the ferryboat men, tugboat men, water-taxi men, etc. This is an old labor organization, having been instituted in 1918, and is affiliated with the American Federation of Labor and the California State Federation, but has never before maintained a local in the San Pedro harbor. Mr. M. Wedekind, general organizer from San Francisco, has been active in the formation of this local. He told the group that if the men were not signed up by June 12th, he would not be responsible for what the International Seamen's Union would do. (So far there has been no action taken). Mr. Melnikow is the respresentative of the Ferryboat men's Union. He operates under the name of the Pacific Coast Labor Bureau and represents several of the maritime, as well as other unions in the matter of negotiations between the members of these unions and the employers. To date we are advised that the Ferryboat men's Union is not yet organized.

*   *   *   *   *   *   *

EXHIBIT 10266

LOS ANGELES POLICE DEPARTMENT
Office of Intelligence Bureau, Metropolitan Division

[Confidential]

Nov. 30, 1935.

Memo. Capt. HYNES.

In regard to call from Capt. MacCaleb of Highland Park Police Station, we interviewed Leslie Jones, who is a trustee and is cook for prisoners in Highland Park Station.

Jones stated he was 37 years of age; stated he was arrested in 1928 for failure to provide, and was sentenced by Judge Bullock to one year in city jail; he served 108 days of his sentence, and then escaped. At that time he was a trustee at the pistol range.

He stated he went East and was employed by various steamship companies as a cook and is a member now of the Marine Cooks & Stewards Union, A. F. of L.; also claims to have joined the Communist Party; and said he was sent by Communist Party to Moscow, Russia in 1929 and received instructions as to being a Party organizer.

He claims that before joining the Communist Party that he contacted Mr. Blanton, head of Dept. of Justice at Baltimore, and was instrumental in aiding the United States Government in various ways by supplying information on the Communist Party movement; and at the same time was connected with steamship companies as under cover agent; ater working himself into a good position as editor of the Marine Crafts Bulletin and exposed the Communist and their set up in the T. U. U. L. and said he was publicity agent for all marine crafts, which catered to the "Marine Crafts Bulletin;" he said that was his business up and down the Great Lakes and Atlantic Coast.

He said he was asked by officials of the Marine Crafts organization to come to the Pacific Coast and start a bulletin here and expose the Communists within the various marine crafts; but in order to be able to do so he was advised by union officials to give himself up here in Los Angeles and finish serving his time; so on July 29, 1935 he gave himself up to the Los Angeles police as an escaped prisoner from 1928, and has now served about 120 days on his sentence, which leaves him about 4½ months still to serve, that is if he serves the full time without any good time off.

He stated he wanted to do the right thing, and that is why he came in and gave himself up, and as soon as he is out he is going to work on the Pacific Coast in exposing Communists within the marine craft unions, and their methods of operating and effecting strikes.

He had several letters from union officials on the Atlantic Coast, also a large assortment of correspondence and Communist literature and bulletins which he claimed he put out on the Atlantic Coast, and they were exposing the Communists.

Jones stated that he was married and that his wife lives at 629 Sepulveda Blvd. San Pedro, that he has two children, ages 8 and 10 years. He said he had put in an application for parole, which comes up Dec. 6th, and that if he was granted parole he certainly would not run away, as he was too anxious to get back into his field of operation.

Jones is very well versed on Communist activities and their tactics, especially within the labor unions, and is certainly qualified for the work he plans to do. It is the opinion of your investigator that this man be encouraged and given a helping hand as I feel that we will obtain from him valuable information within marine crafts here and by Jones carrying on his propaganda program, which will eventually tear down at least a part of the Communists' setup within the various marine crafts.

I feel satisfied that he will not even attempt to escape and will abide by any decision that might be worked out for him and I am sure he can do us much more good on the outside than what he can do in jail.

Respectfully,

LUKE M. LANE, *DL #10.*

L:F.

EXHIBIT 10267

STATE OF CALIFORNIA,
  City and County of San Francisco, ss:

AFFIDAVIT

I, MARTIN GARINER, after being duly sworn, advised as to my constitutional rights and the penalty by law for making false statements under oath, voluntarily state as follows:

I am a marine fireman and occasionally work at other marine engine room work. As of this date I am under shipping articles on the S. S. Paul Luckenbach, which ship I missed at Portland, Oregon, causing me to come to San Francisco to catch the ship when she comes to this port.

I have for some years been a member of the Marine Firemen, Oilers, Water Tenders and Wipers Union until I transferred to the National Maritime Union, where I am a member in the engine room division.

I first met Leslie Jones in the year 1932 in New York City, where I saw him in various seamen's hangouts in the west side of New York. At that time I was working aboard the Motor Ship City of Rayville, of the American Pioneer Line, while the ship was in port for about six weeks between voyages. At that time a marine engineer named Thomas Elli introduced me to Leslie Jones. Jones told me that he was then organizing for the Marine Workers Industrial Union, an organization affiliated with the Trade Union Unity League.

Jones inquired of me as to the names of union men aboard my ship and asked about union activities and any plans for such. I told him that, as far as I knew, I was the only union member in the engine division on the Motor Ship Rayville, and that there were no activities, as conditions were better than on the average ship.

I next saw Leslie Jones in about August, 1933 in Baltimore, Maryland, when I was there on the beach. Jones was a soap-boxer and I saw him frequently on the corner of South Broadway and Thames Street, speaking on behalf of the Marine Workers Industrial Union. He was a fiery talker and advocated militant union activities. He soon had quite a following among the seamen in Baltimore and on the ships calling at that port.

I left Baltimore for a few months and I next saw Leslie Jones, again in Baltimore, around March and April, 1934. At that time seamen had organized in a relief set-up, which they handled themselves through elected committees. Government relief funds were being provided to finance the relief expenditures through these committees, elected by the seamen.

One of the main figures in this relief set-up was Leslie Jones, who acted as Treasurer or Finance Committee Chairman, or something like that, as I understood the arrangements. At any rate, Jones received the money from the Federal Relief Administration and made the necessary payments to landlords, and for the purchase of groceries and the commissary supplies.

While I was on the beach in Baltimore in early 1934 a lot of dissension suddenly started among the seamen with relation to the relief set-up and Jones' activities in it. Auditing committees for the seamen discovered discrepancies in Leslie Jones' accounts and tried to check up on his expenditures, but met with a great deal of difficulty in getting the records.

At the same time that the auditing committee was trying to get the records of Jones' expenditures, a big red-baiting campaign broke out which Jones took the lead in, charging that one or another seaman was a red or communist.

Prior to the beginning of this dissension there had been set up in Baltimore and in operation when I arrived there a centralized Seamen's Shipping Bureau, which served to regulate the distribution of employment and operated in connection with the relief set-up. Jones had nothing to do with the centralized Shipping Bureau. Also during the spring of 1934, because working and wage conditions were very poor on many ships, there were a number of strikes of seamen when ships docked at Baltimore. Consequently, the dissension that started over Jones' activities came at a very critical period for seamen in the port of Baltimore and on the east coast generally.

As the auditing committee, elected to check up on Jones' accounts, secured information they reported a number of incidents where evidence was found indicating that Jones had solicited or been paid rake-off or kick-back money by various business people. They also reported evidence showing that Jones had expended money very freely on certain parties which he attended uptown.

To these serious charges, made by the properly elected auditing committee, Jones and his followers replied by denouncing auditing committee members and many other seamen as being reds. They reported that they had evidence of reds plotting to take over control of the relief set-up, using government money for propaganda and to foment strikes and circulated many similar charges.

Consequently, the dissension in Baltimore became general and the relief funds were not handled properly. Some persons failed to receive necessary clothing, while others had their requirements promptly filled, all of which added to the general dissension already going on.

When this dissension around Jones and his activities was at its height the government discontinued supplying funds, due to the unsatisfactory outcome of the experiment to participate with seamen in a cooperative relief set-up. Thereupon the whole arrangement for seamen's relief was thrown into the scrap heap for a while.

Delegations were elected to go to Washington to try to get the matter straightened out. Jones and his following violently opposed sending such delegations to Washington.

At the time the delegations were discussing matters with the authorities in Washington about the Baltimore relief set-up, I happened to secure some evidence that Jones was serving as an undercover spy but could not learn who was putting up the money for his spy work, nor who was behind all of his movements. I did learn that Attorney Silas B. Axtell of New York City, who was known to have business relations with the International Seamen's Union, of which I was a member, had certain business relations and worked in cooperation with Leslie Jones who, as stated above, had appeared as an organizer for the Marine Worker's Industrial Union, an organization that was a dual union to the International Seamen's Union, which Axtell represented.

When I reported my information to fellow seamen in Baltimore a leaflet was published exposing Jones, but Jones promptly disappeared from Baltimore before any formal action could be taken, either by his union, the Marine Workers Industrial Union or my union, the Marine Firemen's Union, or by the seamen organized in the relief organization. After Leslie Jones Left Baltimore I was informed that the Marine Workers Industrial Union had expelled him from membership in that organization at a duly called membership meeting.

However, the relief system in Baltimore had been completely sabotaged. All relief had been discontinued and friction had been so thoroughly stirred up among seamen in that port over Jones' activities that there never was regained the same unity among the different organizations of seamen that had been in existence before Jones, possibly with the assistance of other undercover operatives, created the dissension.

The Centralized Shipping Bureau was eliminated during the dissension and has never been reestablished in Baltimore. All these developments were to the detriment of sea-faring workers.

Jones disappeared from Baltimore about late April or May, 1934. He returned to Baltimore again in the latter part of September, 1934 just before the date of a scheduled strike, the call for which had been issued by the Marine Workers Industrial Union. He came into town in the company of Silas B. Axtell and made speeches denouncing the Marine Workers Industrial Union as a communistic organization. Jones urged all seamen to get out of the Marine Workers Industrial Union.

Both Axtell and Jones had a number of body guards around them at all times; hence, Jones could never properly be brought to trial or answer to the charges on which he had been expelled from the Marine Workers Industrial Union just after his previous departure from Baltimore.

During the latter part of September or early October, 1934 in Baltimore, both Axtell and Jones in their speeches claimed that they were organizers of the American Federation of Labor on behalf of the International Seamen's Union, of which organization I was a member. I tried to expose Jones again and helped get out another leaflet, but it was not easy to expose a man like that to the new seamen who had come into the port, and who did not know from first hand experience of the things that Jones had done to us before. At any rate Jones, together with Axtell, succeeded in getting a new following among the seamen for a time, but these men in turn finally ran Jones out again.

In early 1935 I frequently saw copies of the Seamen's Journal, official paper of the International Seamen's Union, which carried Leslie Jones' articles. I heard definitely that this Leslie Jones was the same man whom I had known had been spying and disrupting in Baltimore. Jones did not last long as Editor of the Seamen's Journal, as seamen everywhere protested. At any rate, his name was removed from the paper.

Since middle 1935 I have neither seen nor heard anything of Leslie Jones.

Leslie Jones is a man about five feet five or six inches in height, weighed about 135 pounds in 1934, had dark brown hair, was smooth shaven, had a ruddy complexion and had blue or bluish gray eyes. He was rough featured and in 1934 appeared to be about 35 or 36 years of age. When I knew him he had a slight British seaman's accent, or as we say at sea, he talked like a "limey."

I certify that I have read the above statements and swear that they are correct and true to the best of my knowledge and belief.

MARTIN J. GARNIER.
(Martin Garnier.)

Subscribed and sworn to before me this 14th day of January, 1939.

[NOTARIAL SEAL]   VIRGINIA A. BEEDE,
    Notary Public In and for the City and County of San Francisco,
                                                    State of California.

My Commission Expires April 11, 1941.

EXHIBIT 10268

[Intra-Departmental Correspondence]

LOS ANGELES POLICE DEPARTMENT

Office of In. Bu. Metro. Divn.

Nov. 22, 1935, FRI.

Confidential Capt. HYNES.

Lieut. Wellpott phones in from Harbor:

In connection with the dispute in the Fish Cannery Workers Union, confidential informant states that two nights ago Jack Moore and some of his group from the local attempted to attend a meeting of the I. L. A. but were not admitted to same. They then went to the A. F. of L. Painters meeting in San Pedro and were there put out of the meeting.

That same day Jack Moore attempted to see Mr. J. W. Buzzell at Gruver's office (Gruver is secretary of the AFL Council in San Pedro). Jack Moore knocked at Gruver's office and when Gruver found out who it was he slammed the door in his face. Moore told some of his people, "He must think I have smallpox or something." Apparently he did not get to see Gruver neither.

Yesterday confidential operative informed that Jack Moore was on his way to Los Angeles to see Mr. Buzzell to offer that he, Jack Moore and Joy Merwin (alias Mrs. De Campio, alias Alfreda Clary) would resign from Local #18656 provided that Mr. Buzzell would give this local back their charter.

It is further reported that Jack Moore is stepping out and has already made his own selection as business agent for the local, a man named Robertson so that it will be still almost entirely a Y. C. L. setup in the local with Jack Moore in practically direct control as he has been in the past.

It was also learned yesterday from the picket line that Jack Moore has not resigned from the local but is still business agent.

Joy Merwin (alias Mrs. De Campio, alias Alfreda Clary) mentioned above is described as about 25 years old, 5' 8, rather tall for woman, 150 pounds, sort of blonde, not bad looking, probably active in Y. C. L. in harbor, has been assistant organizer among the women cannery workers and assisting Jack Moore.

Sarah Rabkin (Mrs. Gould) who was head of the women's department in the Fish Cannery Workers Union was voted out of the local about five days ago, but she is still secretary of the BOAT PULLERS UNION, of which man named

Ivancovich is president of San Pedro local. This man is known as a Red down there and is a Slovenian; this is a group that were in the Fishermen and Cannery Workers Industrial Union.

It might be said that the cannery workers (of the old F&CWIU) attempted to get a charter from the A. F. L. but were refused because affiliated with the T. U. U. L., and then the T. U. U. L. group went over to the Van de Camp group which was originally a company union and when they applied for a charter from the A. F. L. it was granted some months ago.

EXHIBIT 10269

[Intra-Departmental Correspondence]

LOS ANGELES POLICE DEPARTMENT

Office of In. Bu. Metro. Divn.

FEB. 10–36.

Confidential Memo.

H. E. March, special officer for Coast Cannery Co. Wilmington was in and gave names and addresses of following which were left at 226 W. 6 St. San Pedro room 9, a little hall used by Jack Moore; these names were on slips torn from a notebook and left by Jack Moore, evidently when he left in a hurry; these were found at this place Mon Feb 3–36:

> G. Kaplan
> Marie Temblador, 1256 Hyatt
> Gregario, 2302 E. 115 St Watts
> Piequiro   "
> Lupe Herandez, 2218 E. 105 St. Watts
> Jennie Arias, 11169 Monitor Watts
> Connie Mendoza, 2314 E. 114 St. "
> Nellie, 1420 N. Fries, Wilm.
> Billy (girl) Waterbury, 716 W. "L" St.
> Scott Willard, 1000 block Lagoon St. Apt. 4
> Jonny Hoffman, 1422 E. Denni

F: Mr. March states most of above subjects were active with Jack Moore in strike activities against the Coast Cannery Co.

EXHIBIT 10270

COAST FISHING COMPANY

California Sea Foods—Packers

WILMINGTON, CALIF., *August 15, 1936.*

Lt. RUDOLPH WELLPOT,
    Third Floor, Klinker Bldg., First & Broadway, Los Angeles, Calif.

MY DEAR RUDY: There seems to be a little under-current of turmoil along the waterfront again. We would like to nip it in the bud before it gets a little too active. A second Jack Moore seems to be on the job, and is trying to horn his way into our plant and is slowly issuing some propaganda.

I turned this chap's name over to Officers Hackey and Haley (Haley is now working with Hackey in place of Cole), and they are going to slowly look into this for me, and if you can get a confidential report as to this man's past activities I will appreciate it very much. His name is *A. B. Reser.* I learned through unofficial sources that he is not receiving any salary from the Fish Cannery Workers Union, and they do not seem to know where he is getting his money from, for living expenses.

If you should happen to be coming down to the harbor sometime I would very much like to have a chat with you, or if you are in the up-town office at any time I would like to run in and see you.

With kindest regards, I am
    Yours very truly,

S. HORNSTEIN.

SH:ML
Enc.

P. S.   I am enclosing copy of letter he just sent us, together with copy of my reply.   I am also attaching copy of the last circular we found in the box in the plant a couple of days ago.

EXHIBIT 10271

FISH CANNERY WORKERS UNION

Local No. 20147

769 TUNA STREET, TERMINAL ISLAND, CALIF., *August 14, 1936.*

COAST FISHING CO., BOARD OF DIRECTORS.

SIRS: We are availing ourselves of this opportunity to request an audience with you.   We wish to see you as Union Representatives, on matters pertaining to employee representation.   To some extent this has been taken up with the Superintendent, but since we were unable to arrive at a satisfactory arrangement with him and since he is obviously bound by what seems to be a policy of the company, we consider it necessary to take the matter up with you.

We regard this matter as one of importance to all parties concerned and will appreciate seeing you as soon as possible.

Sincerely yours,

A. GOMEZ   (signed)
A. B. RESER   (signed)

(Penned Note)   If reply is made in writing please mark personal.

EXHIBIT 10272

AUGUST 15, 1936.

FISH CANNERY WORKER'S UNION,
769 Tuna St., Terminal Island, Calif.
(Attention—Messrs; Gomez and Reser.)

GENTLEMEN: Replying to your kind favor of August 14th the officers of the company are available at all times to discuss matters with any of our employees. Will you kindly telephone the office and make an appointment with the writer at any time that is most convenient to you, and if we are at the office we will always be very glad to talk to you, together with a representative number of our cannery workers.

Thanking you, we are

Yours very truly,

COAST FISHING COMPANY,
By S. HORNSTEIN, *President.*

SH:ML

EXHIBIT 10273

[Western Union]

1936 Sep. 13, PM 11 44.

PRA 140 39 NL—TDPR Vancouver, Wash. 13.

Lieut. RUDY WILLPOTT,
Care Red Squad, Los Angeles Police Dept. LOSA—

Understand A B Reser assistant business agent Fish Cannery Workers Union is organizing in Monterey is supposed to have police record in Los Angeles please check and wire me record in detail collect care Cal Pack Vancouver Washington Kindest regards—

OTIS R. BOHN.

(In ink:) "no answer"

EXHIBIT 10274

(In pencil:) "Send to Capt Hynes"

[Western Union]

1936 SEPTEMBER 16.

COLLECT

(In pencil:) "AA 3–19–"

OTIS R BOHN,
    Care of California Packing Corporation, Vancouver, Wash.

No record A. B. Reser have had other inquiries re this subjects activities in and around San Pedro.

JAS. E. DAVIS, *Chief Police.*

"Capt. Hynes ⎫
Intelligence   ⎬ Crossed out.
AJS 9:50 AM" ⎭

(Stamped:) "F. R. PARSONS"

EXHIBIT 10275

FELLOWS AND STEWART

WILMINGTON, CALIF., *August 12, 1936.*

Mr. FRANK A. GARBUTT,
    411 West Seventh Street,
        Los Angeles, California.

DEAR MR. GARBUTT: After talking to you on the phone yesterday I tried to reach Smith of the Wil. Boat Works without success until too late to contact you however I phoned your house and office this morning and left a message at the office for you.

Both Smith and I feel that it would be a little premature to take both the cars away at once, we would like to feel our way by releasing one car and letting the other cruise back and forth between the two plants, at odd times, so that there will be no question but that there is a squad car available on short notice, in the event of anything be started. I am of the opinion that we will have no trouble but Smith has one man who lives in the heart of the union section in San Pedro so he is not too sure but that something may be started if they get the idea that we neither of us have any protection any more.

We will arrange with the one car that is left to make more or less regular calls back and forth for the moral effect. I want to take this occasion to express my sincere appreciation of your cooperation and help in combatting the union gang and defeating their efforts to put us all under the union yoke. It certainly would have been a most galling experience and, without your assistance, it might well have been successful. I am duly grateful. I will also appreciate the favor if you will convey my sense of deep gratitude to Chief Davis for the help he gave us with his "Red" Squad and tell him we congratulate him on the success he has had in the organization of this group.

I will contact you later and will endeavor to get a release of the remaining car if we think it practicable or will call for help again should that remote situation develop.

Sincerely yours,

(Sgd)   V. B. STEWART.

VBS/MH

EXHIBIT 10276

FRANK A. GARBUTT

Suite 712—411 West Seventh Street

LOS ANGELES, CALIFORNIA, *September 26, 1936.*

CAPT. WM. F. HYNES,
    Los Angeles Police Department,
        Los Angeles.

DEAR CAPT. HYNES: I believe our boat builders' strike at San Pedro is practically over and, due to the wonderful protection that you gave us in maintaining law and order, I am happy to say that the shops are running non-Union.

We want to express our appreciation of the fine type of men detailed for this job. They were fair to all concerned and their firmness in maintaining order is responsible for there having been no violence whatever.

If we can reciprocate at any time, kindly let me know.

Sincerely,

FAG–C.

FRANK A. GARBUTT.

EXHIBIT 10277

WATERFRONT EMPLOYERS ASSOCIATION OF SOUTHERN CALIFORNIA

SAN PEDRO, CALIFORNIA, *September 28, 1936.*

To Members:

The following information may be of benefit to you in planning your operations in the event of the interruption in our normal working conditions by reason of a tie-up on October 1st.

It will be optional with each operator to bring his ship or ships into the dock or to leave them at anchor.

If the ships are brought to the dock or allowed to remain at the dock, each individual operator will be expected to arrange for such watchmen and fire protection as they deem necessary. If you wish additional watchmen for use aboard ship or on your piers it is our recommendation that you contact Mr. Bodel at Michigan 8741, Los Angeles. The cost of such watchmen service must be paid for by the operator ordering the service.

In the event ships at anchor should require the services of caretakers they can be secured by calling our Association. The Association will deliver such caretakers and watchmen as you may wish to the particular vessel which you may designate. After that has been done it will be necessary for each individual operator to see that these men are taken care of, protected and fed. It has been suggested that in order to care for a vessel, provisions should be made for not less than ten men exclusive of guards; three in the deck department, three engineers, three firemen, and one cook. The vessel owner or agent must supervise the caretaking of their own ships by means of their own individual port organization.

It is expected that many ships will be fully provisioned upon arrival at anchorage but that others may require supplies. In the event the firm or firms with whom you have heretofore dealt are unable to make delivery of such miscellaneous supplies as may be needed aboard vessels at anchor, by contacting the Association you can secure information as to how such delivery can be effected.

At the present moment it would appear desirable to exert every effort in an endeavor to have a minimum amount of undelivered cargo on the piers on October 1st as it is quite possible that we will be unable to affect deliveries after that date without disturbance. If there should be any change in this situation you will be advised.

Steps should be immediately taken to clean all premises as much as possible from rubbish and debris in order to minimize the danger from fire.

The Police Department has informed us that they will establish a suitable harbor district headquarters through which the assignment of special or additional police patrolmen will be handled, and as soon as this has been accomplished we will advise you whom to contact. Until that time, in the event of any disturbance requiring the services of the Police Department, you will contact them through the already established channels.

Very truly yours,

E. NICHOLS, *Secretary-Treasurer.*

Exhibit 10278

Shipping Companies

American Hawaiian, WI 421 Ber. 175, Stewart.
Banning Co., WI 930. Ber. 188, Miller.
Barge 140, WI 1049.
Camp #2 SP 1592.
Crescent Wharf & Whse SP 2330 230–232, Otto.
Grace Line WI 2100 146, McKenna.
Hammond Lumber Co. SP 1940 Lum. Dock, Term. Isl. Neegaard.
Los Angeles S. S. Co. & Matson WI 241 156–7 Gray.
Luckenback Dock SP 2610.
Marine Exchange SP 3540.
Marine Terminal Co. SP 5600 230–A, Bankston.
McCormick Co. WI 191 B–176 Richley.
Nelson S. S. Co. SP 5500 230–B Tuck.
Norton Lilly WI 372 190, Followill.
Outer Harbor, SP 1900 50, McGowen.
Pacific S. S. Co. WI 401 153–4–5, Germain.
Southwestern Stevedore Co. SP 4417 Christy.

Shipping Companies—Continued

Speed Boat, Harbor Dept. 1st St. Landing.
Soto SP 1951 90 Mowans.
Williams Diamond SP 2710 228.
Woods, E. K. Lumber Co. SP 21 Scaborough.

Detective Agencies

Burns (Chapman) TR 8735, HE 1834, WI 1104.
Harris, Nick TR 8643, PL6789.
Universal, Peterson TU 6660.
Raymond-Miller WH 0647, VA 9433.
Campbell WI 930.

Hotels

Don WI 1481 (Hynes, rm. 211–2).
Cabrillo Hotel SP 5020.
Miramer Hotel SP 3924.

General

I. L. A. Hall (Peterson) SP 2948.
Marine Service Bureau SP 1160.
M & M Employ. Agency WI 260.
Pol. Com. Nuner OX 5544.
Avalon Box Lunch AX 9463 (5939 Avalon).

Exhibit 10279

Roll Call of Members Present   Meeting No. ——— Nov. ——— 1936 [1]

M. M. & P.:
    (R) Doty (Ways & Means)
    (R) Randebert (Relief)
    (R) Johnson x
    (R) Wissing
    (R) Simpler
    (R) Rensher
    (A) Cross
    (A) Kucin (Special Duty)
    (A) Carlson
    (A) Johnson
    (A) Buchtele
    (A) Chaffee

M. E. B. A.:
    (R) Ervick
    (R) Shea
    (R) Corriea
    (A) Himes
    (R) McPhee (Ways Means)
    (R) Norman (General)
    (R) Millett
    (A) Herbert
    (A) Townsend
    (A) Hall
    (A) Opheim (McDonald)
    (A) Nelson (Housing)

A. R. T. A.:
    (R) Jordan (Ways & Means)
    (R) Mathison (Publicity)
    (R) Van Ermen (Picket)
    (A) King
    (A) Robinson (Publicity)
    (A) Loftfield

S. U. P.:
    (R) Hoag
    (R) Russell (Com Publicity)
    (R) Webster (Com.)
    (R) McCluskey (Com. Police detail)
    (R) Christoffersen (General)
    (A) Steveberg
    (A) Greenwald
    (A) Wright
    (A) Pupos
    (A) Morgan (Relief)
    (A) McDermott

I. S. U. Supporters:
    Innes (General)
    Mullins
    Kennedy
    Wegener

[1] Material in parentheses written in pencil on original documents.

I. S. U. Supporters—Continued.
Blackwell
Miritoh
Fays
Lyons
Mendick
(Conners Relief)

M. C. & S.:
(R) Wheeler
(R) Paulson
(R) Munier (Transportation)
(R) McCormick (Housing)
(R) O'Conner (Relief)
(R) Davis
(A) Bowen
(A) Chandler
(A) Hooper
(A) Ryan

M. F. O. W.:
(R) Gardiner (Publicity)
(R) Larkin
(R) Tilley (Relief)
(R) Golden (Special Duty)
(R) O'Sullivan (Ways & Means)
(R) Ferrell
(R) Weston
(A) Johnson
(A) Crocoll
(A) Olinburg
(A) Quinn

I. L. A. 38–119:
(R) Clark (Relief)
(R) Homer
(R) Reintjes (Ways & Means)
(R) Hasley (Ways Means)
(R) Lemon
(A) Vaughn
(A) Sackley
(A) Russell, R.

S. Y. W.:
(R) Farmer (Ways & Means)
(R) Hanvey (Relief)
(R) Reeves
(R) Russell
(R) Schuett
(A) Maga
(A) Albert
(A) Taylor
(A) Parish
(A) Grindle

Port Watchman:
Buffalo
Linnartz
Stephens

I. B. U.:
(R) Benson
(R) Craig (General)
(R) Patterson
(R) Rubelli
(R) Davis
(A) Sarciaux
(A) Kane

I. L. A. 38–82:
(R) Benton (Special Duty)
(R) Johnson, C. (Publicity)
(R) Pugh (Picket)
(R) Patterson (Relief)
(R) Bruce (Credentials)
(R) Ramsdon (Ways & Means)
(R) Donnelly (No Committee)
(A) Culpepper (Relief)
(A) Hansen (Picket)
(A) Fetzer (Transportation)
(A) Hull (Special Duty)
(A) Lindegren (Relief)
(A) Cox (General)
(A) Anderson (Publicity)
(A) Sundegren (for Cox)
(A) Simons (for Donnelly)
(A) Brown (Relief)
(A) Bebo (For Bruce)
(R) Bowen, E. (Transportation)

I. L. A. 38–107:
(R) Meyer
(R) Williams (Relief W & M)

I. L. A. 38–91:
(R) Ortiz
(R) Armanta
(R) Carmona
(R) Sondate
(R) Ayries
(A) Cruz (Relief)
(A) Selazar
(A) Cornejo
(A) Sanora

I. L. A. 38–106:
D. J. Jones

Soap & Edible O. W. U.:
A. Aho

Exhibit 10280

Minutes of the Meeting of the Joint Policy Committee of the Affiliated Organizations

December 5, 1936.

Meeting called to order at the Masters, Mates & Pilots Hall, San Francisco, at 4.30 p. m.

Brother Krumholtz elected Chairman. F. M. Kelley, Secretary.

Moved and seconded the delegate of the Honolulu, I. L. A. Brother Rogers be seated. Quittenton first, Cates seconded. The motion carried.

Roll call taken and the following members present: A. R. T. A., Rathborne; M. M. & P., Charlot, Van Neuuwenhusen O'Grady; S. U. P., Quittenton, Stowell, Cates; M. C. & S., Modin; I. L. A., Bridges, Krumholtz, Mays, Whitehead, Schmidt, Miller, Thomas, Larson, Gholson, Ward, Negstaad.

The Chair ruled there were a sufficient number of organizations present to constitute a quorum.

Brother Quittenton read the minutes of Dec. 4, 1936, which had previously been distributed to the delegates present.

Corrections were noted as follows:

On Page 1 Brother Moore was not seated.

On Page 2 in the motion made by Rathborne and seconded by Quittenton, the second word of the 4th line should be "objection" in place of "object."

Moved and seconded that the minutes be accepted as corrected. Cates first, Thomas seconded. Motion carried.

Moved and seconded that the delegate from Honolulu be given the floor. Thomas first, Cates seconded. The motion carried.

Brother Rogers took the floor and spoke on the situation in the Islands to date.

Brother Modin requested information regarding certain telegrams.

Brother Rogers stated that his organization had received the telegrams which they had refused to recognize as they were thought to be not authentic.

Brother Modin also asked for information about how the money sent from the Marine Cooks & Stewards had been taken care of.

Brother Norman of the M. E. B. A. had sent a letter to the licensed men to stay aboard the ships.

Brother Bridges asks question of Brother Rogers regarding the status of men being pulled off the ships; also the dates of telegrams received and by whom they were sent.

Moved and seconded that Brother Kelley be excused as Secretary. Bridges first, Charlot seconded. The motion carried.

Moved and seconded that Brother Rathborne be elected by acclamation. Charlot first, O'Grady seconded. The motion carried.

Brother Charlot asks Brother Rogers about telegrams received on Oct. 30th from representative of the Sailors Union. * * * "Was any wire received in Honolulu to strike all ships?"

ROGERS. "Yes."

CHARLOT. "Who was it signed by?"

ROGERS. "Signed by Joe St. Angelo, but we paid no attention to it."

CATES. "When was wire received from Coast Policy Committee requesting return of all Eastbound ships?"

ROGERS. "About a week after strike was called."

Cates states that Joe St. Angelo is Secretary of SUP Strike Committee.

VAN NEUUWENHUSEN. "How many ships are tied up in Honolulu now?"

ROGERS. "About 11 ships are tied up in the Islands when I left on Nov. 20th."

Brother Rathborne asks status of radio operators.

Rogers states that approximately 20 radio operators are on board their ships.

BRIDGES. "When ships were struck, did longshoremen come off with ships crews?"

ROGERS. "Yes."

BRIDGES. "Where did they get the word that the strike was on?"

ROGERS. "From crews and from Harry Kealoha."

BRIDGES. "Did they strike at the same time as the crews?"

ROGERS. "Yes, they walked off at the same time as the crews."

BRIDGES. "Did the crews get advice from Coast Policy Committee?"

ROGERS. "No, it was about four or five days before the wire was received from the Coast Policy Committee. Wires were received from various organizations. These wires read to strike all American ships."

BRIDGES. "Now the position is that ships will remain tied up until longshoremen are given preference of employment?"

ROGERS. "Yes, however if the Coast unions release the ships, the longshoremen will not stand in their way."

Discussion by various delegates on this point.

BRIDGES. "What if we sent telegrams requesting the release of East-bound ships, tied up in Honolulu?"

ROGERS. "The ships would stay tied up until the strike is over."

Moved and seconded that Brother Rogers report be accepted and he be given a vote of thanks. Schmidt first, Charlot seconded. Carried unanimously.

The following wire was received from Honolulu:

1936   Dec 5 P. M.   4 36.

759 Honolulu RCA
MERVYN RATHBORNE,
    Secy Joint Policy Committee,
                    San Francisco, Calif.

Regarding move of private party to charter relief ship for Hawaii Stop   discovered today purely selfish motive of individual to profiteer from strike Stop suggest only government chartered ship bring supplies here assuring no profiteering and equitable distribution of foodstuffs among small merchants Stop act immediately Stop can use funds here.

MAXIE WEISBARTH,
          Agent Supec.
HARRY KEALOHA,
Agent Honolulu Longshoremen Assn.
THOMAS REDMOND,
          Agent MFOW.
JACOBSON, W.,
          Agent MC&S.

SAN FRANCISCO NEWS PLAN

Resolution from Public Welfare Committee of the San Francisco Board of Supervisors read: (This resolution is attached to the minutes of the Joint Policy Committee of Dec. 4th).

Resolution submitted by Sailors Union, read.

Brother Lundeberg entered at 5.50 p. m.

Brothers Quittenton, Lundeberg, Stowell, explain the Sailors Union resolution. Brother Stowell states that the SUP Port Committee plan is for the settlement of any and all disputes arising out of an agreement.

Moved and seconded that the resolution submitted by the Sailors Union be adopted. Stowell first, Quittenton seconded.

Discussion by Brothers Bridges, Stowell, Charlot, O'Grady, Rathborne, Schmidt, Quittenton and Gholson.

Brother Lundeberg withdraw Sailors Union resolution.

Moved and seconded that the Coast Policy Committee go on record as endorsing the "a News Plan of Port Committees" as presented December 3rd, as a means of settling disputes arising out of agreements. Stowell first, Rathborne seconded, carried unanimously.

Adjourned at 6.44 p. m.

MERVYN RATHBORNE, *Recording Secretary.*

EXHIBIT 10281

DEPARTMENT OF POLICE
City of Los Angeles California
JAMES E. DAVIS, CHIEF

AUGUST 19, 1937.

To Whom It May Concern:

I have been acquainted with Mr. Lord W. Van Meter, the bearer, whose signature appears below, for approximately two years, and on the occasion of the maritime strike at Los Angeles Harbor during 1936–37 Mr. Van Meter rendered invaluable service to this department, while acting as hotel clerk.

From my personal acquaintance and observation of Mr. Van Meter, he has shown special aptitude for intelligence work and I most sincerely recommend him as highly qualified for intelligence and investigative work.

WILLIAM F. HYNES,
Capt. of Detectives, L. A. P. D., Commanding Intelligence Bureau.

(Signed) LORD W. VAN METER
(Signature of Lord W. Van Meter)

Exhibit 10282

[Intra-Departmental Correspondence]

Los Angeles Police Department

Office of Intelligence Bureau, Metropolitan Division

Dec. 3, 1935.

Confidential memorandum.

It has been learned that Harry Bridges—and a man named Smith will leave San Francisco at 5.00 p. m. this date by United Air Line and will arrive at Union Air Terminal at Burbank, 7.39 p. m.

Two plainclothes officers must be assigned to meet above party and shadow them and determine all contacts made by whom and where, and report immediately, so that this Bureau will be in a position to know what is taking place.

This information must be kept confidential.

William F. Hynes,
Acting Capt. of Detectives, LAPD,
Commanding Intelligence Bureau.

(In pencil:)
Information—Mr. Taylor
United Air Lines—TR 3434—Left S. F. at 2 p. m.   Arrived 4 p. m.
Arrived L. A.—Took company limousine to Biltmore Hotel.   Arrived at Harbor ILWU Hall at 7:30 p. m.
Attached notes:

1. Harry Bridges—TR 3434; Harry Bridges—7:39; Smith; Taylor—MU 4891.
2. Dec. 4–35 9.50 am.   Bill Hynes: Harris phones party due to arrive last night by plane failed to show up; met two planes one arriving about 7 and one about 8, not on them; will see you around 3 or 4 today; can reach him DR 5689.

Exhibit 10283

Don Hotel, Newest and Largest Hotel at the Port of Los Angeles

Wilmington, California.

Mr. Harry Bridges: I called you between twelve and one as agreed.   Decided to come down and find you.

I will stay around this afternoon, as I am very anxious to see you, A mutual S. F. friend has suggested my visit.

C. W. Hunter.

P. S.: If you have to go out, please leave a phone number where I can find and reach you.

D. Transportation Workers Union—Documents Relating to Los Angeles Street Car Strike

Exhibit 10284

Los Angeles Police Department

Intelligence Bureau

Los Angeles, California, *June 8, 1928.*

The following named officers will be detailed to cover Pullman sleeping cars in the south yard of the Southern Pacific depot: E. Kuivanen, W. W. Stewart, John Piening, Charles Evan.

Officer George A. Pfieffer will be in charge of this detail.

Detail will remain on duty, alternating in shifts of two men as designated below, until further notice:

Shift No. 1 2:00 PM to 7:00 PM 5 hours
2 7:00 PM to 1:00 AM 6 hours
1 1:00 AM to 6:30 AM 5½ hours
2 6:30 AM to 11:00 AM 4½ hours

A Drawing Room has been provided in one of the pullmans as sleeping quarters for officers on duty, where they will also receive their meals.

In the event that the shifts conflict with meal hours the officer in charge of the detail will relieve one of the officers while the other eats.

Mr. L. A. Coffin, porter, will be in charge of the Pullman cars in the day time. He can identify porters coming to and leaving the cars.

Mr. E. L. Arnaud will be in charge of pullman cars in the night time. He will assist officers in identifying porters coming to and leaving the cars during his tour of duty.

Officers are further instructed that their duty on this particular detail is to prevent any outsiders, representatives of the Porters' Union or other persons from interfering with the men (porters) occupying these cars. The picketing Ordnance, a copy of which is attached, must be vigorously enforced.

Officers are instructed that in case they are in doubt as to any person entering the cars rightfully belonging there, that pullman porters are required to have their locker keys with a check attached identifying them with the Pullman Company. This will assist officers in determining whether they have any right on the premises.

Officers are further instructed that from time to time various officers of the Pullman Company may visit the various places where police details are in charge. In such cases these officials should be treated with the utmost courtesy and permitted to go about without interference. All such officials have been supplied with a card with a special marking (copy attached) with which they will establish their identity.

Officers are further instructed that they are strictly prohibited from carrying on any conversation with employees of the Pullman Company, such as porters, etc., regarding the proposed strike. This rule must be strictly adhered to.

Officers are also instructed to assist the various special agents of the railroad companies in any manner possible and to cooperate with them to the fullest extent.

In the event of any loitering or congregating on the part of the porters or persons in and about the premises of the railroad or Pullman companies properties, who are not employed by said companies, they should be instructed to leave the premises.

In case of any trouble in any particular place, the officers should at once notify the office of the Intelligence Bureau, phone Westmore 8605. At night, after hrs. Al. 2523.

WM. F. HYNES,
Detective Lieutenant, L. A. P. D., Commanding Intelligence Bureau.

EXHIBIT 10285

LOS ANGELES POLICE DEPARTMENT
Intelligence Bureau

LOS ANGELES, CALIFORNIA, *June 8, 1928.*

OFFICER IN CHARGE,
Pullman Car Detail,
Southern Pacific Depot:

Following a brief consultation with Mr. A. E. Sathren, Service Inspector, the Pullman Company, and with Mr. L. A. Coffin, porter in charge of cars, the following additional instructions will be adhered to:

Arrange with Mr. L. A. Coffin to use only one entrance to pullman cars from which occupants may come and go. The north end of car is most desireable for this purpose because of its being closer to the depot. Through this arrangement all persons entering and leaving the cars can be identified with little or no difficulty.

Previous instructions issued to the effect that pullman porters could be identified by keys and check will not apply to your detail, as porters occupying these cars have not been supplied with porters' equipment. Therefore, there is no occasion for other sleeping-car porters operating from other trains loitering about or visiting with these men. You will strictly enforce this rule, as tactics such as these are usually resorted to in order to make contacts with the men and influence them through some sort of propaganda or another.

You should work in close cooperation with the Pullman and Railroad representatives in all matters affecting your work.

WM. F. HYNES,
Detective Lieutenant, L. A. P. D., Commanding Intelligence Bureau.

EXHIBIT 10286

LOS ANGELES, CALIFORNIA, *June 8, 1928.*

To all Officers on Proposed Pullman Strike Detail:

While it appears that the proposed strike of Pullman porters set for this date has been indefinitely postponed, there is nevertheless reason to apprehend that the announcement of this delay may be a ruse on the part of Eastern Porter Union officials to gain sufficient time to notify union members to the contrary and thus cause as much embarrassment as possible both to the traveling public and the Pullman Company.

Your duty as officers is to protect life and property and to faithfully serve the interests of the Company as well as the public.   In this connection, it is your duty to observe the pullman cars in the yards where you are on duty and see to it that no one is loitering around.   You will also guard against any attempt to commit violence or sabotage, such as the throwing of rock at windows of pullman cars which might result in the breaking of glass, etc.

Officers should suggest to special agents and Pullman Company representatives where they are detailed, that it would be advisable to lower screens in windows so that in the event an outside glass is broken it would not shatter the inner glass. A rigid observance of this precaution might prevent injury to occupants of berths and thereby save the company from possible expense due to annoying damage suits.

Officers are further instructed that their duty on this particular detail is to prevent any outsider, representatives of the Porters' Union or other persons from interfering with the men (porters) occupying these cars.   The Picketing Ordinance, a copy of which is attached, must be vigorously enforced.

Officers are instructed that in case they are in doubt as to any person entering the cars rightfully belonging there, that pullman porters are required to have their locker keys with a check attached identifying them with the Pullman Company.   This will assist officers in determining whether they have any right on the premises.

Officers are further instructed that from time to time various officers of the Pullman Company may visit the various places where police details are in charge. In such cases these officials should be treated with the utmost courtesy and permitted to go about without interference.   All such officials have been supplied with a card with a special marking (copy attached) with which they will establish their identity.

Officers are further instructed that they are strictly prohibited from carrying on any conversation with employees of the Pullman Company, such as porters, etc., regarding the proposed strike.   This rule must be strictly adhered to.

Officers are also instructed to assist the various special agents of the railroad companies in any manner possible and to cooperate with them to the fullest extent.

In the event of any loitering or congregating on the part of the porters or persons in and about the premises of the railroad or Pullman companies' properties, who are not employed by said companies, they should be instructed to leave the premises.

In case of any trouble in any particular place, the officers should at once notify the office of the Intelligence Bureau, phone Westmore 8605; or at night after business phone Albany 2523.

WM. F. HYNES,
Detective Lieutenant, L. A. P. D., Commanding Intelligence Bureau.

EXHIBIT 10287

JANUARY 11, 1930.

Notes Re Street Car Men's Union:

The organizer is alleged to be some Eastern fellow; some fellow from Detroit.

Hyans, Assistant Secretary, Central Labor Council states they held a meeting a week ago last night on East 53rd Street somewhere and took in six members.

These circulars were on the street cars yesterday.

Exhibit 10288

Mr. Street Car Men: This is a personal letter of appeal written at the request of Local Carmen who have held a number of meetings for the purpose of reorganizing the carmen's union on the Pacific Electric and Los Angeles Railways, in order to improve our conditions.

As individuals we are helpless and must tolerate the abuses and low wages imposed upon us, which organized carmen in other cities have long since done away with.

A strong organization of carmen in this city could soon obtain liveable conditions.

The time is ripe for organization. All other crafts are organized. Many are working but five days a week with no reduction in pay. There is no reason why the street car companies should not give the employees who are the backbone of the company a fair portion of what they earn. The mere fact that you are working longer hours for less pay than any organized group of carmen in America is sufficient argument.

Soon an organizer will call at your home; welcome him and talk things over. You need have no fear that the company will identify you with this activity, as we will hold only small group meetings until we are sufficiently organized to protect ourselves.

There will be no dues until the division is fully organized and functioning. You must organize eventually—why not now? The bosses are already well organized. The organizer who calls at your home will have union credentials. Talk to no one else. The bosses are afraid of unions and will send spotters to feel you out.

(Signed) Organizing Committee,
Los Angeles Railway & Pacific Electric Carmen, Union Label #27.

Exhibit 10289

Los Angeles Police Department

Office of In. Bu. Metro. Divn.

December 17, 1934.

Memo. Lt. Lane.

Of. Chas. Evans phones in from L. A. Ry. Bldg. 11th & Broadway that on Mondays, Wednesdays, and Fridays the strikers have their meetings at the Labor Temple from 1 p. m. on and that on other days (except Sunday) are there until 5.30 p. m.

This for office information.

F.

Exhibit 10290

Strike Report A. A. of S. E. R. and M. C. O. of A.

Fri. Dec. 28th.

About four hundred men at the meeting today. Featherstone presided throughout the entire meeting. Morgan was not there.

Announcement was made by brother Featherstone that Armstrong would be here either tomorrow or the day after. He said that he thought he would bring with him some of the relief that the organization and the men need so badly. He got a telegram from Armstrong that the International has taken this fight to heart more than any one they have had for a long time. They'll have to take it quite a bit to heart before they part with very much of the cash which is of course always available for purposes such as this; according to what they claim.

A big argument was started at the meeting this afternoon which took almost the entire meeting; it was over the fact that brother Fiske took the floor and asked that since the Amalgamated did not seem to be getting anywhere with the strike that a committee of the rank and file from among the membership of the local be elected by the men and that their job be the investigation of the methods used by Harry Bridges in the winning of the Longshoremen's strike and that they return here by Monday and give an account of their findings and that the Amalgamated profit by it in the winning of this present strike.

This cause a great deal of dissention among the men as a good many of them, not knowing what was behind the move, seemed in favor of it and the others, knowing that it is motivated by the Communist Party argued against it bitterly. Finally it was brought out by various members that Harry Bridges and the "rank and file" stuff is all communist and a vote of confidence was taken in the officers and the entire body voted to abide by what they say and that no committees be allowed to undertake any kind of business for the union unless authorized by the executive board.

Three men are at the head of the rank and file committee, so called, and they are Brothers Fiske, one of the Executive board members, brother Taylor, an oldish sort of man, very tall, with iron grey hair and wearing glasses and brother Noble. These are the ones no doubt who have been in contact with the Communists and were egged on to get up and make that suggestion at the meeting today. No harm was done at the meeting today but the communists are not going to give up so easily and will be at these fellows again; agent does not believe that they knew what they were getting in for when they were approached by the radicals and they are not to be blamed too much, because those communists are the best bunch of talkers in the business; in fact, that's about all they are very good at.

The time of the meetings has been changed by vote from two in the afternoon to ten thirty in the morning on Mondays Wednesdays and Fridays. They plan to have the meetings over with by twelve o'clock so that all pickets who are not at the moment engaged will be sent to the LA Ry. building at eleventh and Broadway directly from the meeting at the labor temple.

Featherstone is going to look the situation over down there at the building and see just how many pickets the area allotted will accommodate and see to it that there are that many down there every day. The number guessed at, was about one hundred pickets. On the days when there is no meeting at the Temple, the men will come to the temple from their morning division picketing and after having breakfast will go the LA Ry. Building.

Somebody made the motion that the picketing at the building be abandoned but the motion was defeated by a vote of about ten to one.

Division four will be picketed tomorrow morning.

This was the first dissension which has come up in the ranks of the union to date, and although it was smoothed over today, it is no good for the morale and there is no doubt in agent's mind that it will recur again in the near future.

The meeting voted to support the move to have the Anti-jitney bus law repealed. There was a great deal of discussion among the men however, after the meeting about the advisability of the move as it would in the first place take so long for it to be put in operation and secondly it would take about the same length of time to do away with it when this strike is settled. The same thing applies if the municipal busses go through. Agent does not believe that the men are all in all so fond of the idea after all, and will become less so the more they can think about it.

#3 says that the ranks of the bus driving strikers are becoming demoralized. He said today that he knew of three of them with families who have not been home for several days and who have been drunk practically all the time. They don't, he said, show any inclination of going back to work, but are beginning to lose faith in the Amalgamated.

EXHIBIT 10291

(In pencil:) "LA Ry. 1060 S. Bdwy. to Lt. Luke Lane."

LOS ANGELES, CALIFORNIA *January 11th, 1935.*

The boys seem to be getting discouraged, and Armstrong made the statement, before he went to Omaha, that the strike was practically washed up. However, Morgan said today that regardless of the attitude of the International Amalgamated Association, the local boys will fight to the finish. They are getting all the unions and citizens in and the strike will last four years is necessary before it will be given up.

The Executive Committee meeting held today decided that the Committee itself would stand together even if all the other members drop out. The Strike will be continued indefinitely.

Morgan said that as a last resort he would call in the Communists to handle the situation and that the Company isn't going to get away with anything this time.   He said that the Central Council and all the other Councils are with him in this movement.   That is with the exception of the Communistic part of it, which he didn't tell them anything about.

Morgan is going to take his old place on the People's Anti-Franchise Committee and fight like the devil.   He is also lending all his support to the Municipal Bys Movement.   This is one movement that the union thinks will put the L. A. Railway Company out of business for all time.   It is a least a straw for them to grasp.

Coleman is busy as Hell, and Agent hasn't been able to see him for the last day and a half, but will contact him over the week-end.   He has something up his sleeve which he is being secretive about but Agent will uncover his purposes over the week-end.

(Written in ink:) "Luke—thot this may be of value to you.—R. H. H."

Exhibit 10292

Annual Report of Los Angeles Railway Corporation, Los Angeles, California, to the Railroad Commission of the State of California For the Year Ended December 31, 1934

[Page 405, Schedule 419 Attached]

This is to certify that attached is a true and correct copy of Schedule 419 on page 405 of the Annual Report of Los Angeles Railway Corporation, Los Angeles, California, to the Railroad Commission of the State of California, for the year ended December 31, 1934.

[SEAL]   H. G. Mathewson,
                             Secretary, Railroad Commission, State of California.

419. PAYMENTS FOR SERVICES NOT RENDERED BY EMPLOYEES

In the form below give information concerning payments, fees, retainers, commissions, gifts, contributions, assessments, bonuses, pensions, subscriptions, allowance for expenses, or any form of payment amounting in the aggregate to $5,000 or more during the year to any corporation, institution, association, firm, partnership, committee, or any person (other than one of respondent's employees covered in Schedule 418, or management fees and expenses covered in Schedule 325 in this annual report) for services or as a donation.

To be included are, among others, payments, directly or indirectly, for legal, medical, engineering, advertising, valuation, accounting, statistical, financial, educational, entertainment, charitable, advisory, defensive, detective, developmental, research, appraisal, registration, purchasing, architectural, and hospital services; payments for expert testimony and for handling wage disputes; and payments for services of banks, bankers, trust companies, insurance companies, brokers, trustees, promoters, solicitors, consultants, actuaries, investigators, inspectors, and efficiency engineers.   Payments to the various railway associations should also be included.   *The enumeration of these kinds of payments should not be understood as excluding other payments for services not excluded below.*

To be excluded are: Rent of buildings or other property, taxes payable to the Federal, State, or local governments; payments for heat, light, power, telegraph, and telephone services; and payments to other carriers on the basis of lawful tariff charges or for the interchange of equipment between carriers.

If more convenient, this schedule may be filled out for a group of roads considered as one system and shown only in the report of the principal road in the system, with references thereto in the reports of the other roads.

If any doubt exists in the mind of the reporting officer as to the reportability of any type of payment, request should be made for a ruling before filing this report.

Line No.	Name of Recipient. (a)	Nature of service. (b)	Amount of payment. (c)
1	Nick Harris Detectives & World Wide Detective Agency.	strike guards	$159,960.22
2	Captain Wm. F. Hynes	strike detail	7,393.68
3	Fusco & McDonald	auto hire account strike	26,944.02
4	Hertz-Driv-Ur-Self Stations	auto hire—strike	14,327.65
5	Walter Jackson	Consultant, (weekly passes)	7,702.00
6	Gibson, Dunn & Crutcher	Retainer fee, legal and other expenses	96,106.24
7	California Hospital	Employers' hospitalization expenses	5,472.68
8	Community Chest of Los Angeles	Donation	8,875.00
9	Electric Railway Presidents' Conference Committee.	contribution in connection with the "Hirshfeld" car.	6,700.00
10	Total		333,481.49

Certified as a True Copy:
[SEAL]

H. G. Mathewson,
Secretary, Railroad Commission, State of California.

Exhibit 10293

Elden, George Z.
324¾ N. Soto St.

Reported by MR Ventor ("Ventor" written in pencil) Lt. Auxiliary Police 1/14/37 as suspected Com. employed as Motorman L. A. RY CO described 175#, 5′ 8½″, gray eyes dark hair, smooth shaven; said to be organizing among St. Ry employees.

Exhibit 10294

Payments of Los Angeles Railway Corporation to P. Edward Wish Detective Agency for Undercover Services, January 1, 1934 to November 24, 1939

(Prepared by the staff of the subcommittee from data received under subpena from the Los Angeles Railway Corporation)

Vo. No.	Date	Amount	Vo. No.	Date	Amount
63880	Jan. 5, 1937	$1,910.85	80845	May 6, 1938	$3,246.21
65270	Feb. 10 "	4,080.57	81891	June 8 "	2,041.19
66285	Mar. 10 "	3,077.84	83137	July 13 "	1,966.04
67068	Apr. 5 "	3,514.60	83755	Aug. 8 "	2,248.12
68213	May 6 "	3,380.40	84552	Sept. 6 "	2,285.92
69650	June 10 "	3,400.90	85672	Oct. 6 "	1,841.00
70426	July 9 "	2,974.38	86557	Nov. 4 "	1,909.13
71407	Aug. 6 "	3,193.84	87498	Dec. 5 "	1,883.90
72333	Sept. 3 "	3,116.73	88542	Jan. 5, 1939	1,809.49
73390	Oct. 8 "	3,142.84	90112	Feb. 13 "	1,951.83
74399	Nov. 4 "	3,825.57	90849	Mar. 9 "	1,577.70
75660	Dec. 7 "	3,655.94	91879	Apr. 11 "	1,869.04
76547	Jan. 6, 1938	3,411.18	92593	May 5 "	1,778.48
77771	Feb. 9 "	3,440.37	95092	July 18 "	673.63
78701	Mar. 8 "	3,088.70			
79781	Apr. 7 "	3,383.06	Total		79,679.45

E. Upholsterers Union

Exhibit 10295

Los Angeles, Cal., *June 6, 1933.*

Re: Scheduled Upholsterers' Strike.

Capt. Wm. F. Hynes,
  Commanding Intelligence Bureau.

Sir: Together with Officers Pfeiffer, Abbott, Phelps and myself, we went to Universal Furniture Mfg. Co. 1617 McGary St. PR 4068, yesterday at 3 p. m. and stayed there until 5.15.

During that time several carloads of men and others on foot were about the vicinity of the Universal plant, and in questioning some of these men, found that most of them were from Brown & Salzman Furniture Factory, which is a Union shop. They stated their purpose of being at the Universal plant was to inform the upholsterers at the Universal that there would be a meeting of the Upholsterers' Union last night at which they would discuss their labor conditions and at which a vote would be taken as to whether the Union would call a general strike of the upholsterers in this city.

We told them that owing to assertions made by Tom Mayhew and others of the Union, that men working at the Universal would be forced to join the strike if one were called and that violence would be committed against some of the people at the Universal if they failed to accede to the demands of the Union, therefore, we would not permit them to loiter about the premises, we knowing their purpose for them being there.

We moved and dispersed between 20 and 30 Mexicans and about 5 white men in that vicinity, and informed them that if a strike was called and picketing was resorted to or any violence committed against men who were working, that drastic action would be taken against them and that we would not stand for any monkey business.   These men that had gathered about were easily dispersed and only about 6 showing any reluctance about moving on when asked to do so.

This morning (June 6) at seven, Officers Pfeiffer, Abbott and myself went to Universal Furniture Mfg. Co.   No picketeers showed up in that vicinity and we learned about 8 o'clock that it was decided at the meeting last night that a strike would not be called at this time, that they would await the outcome of a Federal Bill that was being passed in Congress some time this week pertaining to the industrial control bill governing wages, hours, etc.   Therefore, we returned to this office.

  Respectfully,

R. A. Wellpott, #1533.

W:F

Exhibit 10296

Los Angeles Police Department
Office. of In. Bu. Metro. Divn.

Oct. 3, 1934.

Re: Pending Upholsters' Strike.

Lieut. Luke M. Lane,
  Commanding Intelligence Bureau.

Sir: Telephone report from Archie Smith is that a general walkout of upholsters will likely occur next Monday morning in Los Angeles.   This upholsters' strike will be Coast-wide, the upholsters having been called out yesterday at 11 o'clock in San Francisco and in Oakland they were called out at 12 noon; strike is also in progress at Portland and Seattle

Efforts are being made here locally by the local office of the National Labor Board to call representatives of the Union and furniture manufacturers association into a conference to reach some agreement to avert the strike.

  Mr. Smith said he would keep me posted, as to any developments.

  Respectfully,

R. A. Wellpott, DL 131.

W:F

EXHIBIT 10297

[Intra-Departmental Correspondence.   Form 235]

LOS ANGELES POLICE DEPARTMENT
Office of In. Bu. Metro. Divn.

OCT. 6, 1934.

Memo. Re: Proposed Strike of Upholsterers' close of business Monday, Oct. 8–34.

Mr. Smith of Universal Furniture Co. 16th & McGarry Sts. phones in that at a meeting of the Local #15 of Upholsterers' International Union, held at Labor Temple on Maple Ave. last night, they voted to go on strike *next Monday evening;* this in support of the Bay Region and other Pac. Coast points, and that there will be no arbitration until there is some sort of an agreement as to their wages and hours.

Mr. Smith informed us that employees in his factory are not going on strike, that they are organizing a Union within their own shop, and that they are being advised by the Federal Labor advisors to make their organization bonafide.

Mr. Smith requested that 2 officers be detailed to his factory Monday noon, Oct. 8–34, because an effort will be made to have his employes join the general walkout of the upholsters.

RAW:F

EXHIBIT 10298

[Intra-Departmental Correspondence.   Form 236]

LOS ANGELES POLICE DEPARTMENT
Office of In. Bu. Metro. Divn.

OCT. 10, 1934.

Confidential Memo.

Opr. B–20 phones that,

He talked to Rubin last night re the strike, who claimed the AFofL Loca 15 Upholsterers is arranging for arbitration but that the TUUL Rank & File are trying to continue with the strike.

Weekly Org. meeting held TUUL Hall 8 p. m. last night.   There is to be a general membership Meeting held Thursday night, Oct. 11 at TUUL Hall at 8.30 for the Downtown Sub-section, this is the first one in a long time,—3 or 4 months, expects about 130 to be present.

RE The YCL, this girl, Lucille Gordon sort of a sub-section YCL assistant to Jack Moore, came to the meeting last night.   She wants the sub-section to furnish this YCL Red paint and the agreed.   The YCL is going around in a few days and paint Sam Darcy election slogans and hammer and cycles on empty buildings in red paint—probably mostly up around Bunker Hill.

Bill Dunn, nationally known Com. leader, is coming here from New York, due to talk at 732 So. Grnd. Oct. 21, 8 p. m.

Ezra Chase is the organizer of the SERA Grievance, a new orgn. started up for SERA members have any grievances are supposed to report to him at 3015 So. San Pedro St.   He is to take up all SERA grievances.

EXHIBIT 10299

[Intra-Departmental Correspondence.   Form 236]

LOS ANGELES POLICE DEPARTMENT
Office of In. Bu. Metro. Divn.

OCT. 13, 1934.

Confidential Memorandum.

Opr. B–20 phones that, attended Upholsterers' Union meeting last night at Labor Temple, started about 5 o'clock and ended about 7.20.   Herman White was chairman, he is president of Local 15 Upholsterers' of AFofL and first order of business was reports of different people on the strike list.

A big, tall fellow, about 170#, wears a white shirt is picket captain. The Red Squad asked him yesterday if he was a picket captain and he said no, there was no leader, but he is. He made a motion to go up to Mayor Shaw and prevent the police from interferring with the pickets—they didn't mentioned specifically the Red Squad.

There were several men got up and talked on different individual agreements made by different shops who want them to go back as individuals, and this seemed nearly to carry, until CHAIT got up and gave the people a talk told them the upholsterers were waiting for years to get the bosses in this position and they must stand for a united front and accept no agreements without the single Strike Committee. Also different people talked suggesting that they not let any violence take place, that the pickets wouldn't make any remarks to the police as they passed them and further wouldn't holler through the windows "scabs" at people work. These statements were not formally put up but more as suggestions and they seemed to be approved by the large majority of applause given them.

As a whole Chait seems to have made a large following among the upholsterers and furniture workers among AFofL members. He received large applause on his remarks. He got up and praised the solidarity of the united front and for the part taking in picketing. He said "If we haven't got enough men to picket we will get 10,000 more pickets" and he was applauded on that. He said they should accept no individual agreement, that they should all stay out and should keept a united front and to get large applause.

Also present at this meeting were 15 men from Angelus Furniture Co. who are supposed to belong to Local Union #1 of the Independent Furniture Workers Union (Busick's outfit) and some of them got up and said they had quit from today and were coming in and joining the F. W. I. U. These 15 came in a body and they said they were now joined with the F. W. I. U.

Opr. further said that trouble was avoided yesterday when the Red Squad took Meyer Baylin off the line and that trouble was averted over this by the picket captain, a big fellow called Johnny, about 6', who stopped the racket among pickets.

Said further plans are to contact Barker Bros and Bullocks upholsterers' and bring them out by Monday. There are two or three more little shops that have from 6 to 8 people and they plan to contact them at their homes and trying and get them out by Monday also.

Said main points of pickets are Roverti's, Universal and Turner's. He said there was no indication of any violence or disturbance that Local 15 seems to want peaceful pickets, but CHAIT wants mass picketing, shop by shop and if the scabs don't come out, he wants to go in and bring them out. He was going to try and get that over at the meeting; however, he didn't come out openly with that, but told them to stand together in mass picketing in a united front.

About 300 people present at this meeting.

Opr. Further said that Voulich who was active during the Milk Strike last winter and then beat it to Seattle is back now in Unit 9; also came in unit 9 old man George Paff, 531 Aries St. 70 years old (an old ex-wobbly known in San Pedro in 1922 and John Nordmark who was active in RWPU.

Said unit 11 is now under Steve Somers as organizer who is building the unit up, now has about 24 members.

Said re the Unemployed Convention at Fresno, T. H. Randel, young fellow and Burns are to be present at this convention; Chase and Sanders who were elected for the RWPU both declined. Rendel and Burns are to leave this morning.

A YCL girl named Kress is getting up YCL campaign bulletins, they are to be printed by Nick, putting out in name of Young Voters League.

Said the Party Organizer for Oct. has instructions on roll of YCL in elections, etc.

Exhibit 10300

BILL: These are not quite all the members. Mayhew claims they are practically all organized and he is taking them in every day.

I have taken these names from the ledgers, day books and got fifteen of them out of Mayhew's note book. I tried to list them all alphabetically so they would be handy for you. I am sorry that it took so long but no human could have gotten them any faster with several strikes on and the Business Agents terribly busy and afraid to let out any information.

I had to copy the names by hand out of the books myself and some of the writing is poor and almost impossible to make out so some of the names may be slightly mispelled but they are about ninety per cent correct.

I just took it for granted that the list of names I got out of his book were newly obtained members and listed them herewith as such.

The officials claim that since the Jews got into this business they cheapened everything and make so much shoddy that it is up to the unions to make them come to time. Mayhew claims that they are going to continue pulling strikes and keeping the bosses in hot water.

I was also tipped off that sabotage is going to be attempted is certain spots.

I spent almost a whole week in the little office in the alley on south side of Labor temple getting this dope so naturally heard much of the talk that went on.

X50

There are some more, perhaps about fifty which I'll mail you special tonight as I could not get the ledger to copy them. I go as far as the letter S. I would have had them long ago but for the strikes etc. Everything is fine.

Also enclosing all the firms you may have use for them.

Exhibit 10301

[Intra-Departmental Correspondence   Form 235]

Los Angeles Police Department
Office of In. Bu. Metro. Div.

9/30/35   4.10 p. m.

Re Strike at Ziem Upholster Co. 310 No. Ave. 21
Memo. Capt. Hynes

Per instructions went to above concern where we learned six men who worked in shop there went on strike this morning and were sitting parked in car near corner of factory during morning and until this afternoon, stopping people who came to the plant to secure work from an ad firm had placed in paper.

Mr. Ziem hired 2 new employees while we were there and we advised him to pick them up in the morning; that if he had further trouble to phone in.

ROGERS, L. E.
CATHERMAN, C. D.

Exhibit 10302

Recd 3/3/37.

Report on Upholsterers Union

Have been following your suggestion of stirring up the membership about too much secrecy and the absence of financial reports.

The result was—at the last meeting they reported the finances as a little more than $500.00 and promised a detailed report in the near future.

They also elected a full time secretary and treasurer at a salary of $40.00 per week and expenses—Charlie Yost is holding the office.

This brings the pay roll to about $400.00 per mo. The estimated expenses per month are as follows:

Salaries	400. 00
Per Capita Tax (This is to the Central Labor Co. Per Capita Tax to the International is exempt because of the Kroehler Strike)	40. 00
Hall rent	25. 00
Utilities	15. 00
Strike Benefits	1200. 00
Misc	100. 00
Approximate Expense per mo	$1780. 00

Dues 400.00 per mo or less.

Assessments—there has been no report whatever. However, the union is spending far beyond its income. It is in a bad state of affairs, and should they become involved in a fairly good sized strike, their condition would be critical.

In the election for a delegate to International Convention the vote was as follows: Chase, 52; Yost, 37; Bruner, 19.

The result—election won and then—reported the San Diego members were voting by telephone and they called up and reported San Diego had cast it's 26 votes for Yost giving him a total of 63.

I didn't look for such a rank act and I was sure the members were pretty sore, so before they could protest Chase jumped to the floor and declared the election to be fair and square and I made a motion to elect Yost unanimously.

Now the members are wanting to reopen the elections.

The manner in which Chase was defeated was helpful to me.

Investigated the San Diego vote and Westfall went to San Diego and lined up the boys for Yost. He also split the fraction and defeated them. Yost is a re-actionery.

The party is calling an investigation of the affair. So I am certain Chase will gain ground there.

The party is disgusted with the fraction and they will soon take action, so I am moving with the party, and soon expect to get Westfall, Staudera & Silva out of the fraction, then I will have complete control and then I can rebuild it with material of my selection.

We are about to start picketing furniture stores.

Exhibit 10303

[Intra-Departmental Correspondence. Form 235]

Los Angeles Police Department
Office of In. Bu. Metro. Divn.

Oct 1–35, 4.30 p. m.

Re Upholster Strike Situation.
Memo. Capt. Hynes.

Mr. Iske phones in that following 3 firms are going to put up a fight with union, viz: Roberti Bros (plan hire new men tomorrow in place of men who struck); Ziem; Bay Murray (already hired new men).

These are only 3 firms they have involved now.

F

F. Furniture Workers Union

Exhibit 10304

[Intra-Departmental Correspondence]

Los Angeles Police Department
Office of _____

B–50
Capt. Hynes or Lt. Wellpot

We called a strike tonight 9/16—All workers will go out at 7:30 A. M. tomorrow. Moody Bed Co., 154 East 57 St. If you have any special instruction for me leave note with night man at office and I will call in tomorrow night.

B–50
Catherman   12 M 9/16.

EXHIBIT 10305

[Intra-Departmental Correspondence. Form 235]

LOS ANGELES POLICE DEPARTMENT
Office of In. Bu. Metro Div.

DEC. 16, 1933   10 a. m.

Memo. Re Strike against Soronow Furniture Co. 905 E 59 St.

Officer Chas J Evans phones in from above concern phones in that he learns re this dispute as follows:

Mr. Soronow said that 8 men working in upholstery dept. on chairs and daven-ports walked out due to dissatisfaction on apportioning particular kind of work out; said that on expensive chairs, etc. it was necessary to assign especially expert men; apparently no Union involved in this strike.

Of. Evans phoned in a few minutes later that he had talked to some men picketing outside and they told him there was a strike on that it had something to do with wages.

Of. Evans advised Sam Evans that 14 men were out; expects may be some difficulty Monday morning.

F

EXHIBIT 10306

[Intra-Departmental Correspondence. Form 235]

LOS ANGELES POLICE DEPARTMENT
Office of In. Bu. Metro Div

Memo. Re Strike Saranow Furniture Co. 905 E. 59 St.

Dec. 18–33, 3.30 p. m.—Officer Chas. Evans phones in that he learns strike this firm evidently called by the Upholsterers' Industrial Union of T. U. U. L., an application blank for this having been found inside the shop. He said 6 shop workers were out, but they have from 15 to 20 pickets around; also that large tacks are being thrown in the street; he said there are about 4 or 5 men employed in the shop, not counting office employes. No handbills being distributed.

EXHIBIT 10307

[Intra-Departmental Correspondence]

LOS ANGELES POLICE DEPARTMENT
Office of In. Bu. Metro Div

DEC. 21, 1933

Re: Strike Situation, SORONOW FURNITURE CO., 905 E. 59 St.
Capt. WM. F. HYNES,
Commanding Intelligence Bureau

SIR: In connection with strike called on above concern, wish to report as follows:

Men who went out on strike effective Thursday, Dec. 14, 1933 under auspices of the Furniture Workers Industrial Union of the T. U. U. L. are as follows: P. Conte, F. Conte, C. Tucciaidi, F. Dewhe, S. Glembot, S. Sato, S. Diamond, F. Soto, H. Lopez, A. Seiber, D. Corellone, E. Rivers, B. Grozes.

Of the above listed names, most all are upholsters and Sid Diamond and Sam Glembot are the most active, Mr. Soronow has a full crew working now, mostly American help. There are other members of this Union picketing this shop, in addition to the above, of which one is Joe Daw. We question new pickets as they arrive on scene, and finding they have no business there we advise them to leave. So far we have made no arrests or had any serious difficulties.

CHAS. J. EVANS.
SAM EVANS.

CJE:F

EXHIBIT 10308

[Intra-Departmental Correspondence. Form 235]

LOS ANGELES POLICE DEPARTMENT

OFFICE OF INTELLIGENCE BU. METRO DIV

JAN. 3, 1934

Re: Termination Strike Duty at Soronow Furniture Co. 905 E. 59 St. AX 9293.
Capt. WM. F. HYNES,
    Commanding Intelligence Bureau.

SIR: Wish to report that in view of the fact that no pickets whatsoever have appeared at this concern the last three or four working days, Mr. Soronow feels as though he does not need us any more, as he believes the strike is over, as most of the men who struck have collected their tools and checks.

Therefore, we terminated our tour of duty there effective 6 p. m. last night, Jan. 2, 1934. We advised Mr. Soronow in case pickets cause further trouble, to advise this office at once.

The firm now has a full crew working, about twenty employees—none of them strikers.

Respectfully,

C. J. EVANS.
S. G. EVANS.

CJE:F

EXHIBIT 10309

LOS ANGELES, CALIF.,
Mon. July 1st, 1935.

Confidential Memo.

Oprs. report re activities of the Furniture Workers Union Local #1561 (A. F. of L.)

Opr. reports that all activities of the union will be directed against the Gillespie Furniture Mfg. Co. Talk among the union officials is that four furniture manufacturing companies are willing to sign an agreement with recognition of the union, but are unable to do so because Mr. Forest Gillespie has organized several of the manufacturers to fight the union in this strike, and in so doing each member who had entered into an agreement with Mr. Gillespie had to post $1,000 bond, so that in case one of the manufacturers withdrew from this group, his bond would be forfeited. Therefore, if the union is able to force Gillespie Furniture Mfg. Co. to recognize the union and meet their demands the other manufacturers would be more than glad to fall in line.

Opr. also reports that Mr. Fitzgerald, some sort of Federal Labor Concilator has told them that Gillespie is tough and is the only manufacturer that is blocking recognition of the union and, therefore, the union should direct their efforts towards bringing this firm into line.

Practically all picketing will be directed against the Gillespie Furniture Mfg. Co.

Opr. reports that Sitkin of the Angelus Furniture Mfg. Co. has been endeavoring to organize a shop union, that out of 350 employees, 150 were members of Furniture Workers Union Local #1561. It is talked about the union hall that Sitkin was not very successful in this move and that 50 additional employees of Angelus Furn. Mfg. Co. joined Local #1561, and that a great many of these had joined the company union are or were members of the Furniture Workers Industrial Union, that the Reds practically have control of the company union. Opr. further reports that the officials of Local #1561 are quite amused at the fact that Mr. Sitkin of Angelus Furn. Co. has asked the aid of them to clean the Reds out of the company union.

EXHIBIT 10310

[Intra-Departmental Correspondence]

LOS ANGELES POLICE DEPARTMENT
Office of In. Bu. Metro. Divn.

7–11–35   noon.

Memo. Re Communist Agitator among Martin Young Furniture Co. employees.

Mr. Martin Young of above firm phones in complaining an agitator appears at his plant 2 or 3 times a week during noon hour and harangues his employees when outside for lunch; this subject is J. A. Silva (former employee) and he believes an assistant of Hymen Chait. Said subject is out there now; described as big nose, sort of closed eyes, 35 years old, now wearing straw hat, white shirt color open.

Said his firm has no trouble but don't want any worked up by agitators; said talked to Chief Davis at range meeting and the Chief advised him contact this Bureau re any agitators around his employees; would like something done re this.

EXHIBIT 10311

JULY 27, 1935.

REPORT OF UNDERCOVER OPERATIVES

Subject: Meeting at Labor Temple, Maple Street July 26, 1930, 7:30PM.

This meeting was an advertised, open meeting, of the Furniture Union #1561 held for the benefit of the general public that they might learn the facts of the strike.

The first speaker was a man named Murray, an organizer for the furniture union and he spoke on the general conditions in the unions and gave the causes for the strike.

Next Antonio Entenza, also spoke of general condition of all unions and labor organizations. He stated that the strikers were right and should hold out indefinitely.

He was followed by Saul Klein, Los Angeles attorney, who spoke on general labor conditions. His topic was: "As Milk from contented cows makes a good sales talk, furniture from contented workers should also make a good sales talk." Klein exhibited a poster received through the mail, which was a photograph of Tom Mooney, commemorating today as the nineteenth anniversary of his incarceration.

The last speaker was Bill BUSIC, Communist organizer, who ran down every form of government from the local police to the President of the United States. He insisted that the workers should not be satisfied with shorter hours but should continue their efforts until they actually owned the business. He stated that Mayor Shaw and his tool, Chief Davis, had been put in office by the labor party, but that they had, since being in office, only aided in the betterment of the owners and the capitalists. He also stated that he was against the constitution and all present political organizations. He called attention to the fact that Chief Davis had mailed a letter to the strikers in the clothing and furniture industry, advising them not to strike, stating that in the event of a strike he would take stringent means to aid the manufacturers put down any strike or labor difficulty that labor might develop. He argued that the present form of government is controlled by the Supreme Court, which is composed of past members of the Capitalist party, and they have declared unconstitutional every bid of labor legislation. He stated that the present strike will be aided by other organized unions.

There were no resolutions passed at this meeting.

The meeting was quiet and orderly.

Respectfully

OPERATOR A–10 AND B–6

EXHIBIT 10312

FURNITURE WORKERS UNION, INCORPORATED

LOS ANGELES, CALIFORNIA, *November 19, 1937.*

To all Applicants and Members.

Our first regular meeting will be held on Monday evening, November 22nd, next at the Polish Hall, 608 East 42d Street (opposite Wrigley Field, on Avalon Blvd.).

Offices open for payment of dues at 7:30, meeting called to order at 8:00. We will have as speaker of the evening Mr. Wilahan, one of the founders of the Independent Union Movements, and address which you cannot afford to miss. Membership credentials will be ready for you, and plans made for election of your Representatives on the governing board.

We will also be able to tell you some of the latest obstructionists methods to keep you from working, notably on the Biltmore Hotel job, rumors of which you have no doubt heard.

Rumors have come to our ears of dire threats of strike, boycott, etc., being made by certain union interests. Don't let them kid you. I think we will have a theme song, "Who's afraid of the big bad wolf."

————— —————, *Secretary.*

Please sign your name below, and present this slip at the door for admission.

(Pencil notation) "MILAKEN, *Speaker*
JE 2400"

G. GARMENT AND TEXTILE WORKERS

EXHIBIT 10313

LOS ANGELES, CAL., *Sept. 8, 1933, 4:15 pm*

Memo: Re Request DETAIL 939 So. Broadway 7:30 a. m. Sat. Sept.9–33.

Mr. Jos. Zukin of 939 So. Broadway, TR 7557 calls in asks for Capt. Hynes, and states re matter he previous spoke about he would like a detail of 3 plain clothes officers at his address in the morning, as they intend to work to make up for Monday, a holiday; he said they intend to work all day.

F (In pencil:) "HYNES & ABBOTT"

EXHIBIT 10314

LOS ANGELES, CAL. *5 pm SEPT 8–33*

Re Request DETAIL Sat morning at 217 E. 8th St.

Mr. Bardfield of J. BARDFIELD Co. ladies garments, room 1106—217 E. 8th St. TU 4778 phones in that his shop intended to work tomorrow SAT. to make up for Monday, a holiday, said three or four of his employees, whom he states are Reds, have told him he could expect trouble, that they did not intend to work tomorrow. Asks protection. He opens at 8 a. m. and expects to be open all day.

(In pencil) PHELPS & EVANS
YO 3273

EXHIBIT 10315

LOS ANGELES POLICE DEPT

SEPT 12–33.

Memo. Re Picketing: GLICKMAN & Co. (uniforms) 128 E. 9th St. TR 6536.

Mr. Glickman above firm phones in requesting detail to prevent interference his employees entering building to work. Said this trouble been going on about a week; said they had signed up with the Journeyman Tailors, complying with NRA, shorter hours, 20% increase; said Amalgamated was causing the picketing.

Said hours most needed officers: 7.15 to 8.30 am; 11.30 am to 1.30 pm.
Employees quit at 4 pm.
Said occupied entire top floor of two story building. If he is not in will leave data with girl in office.
F

Note for Capt. Hynes Sept. 13–33: Yesterday, about 11 am, Officer Abbott and I called at above mentioned shop and talked with Mr. Glickman, and he informed us that a week ago one of the men that was a go-between the Amalgamated Union and his shop quit because of a little dispute. Twelve other employees quit and left the shop during the next three or four days. A strike was not declared until Friday, Sept. 8, and picketing was at that time started by the Amalgamated Clothers' Union.

Mr. Glickman said he began replacing employees who had quit their jobs, and these new employees were contacted by the picketeers, and four or five of them failed to return for work; therefore, Mr. Glickman called our Bureau yesterday and asked for assistance.

Officer Abbott and I started policing yesterday noon, and just before 12 noon, about 12 pickets appeared and began walking back and forth before the shop. When journeymen from Mr. Glickman's shop came down for dinner, we saw to it that they were not molested by the picketeers. Our action had a tendency to discourage their picketing and yesterday at 4 pm a committee of four went to Mr. Glickman to negotiate the return of those who had quit their jobs with him. A final agreement was not reached until today (Sept. 13) noon when another committee of three went to Mr. Glickman and on agreement was reached regarding their return to work and the strike was officially called off.

Mr. Glickman has signed up with the Journeymen's Tailoring Union, affiliated with the A. F. of L. Mr. Glickman was informed the Journeymen's Union voted on his application last night's meeting, accepting same.

W:F   R. A. WELLPOTT $1533.

EXHIBIT 10316

LOS ANGELES, CAL., *Oct. 6, 1933, 9.50 am.*
Memo. Re Strike at Golden State Tailoring Co. 1042 So. L. A. St. PR 0288.

Mr. Jack Munzo of Clothing Mfgrs. Asso. phones in and reports that strike is in progress at that concern, 11th & Los Angeles Sts. Mr. Keen and Mr. Cohn are owners of this concern. The organization calling the strike is the Amalgamated Clothing Workers of America.
F
Officers Wellpott & Abbott, DETAILED to cover this.
By direction:
WM. F. HYNES,
Actg. Capt. Dets, LAPD, Comdg.

NOTE 10–6–33, 11 am: Called on above firm and talked with Mr. Keen and Mr. Cohn, also Mr. Munzo, who was present. Mr. Munzo stated that their Board is meeting with a delegation from the Amalgamated Union and an N. R. A. Mediation Board this afternoon to arbitrate the differences between the manufacturers and Union.

They said it would all depend on the outcome of this conference as to reaching an agreement, that at present there was no need for any police protection because their place was not being picketed. However, if an agreement was not reach and strike continued, undoubtedly the Union would picket their place and they were advertising for new help which would be prevented from applying for jobs, if they did not have necessary police to prevent this action of strikers.

Mr. Munzo will phone this office if it is necessary to have a police detail after today.

The entire shop went out, except foreman.
W:F   WELLPOTT-ABBOTT.

Exhibit 10317

[Intra-Departmental Correspondence. Form 235]

Los Angeles Police Department

Office of Metro Div. in BU

[Confidential]

Oct. 16–33 5.30 pm.

Memo. Re Strike Plans.

Mr. Booth of Associated Apparel Asso. phones in he was delivered an unsolicited report from the Pinkerton people today that an executive member of Communist Party attended a secret meeting of all organizers of the Needle Trades Workers Ind. Union at 755 So Main where they said that *starting tomorrow* all Los Angeles dressmakers, men and women are to form pickets, members of CP mingling with the strikers to see that no non-union workers take the place of the strikers, all pickets to report tomorrow morning.

Exhibit 10318

[Intra-Departmental Correspondence. Form 236]

Los Angeles Police Department

Office of In. Bu. Metro Div

Oct. 17–33 5.35 p. m.

Memo. re Officer, Special Duty, Connection Strike.

Call from Mr. Bloom who says with Bureau Investigation for Govt and NRA phones in re furnishing an officer special duty connection strike.
Says can get him 9 to 5 daily MA 2751, at nights NA 2493.

Exhibit 10319

[Intra-Departmental Correspondence. Form 236]

Los Angeles Police Department

Office of Intelligence Bureau, Metropolitan Division

Statement of Mr. George Jennings, 450 So. Benton Way, FE 4696 (landlady's phone) taken in office Intellgence Bureau, LAPD Saturday, Oct. 21, 1933, 1:06 pm; in connection with transporting a "load" of non-striking emplloyees from 860 So. L. A. St. to Pico & Main, Friday, Oct. 20–33;

Present: Officer R. A. Wellpott, Mr. Geo. Jennings; Frank H. Folsom, stenographer.

Mr. Folsom. Mr. Jennings, give a general statement of your order to haul some girls away from So. Los Angeles St. yesterday?

A. At 2.30 p. m. Friday, Oct. 20th I received a waybill and Car #41 from the garage at 2500 West 6th, Bristol Limousine, and was ordered to go to 860 So. Los Angeles St., orders being issued to me by Mrs. Bristol, and told I was to be there at 2:45 p. m. and be sure and have the waybill signed.

I arrived at my destination and lined up with other cars from same company, with which I worked, and at about 3 o'clock had eight women placed in my car (which is a Cadillac limousine, bearing license PCJ–41).

I was told by a gentleman wearing a light gray suit and who wore a little black mustache, a light gray felt hat, about 32–3 years old, to take my party around two or three blocks to be sure that the car was not being followed and then to take them to their respective carlines where they could get street cars to go home. He said, "You don't have to take them very far and hurry back for another load." After we started out a motorcycle officer followed the car north on Los Angeles St. to 7th, east on 7th to Maple, south on Maple. Here, I want to correct a statement I made to Capt. Hynes last night over the phone. He asked me if at any time I was on 11th St. and I believe now, as I recall, that I did turn and go west on 11th St. one block, when one of the women mentioned the Union Hdqrs was on that st. some place so I turned off at that st. and went south to Pico on Wall St., I believe it was.

The motorcycle officer only followed me to about 9th St. and Maple, I think it was, and I continued to glance back to see if I was followed, by another car, and no other car was following me. I then proceeded west on Pico to Main St. to the northeast corner of the intersection, pulled up to the curb and discharged the load.

Q. At their request or what way?

A. Not particularly their request, they said all going south on Main St. and that was the carline there.

Q. After discharging the load, what did you do?

A. I waited on the corner for about 30 seconds or so while traffic signals changed and at no time did I see any suspicious loiterers or see any commotion of any kind. The women walked towards their various street car locations and I drove north on Main to 9th, east on 9th to Los Angeles and south on Los Angeles to 860 So. Los Angeles St. to pick up my second load, arriving there about 3.10 p. m. Some man dressed in a reddish brown suit, a man I judge to be around 50 years old, stepped out from the curb and asked me where I had taken my load to. I told him and he told me that then I was supposed to take the parties any place they wanted to go and asked me why I didn't do it. I informed him of my prior orders and he wanted to know who gave me those orders. I told him I didn't know the gentleman's name but I described the gentleman to him and he informed me he was the boss and he was giving me orders. He gave me no name.

I then took my load to 7th and Hill and 7th & Broadway and then proceeded back to 860 So. Los Angeles St. When I arrived, about 3:20 p. m., the same gentleman that gave me my orders to take the passengers to any place they wanted to go, stepped out from the curb, asked me my name and wanted to know why I drove the load in front of Union Hdqrs. 11th and Main. I informed him I did not drop any load in front of the Union Hdqrs. at 11th and Main, nor did I go pass the intersection of 11th and Main while carrying passengers in the car. While he was talking to me, the first gentleman, the one wearing the gray suit, came up to the car and I tried to inform the second gentleman of the orders that the first one had given me and pointed him out as the man had given those orders, but he disregarded me entirely, turned his back on me, told me that was all, I could go.

I proceeded back to the garage at 2500 West 6th St. and was there informed by Mrs. Bristol that the load that I had dropped at 11th and Main had all been beaten up and taken to the hospital, and that the police department was looking for me. This was about 3:45 p. m.

As I was supposed to return to duty at 7 p. m. I told Mrs. Bristol that I would go home and would be back at 7 o'clock, that I did not drop any load at 11th and Main, that possibly they had the drivers mixed up. When I arrived at the garage at 7 p. m. I was informed that I would not be allowed to work, that Capt. Hynes had made repeated efforts to get hold of me. I then asked Mrs. Bristol why she hadn't given Capt. Hynes my address. She made no excuse, so I told her I would then call up Capt. Hynes and get in touch with him by telephone. She said, "no, no, don't do that." I said, "all right then, I will go home but if Capt. Hynes calls for me tell him where I am." After I got home I got to thinking the matter over and I called up Capt. Hynes. Until this time, my boss, Mr. Bristol, has not talked with me concerning this affair, nor has anyone named to me the accuser or have I been identified as the driver that dropped the load at 11th and Maine.

Q. How are you identified with the company?

A. As Driver #2, wearing a uniform cap, with chauffeur's uniform.

Q. When you left the garage, did you have knowledge of the nature of the load you was to carry at all?

A. Not directly, except recognizing the address as being in the zone of the garment strike, and knowing that other cars from the same garage had taken loads away from this locality on the preceding day. I work nights and on the day in question I was asleep at noon when the telephone call came, my wife answered the call, and it said Mr. Bristol wanted me to be over at the garage not later than 2:30. That is not unusual because they have called me at various times to come over and be there when the other drivers were all out in case somebody else wanted a car and they had no driver there. But when I reported to the garage Mrs. Bristol had waybill made out, told me to hurry.

Q. How long did it take you for your car down to 860 So. Los Angeles?

A. I imagine about 12 minutes.

Q. You proceeded direct, without stopping at all?

A. Yes.

Officer WELLPOTT. I understand you to say you took your first load out at 3 o'clock?

A. Yes, I didn't look at my watch, but as near as I can estimate the time it was about 3.

Q. You left your garage at 2:30, I understand you to say?

A. The ticket was punched at 2:30, but I had to go upstairs to get the car, which took about 2 or 3 minutes to warm up the motor. The ticket was punched out, given to me and I took it up to get the car; I didn't go by the office; went on the ramp and right on out.

Q. You went and got your car and it took you about 30 minutes to get——

A. About 15 minutes. I was sitting in the line up about 15 minutes, as I remember.

Q. Did you have any conversation after you left the garage until you arrived at 860?

A. No.

Q. Did you have any conversation with any of the boys that delivered the loads the previous day from there?

A. Yes.

Q. Regarding the strike?

A. Yes.

Q. Was there anything in the nature of these conversations that any of these boys are in sympathy with the strike?

A. No.

Q. Just, in substance, what was the general conversation you had regarding the strike with these boys?

A. They just told me voluntarily they were down to take some of the strike-breakers home and I said didn't it take a lot of nerve to pull it down there where there are mobs on the street, and they said everything was orderly, there is policemen there, plenty of policemen and they line up and load your car, right with you all the time, and they said in case you ever do go down there keep the door locked on your side and the window up.

Q. Did you have any further conversation regarding the strike with these other drivers?

A. None that I recall, no.

Q. Did you at any time previous to that have any conversation regarding the strike, in case you went there?

A. No.

Mr. Folsom: Are you a member of any Labor Union?

A. No.

Q. Have you ever been a member?

A. Yes.

Q. What Union, where and when?

A. The Chauffeur's Union here in Los Angeles, that was a year ago last February, I think it was, no before then, probably Jan. or Dec. preceding that, I only belonged about 3 or 4 months, if I remember correctly.

Q. What other Unions have you belonged to, if any?

A. That is the only one, I belonged to, this particular Union on two different occasions.

Officer WELLPOTT. Who was business manager of this particular Union?

A. George Baker.

Mr. FOLSOM. You say you belonged on two occasions?

A. The occasion before that I was driving for the Red Top Cab, but I have forgotten the year, and the Union blew up shortly after I joined, lots of internal strife in there and I got out, and later on reorganized. George Baker asked me to come back again, I went back into the Union and I got driving for the Red Top Cab Co. and I didn't keep up my dues, I was automatically dropped.

Officer WELLPOTT. What was the reason of not keeping up your dues?

A. The Union couldn't do me any good where I was and insufficient money to carry the dues.

Q. You dropped out about how long ago?

A. I think it was a year ago last February.

Q. How many cars from the Bristol Cab Co. went down there?

A. I don't know exactly, there was 3 limousine and I think 3 small sedans.

Q. Did you all go to 860?

A. Yes.

Q. Were they all reporting to the same that you (were) at 860?

A. Well, Mr. Bristol himself was there, I don't know as to that. I don't know whether all loaded out of this particular place; Mr. Bristol was there himself, he was driving one of the cars.

Q. How many cars went out ahead of you from the garage, were they all checked out ahead of you?

A. Yes, I think they were. I think I was the last one out; they were all gone when I went over and got my car.

Q. The other cars had loaded and pulled out ahead of you at 860?

A. At 860, I don't remember whether I was the last car or not. I distinctly remember seeing three cars loaded out ahead of me; one of the small and big ones, the Pierce Arrow and Cadillac loaded out ahead of me and one of the small cars loaded out ahead of me.

Q. I will ask you the the question, at any time enroute from 860 S. Los Angeles St. until the time you arrived at Pico and Main, did you stop to let these people out?

A. No.

Q. Had they asked you to stop to let them out previous to the time of arriving at Pico and Main?

A. No.

Q. Did they ask you to leave them at Pico and Main?

A. No.

Q. Did they make any objection to being let out at Pico and Main?

A. No.

Q. Did these women tell you they wanted to take the street car south on Main St.?

A. Yes.

Q. About where were you in this roundabout route you took these women?

A. They didn't ask me to leave them at Pico and Main, but I was merely following my orders from 860 was to take them to their street car line and get back as quickly as possible.

Q. Did you see any group of people anywhere in the vicinity of Pico & Main?

A. No, I did not.

Q. Did you see any group of people north of Pico and Main after you left?

A. No, not in the next block and from then on I didn't pay any particular attention, because I was watching traffic, but I don't recall seeing any group of people at all until I got back to the strike zone again. If there had been any group I would have noticed it.

Mr. Folsom. What did you know about this strike in progress and where did you learn concerning same?

A. Don't know anything about it, only I have read one or two headlines in the newspapers of the garment workers having a strike and I never paid enough attention to it to read the items in the paper.

Q. Are you acquainted with any officials or employes of the Union?

A. Not outside of George Baker and I don't know whether he is still in town. I haven't seen him for a year, I guess.

Q. Are you acquainted with any employe affected by this strike in any way?

A. Not that I am aware of.

Q. What is your attitude as to the strike?

A. I have no attitude at all. I am strictly neutral, it doesn't concern me at all, I am not a garment worker.

Q. Do you know where the headquarters of the International Ladies' Garment Workers Union are?

A. No, I don't.

Q. You mentioned in your statement awhile ago about some Union Hdqrs. around 11th and Main, clear that up?

A. One of the women passengers in my car mentioned the fact the Union Hdqrs are on this street. There was some discussion in the car after that statement, some of the ladies saying, no, it was in another street; however I immediately turned off of 11th St. and said "we are going south a ways."

Q. That is about all you know about it then?

A. I did hear a statement that there were 6 women hurt; there were 8 women in my car. I can't understand how 6 of them could be hurt and the other two not mentioned, if it was the passengers I carried were the ones involved; also that I was accused of dropping my load at 11th and Main, when I denied it and said it was at Pico and Main I dropped my load, this man said "Yes, that's it, you're the fellow." Another point sticks in my mind is how the information of a fight could get down to 860 So. Los Angeles St. in so short an interval of time, in less time than it took me to drive down in the car.

Q. What is your opinion of people who continue to work at a shop against which a strike has been declared by a Union?

A. I consider that as that person's personal affair, because my record will show that I have worked under strike conditions. I worked for the Pacific Electric during their strike under strike conditions, knowing what I was doing, but because I wanted to work and I feel any other man has the same privilege to do likewise.

Officer WELLPOTT. In connection with your statement you have no knowledge where the headquarters of the Garment Workers Union are, did you know that you dropped this load within one block of the Hdqrs. of the Ladies Garment (Workers Union)?

A. No, I dian't.

Q. Then you were ignorant of the fact you dropped them within a (block) of the Hdqrs. of the Union.

A. Absolutely.

Exhibit 10320

[Intra-Departmental Correspondence. Form 236]

Los Angeles Police Department

Office of In. Bu. Metro Div

Oct. 30–33, 5.25 p. m.

Memo. Re Picketing Activities 850 So. Broadway & Along Broadway between 8th & 9th this afternoon.

Officer Wellpott phones in that they had quite a bit of congestion on So. Broadway this afternoon, especially at 850 and when the delegation of the Congress of Youth moved in, along with the regular pickets, etc. it became necessary to move group up to 9th and direct them east on 9th to relieve the congestion.

When they wouldn't let the Cong. of Youth parade they took their little emblems off and started picketing anyway, and when moved from there a lot of them evidently went up to 939 So. Bdwy.

Busick was in the crowd and was moved along 9th and East along with the rest, and it is understood he plans to lead a delegation of protest to the Mayor.

He also said Scott came up the street and W. told him re the Congress of Youth delegation being there again and congesting things up; and he said he would have an understanding re that, seeming provoked.

F

Exhibit 10321

[Intra-Departmental Correspondence. Form 235]

Los Angeles Police Department

Office of In. Bu. Metro Div

3.15 p. m., Oct. 31–33, Tues.

Memo. Re Strike Situation Broadway between 8th & 9th.

Of. Wellpott phones in that there is a large congestion there now, between 400 and 500 pickets, with Busick going among them passing instructions, etc. as if the "General." Said he would do best he could to handle same, but thinks Union officials should be advised re understanding of not having more than 100 pickets in this area.

F

EXHIBIT 10322

[Intra-Departmental Correspondence. Form 235]

LOS ANGELES POLICE DEPARTMENT
Office of Intelligence Bureau, Metropolitan Division

Nov. 9, 1933, 4.45 p. m.

Assignment Officers Garment Strike Detail: Two Officers.

Cover building 939 So. Broadway, Effective 6.45 a. m.

Friday Nov. 10, 1933, Tour of duty: (Daily) 6.45 a. m. to 9.15 a. m.; 11.00 a. m. to 1.30 p. m.; 2.45 p. m. to 5.00 p. m.

(To prevent picketing and molestation of non-striking employees entering and leaving building; to remain on duty at above location until such time as all non-striking employees are safely in or out of building.

By Direction:

C. B. HORRELL,
Capt. Commanding Metro. Div.

H:F
Copy Metro Div

EXHIBIT 10323

[Intra-Departmental Correspondence]

LOS ANGELES POLICE DEPARTMENT
Office of In. Bu. Metro Div

DEC. 4, 1933, 1 p. m.

Memo. Request Detail 834 and 850 So. Broadway.

Mr. Booth of Associated Apparel Mfgrs. Asso. phones in says some picketing expected this afternoon both above locations, refers to complaint of Mona Lisa Shop, 203–850 So. Bdwy (this is same location as Lowe Bros. Shop).

NOTE: Sam Evans will cover, 3 pm as well as 3 men from Vag Squad
F

EXHIBIT 10324

Date of Arrest	Defendants	Location Arrest	Offense	Remarks	Disposition of case
1933					
11–10	Mrs. Lena Rosenfeld, 1311 Talmadge.	9th & Broadway__	Ord 20586 Sec. 1, 2. Ord 38161/16449 Sec 1.	Passing out Handbills of NTWIU.	Up in Div 7, Dec. 5-33.
11–9	Mrs. Cline Katzman, 441¼ Fickett.	818 So. Broadway_	Ord 20586 Sec 1, 2. Ord 38161.	Call out "scabs", bl. sidewalk.	
	Mrs. Anna Weiser, 336 No. Ficket.	"	-----Do------------	-----Do---------	
	Mrs. Francis Goodwin, 925 Georgia.	"	"	"	
	Mrs. Frieda Lance, 3040½ Lan Franco.	"	"	"	
11–13	Miss Stella Sherman, 2708 W. 5th St.	818 So. Broadway_	Ord 16449 Sec 1____	Passing out Handbills of NTWIU.	
	Clara Stein, 1400 No. Occidental.	"	"	-----Do---------	

Exhibit 10325

Los Angeles Police Department
Office of In. Bu. Metro. Divn.

Sept. 18–34.

Memo. Re Termination Regular Detail Mission Hosiery Mills.

Of. Chas. Evans phones in that effective close of business tonight will discontinue regular detail this concern; he and Officer Hames will report to office for detail at 1 p. m. tomorrow; said have an understanding with Mr. Whittenberg, proprietor, that if they are needed he will phone office for officers to handle any pickets who may cause trouble.

F

Exhibit 10326

Los Angeles Police Department
Office of In. Bu. Metro. Divn.

Sept. 28, 1934.

Confidential Memo.

Mr. George Goldman, house RI 1428 came in and said that one RUDITES, is the chairman of the local Needle Trades Workers Industrial Union, and the main agitator, with hdqrs 755 So. Main. He described subject as apparently Russian Jewish, slight accent, wears glasses, about 5′ 8, stout built, ruddy complected; he is a tailor, formerly employed by Carver's on Hill St. but is now blacklisted from custom tailors for agitating.

He asks us to let him know local address of Joyreneman Tailors Union, phone, organizer.

Exhibit 10327

[Intra-Departmental Correspondence]

Los Angeles Police Department
Office of In. Bu. Metro. Divn.

Oct. 12, 1934.

Confidential.

Mr. Goldman (in office 10 days or so ago) reports confidentially there may be something doing in the Custom Tailors Industry in the next few days; he states a circular has been printed for quiet distribution among all custom tailors employees calling for a mass meeting next Wed. night Oct. 17, 7 p. m. at 755 So. Main St. and issued by Custom Tailors Industrial Union, 755 So. Main St. This circular is addressed "To All Custom Tailors, helpers, everybody in the custom tailors industry" regarding this mass meeting to get the bosses to meet their demands. Said as far as he can learn this has nothing whatever to do with the Algamated Clothiers Union, which is more or less among the cheaper priced men's suits, whereas custom tailors is for suits say from $90 up.

Exhibit 10328

[Intra-Departmental Correspondence. Form 235]

Los Angeles Police Department
·Office of Intelligence Bureau, Metropolitan Division

Aug. 21, 1935.

SPECIAL DETAIL, 3.30 p. m. Wed. Aug. 21, 1935

The following named officers will be at the CAL-TEX SPORTS WEAR CO. Beverly and Lake St. in connection with possible picketing of this concern by the

International Ladies' Garment Workers Union, or possible distribution of handbills in violation of City Ordinance.

Officers Cartwright, J. J.; Mathews.

By Direction:

WILLIAM F. HYNES,
Acting Capt. Dets, LAPD, Commanding In. Bu.

W:F

EXHIBIT 10329

[Intra-Departmental Correspondence Form 235]

LOS ANGELES POLICE DEPARTMENT

Office of In. Bu. Metro. Divn.

THURS., NOV. 14–35.

Memo. Request Police Protection, GLICKMAN & Co. (uniforms, men's clothing) 128 E. 9th St. TR 6536, connection labor trouble

Mr. Fysh of M&M phones in about 9.50 a.m. has report through Cham. of Com. to be strike there about 10 a.m. today; asks if we will investigate; said trouble is expected.

Contacted Capt. Justin, Metro. Divn. requesting he detail officers to handle; advised him would contact Glickman & Co. and learn more about trouble and let him know. Then phoned Glickman & Co. talked to Mr. Glickman who said he was making uniforms, etc. on an open shop basis, occupying 2nd floor s.w. corner of this two-story bldg.; said from time to time has had trouble with the Amalgamated Clothiers Union of America, Blumberg, organizer; that his firm has about 30 employees, hours 8 to 5 p.m., lunch 12 to 1 p.m.; this morning before 8 said 8 or 10 pickets in front of place stopping all the employees and trying to cause a walkout; they promised to be back at 11 a.m.

Advised Capt. Justin, who is detailing Officers *F. L. Mitchell & J. J. Cunningham* to handle from 11 a.m.

EXHIBIT 10330

[Intra-Departmental Correspondence]

(In ink:) "hours 7:15–8:30 a; 11:30 a–2:30; 4:15–5 p"

LOS ANGELES POLICE DEPARTMENT

Office of Intelligence Bureau, Metropolitan Division

WED. SEPT. 15, 1937.

Request for Officers: Beverly Knitting Mills, 5th floor, 1240 S. Main St. Ri 6396.

Mr. Onthank special agent of M&M phones he has been requested to arrange for police protection above firm today;

Asks officers be there 4 p to 5 p today;

Tomorrow 7.45 a–8.45 a and again 4 p to 5 p

(In ink:) "3.45 pm PL Philps EW Ford"

States this is rather large knitting mfgr. firm about 75 employees, MR. GRIFFIN mgr, that last night employes had a vote whether or not to go on strike and turned it down; however, that Bill Busick of ILG.W.U. CIO said there was a strike there right now; and that this morning union organizers induced employes to go down to Union Hall where they were talked to, resulting in no one showing for work; all are now out and mgr. decided to close production until NEXT MONDAY; when he will issue a call for his employes to return. In ink: "Becktel Mfg. Co. Pr8465"

However on 6th floor same bldg. is another firm works with Beverly, making sweaters, etc. for them; there employes are working now and it is feared union picket line may intimidate them into quiting work also; hence request for immediate detail Two UNIFORM OFFICERS TODAY & TOMORROW.

Advised Mr. Onthank if not possible to cover would have Lt. Wellpott phone him by 3.30 at M&M TU 6244.

F

EXHIBIT 10331

"DARLING SPORTSWEAR"

W. R. DARLING, MANUFACTURERS OF WASH DRESSES, BEACH AND SPORTSWEAR

Harris Newmark Bldg., 127 East Ninth St.

LOS ANGELES, *September 25, 1937.*

Captain HYNES,
  Los Angeles Police Dept., Los Angeles, California.

DEAR CAPTAIN HYNES: We would like to take this opportunity to express our appreciation for the cooperation you have given us during the strike.

Your men have one and all been cooperative in every way and with out them, we never would have been able to keep going.

At present, there appear to be no pickets around and we are hoping they will not bother us any further.

Our thanks and appreciation are extended to each one individually who had anything to do with the situation in any shape or form.

Yours sincerely,

W. R. DARLING,
By W. R. DARLING (sgd.).

EXHIBIT 10332

[Intra-Departmental Correspondence]

LOS ANGELES POLICE DEPARTMENT

Office of In. Bu. Metro. Divn.

FRI., OCT. 22, 1937.

Memo assignment of officers, JONES KNITTING MILLS, 1013 W. Santa Barbara, PA3115.

About 10 a. m. this date Mr. Onthank spec. agent of M&M phoned there was a picket line at above location, about 35 men, supposedly members of CIO under direction of Wm. Busick, an organizer for ILGWU pickets were there at 7:30 A. and later taken away to a meeting, and they returned at 10 a. m.

Mgr. of plant Mr. Ellis Jones.

ASSIGNED: Officers L. P. Walter & W. C. Hayes.

EXHIBIT 10333

[Intra-Departmental Correspondence]

LOS ANGELES POLICE DEPARTMENT

Office of In. Bu. Metro. Divn.

OCT. 16, 1937.

Memorandum assignment of officers: Gilfillan Bros. Inc., 1815 Venice Blvd. EX 1291, for 8 a. m. Tues. Oct. 19, 1937.

Mr. Peter Heiser, sales mgr. above co. requests two p. c. officers to be at their premises in connection with a demonstration by members of the C. I. O., to swing over employes of their concern to a C. I. O. union.

ASSIGNED I. M. Deaton, I. B., L. P. Walter, I. B.
D:F

H. BUTCHERS AND PACKING HOUSE WORKERS

EXHIBIT 10334

OCTOBER 26TH, 1933.

TODAY IN LOS ANGELES

The regular meeting of A. M. C. & B. W. Local 244 was called to order at 8 o'clock this evening with an average of about 120 men and 5 women at the meeting, 10 colored workers from Wilson's and 40 Mexicans.

One of the N. R. A. officials was the main speaker, who gave President Roosevelt a good send off and pointed out what the N. R. A. was doing and what it will do in time for the working class, how it was going to handle the "chiselers" etc etc.

District Organizer Hobart made a short talk on how he was organizing the meat cutters etc., poultry workers and asked how many Wilson employes were at the meeting; about 30 got up and he then told how he and Sec-Treas. Saunders went to Wilson's to look into their grievances and that Mr. Peterson refused to hear them, saying they did not represent a majority of their workers; this kind of hurt Hobart. He also asked how many workers at the Wilson plant were asked to join the Company Union by the Supt. and about 5 stood up whereupon Hobart asked them if they would back him up in statements on this matter and they replied "Yes."

Hobart then put up the question, how many present from the Wilson plant are ready to strike, to stand up; he then said "All right, we will call a strike in the morning, I will be at the gate at 5:30 A. M. with you boys to keep everyone out if possible and I will stay there until chased away." At this point, he said "Now Brothers and Sisters, I have a real surprise for you, a very important official of the N. R. A. has been sitting in the rear of this meeting, taking in everything and now I will introduce Mr. Bloom who did write a letter to Wilson & Co. on your grievances and did bring this company to time very fast. Mr. Bloom then told about the good work he was doing, how the Government was going to act very soon on some of these "chiselers" and on one case in particular, you workers all know about, Wilson & Co. He said he was glad to see how the Wilson workers stood up tonight and stuck together and he hoped they would all stick together like this when they were right as they are right now. He also advised them to be right all the time and take all their cases up with the N. R. A. through their officers of the union at all times; he also said he run a good bluff on a big company you all know about and there is no doubt you workers can also; he again advised all present to be sure and take their N. R. A. cases up through the Union officials.

Hobart then advised all union members present as well as packing house workers of the Vernon district to stay away from the new employment office which was started up in the Vernon Packing district, that the packers were probably in back of it, even to stay away from the corner where there is generally some loafing going on so that the bosses cannot come out and pick you up, all union men should stay around their own headquarters and all butchers should be hired through Saunders, Sec.-Treas., that if they did not stay away from this corner and were picked up by the bosses there, they would be cutting their own throat.

Hobart going back to the Wilson & Co. subject, urged all present to be sure and get to the gate good and early and to instruct all their friends to be there so as to keep everyone out of this plant, that there would probably be some special meetings called for Wilson workers soon; he said he had some stickers ordered which he was going to hand out to be posted on trucks, in meat markets, in fact everywhere so as to be noticed.

Howard, who is the Rec. Sec'y. of the Union, is an employee of Wilson's but was not at the meeting tonight.

Respectfully submitted.

Operative got in touch with Wilson & Co. official at 9:50 P. M. and conveyed the information about a strike going to take place at the Wilson plant in the morning and reported that there were 130 employes in the union, Dist. Org. Hobart making this statement in open meeting, who work at the Wilson plant.

It is respectfully suggested that Wilson & Co. have nothing to do with the N R A officials otherwise they will get in bad in more ways than one as butchers only seem to be the troublemakers at Wilson's and this strike could be beaten quickly if handled in the proper way, otherwise it might involve others.

Exhibit 10335

[Confidential]

10/27/33 (In Pencil) 5–Packing house Strike (Wilson).

Captain Hynes,
   Los Angeles Police Department,
      Los Angeles, California.

Dear Sir: A Brief on the Butchers Etc. of Los Angeles. The name under which the local union operates is the Amalgamated Meat Cutters and Butchers of America. The President is P. Gorman, and the Secretary is Dennis Lane. The Headquarters, Cincinnati. The Pacific Coast representatives in San Francisco are: Maxwell, President; and Henderson, Assistant. The Local Organizer is George Hobart, who represents both the Meat Cutters and the Butchers. The Business Agent of the Butchers is Sanders. The local headquarters are in the Musicians Building on Georgia Street; but the butchers have an office just on the outskirts of Vernon.

The Meat Cutters hold their meetings every Monday evening at Musicians Hall, Georgia Street. Their local is No. 421. The Butchers hold their meetings in the same hall on Thursday evenings at 8 p. m. and their local is No. 244.

There are some thousand members estimated in the Butchers Local No. 244; and 1200 Meat Cutters in Local No. 421. Each group has its President, Secretary, etc. The President of the Butchers is named Barger. However, because of a difference of opinions, the local was suspended as far as their officers were concerned, by President Gorman, and Hobart is now in full charge of both groups, the Meat Cutters and the Butchers.

There is, at this time, something like 5,000 employees in the packing industry and something like 2,000 to 2,200 in the various unions. These groups are affiliates of the A. F. of L.

Exhibit 10336

[Confidential]

Los Angeles Police Department
Office of In. Bu. Metro. Div.

Oct. 27–33 4.15 p. m.

Re: Purported Mass Picketing at Wilson Packing Co. Macy & Lyon St. from 5 to 6.30 p. m. Fri. Oct 27

Capt. Hynes:

Mr. Lucien Wheeler calls re the situation at Wilson Packing Co. wants advise Capt. Hynes he has information there is to be a big crowd there around 5.30 p. m. tonight in order to get employes leaving the plant 5 to 5.30 and on. He learns from confidential sources that a large group is to be there tonight from 5 pm (quiting time) until all employes have left, presumably which would be around 6.30 p. m. Asks, if possible to have a large enough group of officers on hand to handle situation and that they cover until all employes have left.

Also he advises that he understands the Cudahy Plant is the next one to be on strike, this within next few days.
   F
Copy Capt. Horrall

Exhibit 10337

[Intra-Departmental Correspondence. Form 235]

Los Angeles Police Department
Office of In. Bu. Metro. Div.

4:30 p. m., Nov. 20–33.

Memo. Re: Expected Picketing 724 Salino St.

Capt. Lofthouse of Speed Squad phones a friend of his with Sterling Packers, Vernon, asks for help tonight 5.00 p. m. at 724 Salino St. (Off No. Broadway) that cars with striking packing house pickets expected concentrate on this place tonight.

He is sending 4 of his men; asks someone from Bu. also be there if possible.

F

EXHIBIT 10338

LOS ANGELES POLICE DEPARTMENT
Office of Intelligence Bureau, Metropolitan Division

MARCH 13, 1936.

Memorandum for Chief DAVIS.

With reference to your request for such data as we have regarding FRANK KRASNESKY of the Butcher's Union, please be advised subject is Organizer and Secretary for the Amalgamated Meat Cutters Union Local #551 of San Pedro and vicinity. He resides at 1503½ Weymouth Ave. San Pedro, phone San Pedro 1278-R. He is also said to be a member of the Central Labor Council of San Pedro. He has been in charge of picket line at Smith's Market, 529 S. Pacific Ave. San Pedro for the Butchers union.

Subject is described as a man 48–50 years old, dark hair, streaked with gray, about 5′ 9″ dark eyes, about 170# apparently Polish; drives an old sedan; wears a moustache.

Officers who have covered labor difficulties at Smith's Market 529 S. Pacific Ave. and the Savings Center Meat Market, 627 S. Pacific Ave. San Pedro, state subject has cooperated fairly well with them in their duty of maintaining law and order.

So far as known, Mr. Krasnesky has no Red tendencies, but is simply considered as a regular union organizer under the American Federation of Labor.

There is no record on subject in our Bureau of Records & Identification.

Respectfully,

WILLIAM F. HYNES,
Acting Capt. of Detectives, LAPD,
Commanding Intelligence Bureau.

H:F

I. FUR WORKERS

EXHIBIT 10339

11.40 a. m., DEC. 21, 1932.

Memo. Re Picketing and Molesting Employees of ROSE ANN SITKINS GARMENT SHOP, 339 So. Western Ave. EX 4638.

Received phone call from Radio Car 71 (Of. Quino) he was on call above shop re picketing. I then talked to Mrs. Sitkins, manager, who said that last week she discharged a furrer and he is now around trying to get her other employees to quit and has assistants with him, trying to follow them home and picket them when going to and from work and the like. She believes it has some connection with Communistic activity.

She employs four girls and two men in the shop making furs.

She opens the shop at 8.30 a. m. and closes at 9 p. m. but the help leaves at 5 p. m. She wants protection.

Told her officers would call today.

F

DETAIL: Officers Phelps & Schulz.

Note: Cover above shop 8 a. m. to 9.30 a. m. Dec. 22 about 6 pickets left on approach of officers.

Exhibit 10340

Los Angeles, Cal., *Dec. 30, 1932.*

Report on Picketing at Shop of Rose Ann Sitkins Fine Fur Shop, 339 So. Western Ave.

Capt. Wm. F. Hynes,
Commanding Intelligence Bureau.

Sir: We have been covering this shop to afford protection against picketing or molestation of employees since morning of Dec. 22 (Thurs.)   The first four mornings we escorted a Mr. Braudsky, foreman in the shop, from his home at 1050 No. Ficket St. over to the shop, as he had advised us that communists had gather at his home one morning about 6.30 and heckled and embarrassed him in front of neighbors; however during the time we escorted him we observed no communists.

During our details covering this shop we have observed only two communists around the vicinity, one J. Sonneshine, 2754 Houston St. who stated he worked at Margolis's, 806 So. Vermont and the other M. Suroff, 2201 City View Terrace, he stating he worked for Sigmon at 117 E. 9th St.; both said they were garment workers.   We advised these men to stay away from vicinity of shop unless they were around the district on lawful business, and that if any picketing was attempted or approach made to the employees, we would take action.   Since this warning they have not been around.

It had been reported to us that Suroff was the man who had accosted one of the women employees of the shop and told her she should join the Union; but no further remarks were made by him.

We also learned that a Miss Margaret Coeber, 1138 W 29th St. former employe of Miss Sitkins had been approached by members of a communist organization and threatened if she did not quit as the shop was on strike.   This was reported to us by Mrs Sitkins.   We then went to 1138 W 29 where we met the landlady, who told us that Miss Coeber had confided in her and told her she had quit her job as she knew that after Christmas work would slack up and she would be laid off; she said she had not been intimidated, that she used to belong to the Union back in New York and did not want to antagonize the local union.

While we were on duty covering shop this morning, Mrs Sitkins phoned in from her home and talked to me and asked why we had not made some arrests, that she was tired of being annoyed in the manner that she was.   Advised her that in order to make an arrest a person had first to violate the law and that if we made an arrest without sufficient evidence to prosecute successfully that it would cause more communists to congregate at her place, by not getting a conviction.   She also complained of people going up and down the alley in rear of her shop and wanted us to stop this practice; however as this is a public alley the public has free access to same.

Pending your further instructions, we will continue to cover this shop from 8 a. m. to observe for any possible picketing or molestations, and if any violations of law occur will take prompt action.

Respectfully,

C. J. Evans & C. R. Abbott.

E:F

Exhibit 10341

[Intra-Departmental Correspondence.   Form 235]

Los Angeles Police Department

Office of In. Bu.   Metro. Div.

Memo. Re Termination Strike Detail L. Rifkin & Sons, 719 So. L. A. Close Bus. Sat. Jan. 20–34

Capt. Just in, Metro. Div. comes in and says Officers Hugoboom and Murphy who have been on strike detail above location, the last few weeks, report that manager above firm told them Sat. he would not need them any more, after Sat. Jan. 20–34.

Capt. Hynes wants check made with Rifkin on this.

F

EXHIBIT 10342

FURRIERS' MEMBERSHIP REPORT, MARCH 20, 1934

Adler, Nathan	Init. 8/28 $4
Albright, Myrtle	1 wk. Jan.
Altman, Clara	Init. 10/10 $2.
Alterescue, Ben	End Oct.
Aronson, Wolf	Init. 9/27 $1
Baranzic, C	3 wk. Sept.
Baron, L	2 wk. Nov.
Baumfield, C	2 wk. Oct.
Berger, S	2 wk. Jan.
Berlin, Mrs. T	3 wk. Oct.
Blue, Minnette	3 wk. Oct.
Blum, Joe	Init. 7/31 25¢
Boardman, Betty	End July
Boschan, F	End Feb.
Brandstatter, M	1 wk. Sept.
Branfmuir, Jack	Init. 8/14 $3.
Bregman, Clara	3 wk. Dec.
Brenner, M	2 wk. Feb.
Bricker, Abe	End Sept.
Brill, Dora	1 wk. April
Brown, Mary	4 wk. Sept.
Brownstein, Frank	End Oct.
Bruckman, H	Init. 5/18
Butman, Jack	2 wk. Feb.
Cantor, Pauline	1 wk. Mar.
Cline, Anna	End Oct.
Cohen, Harry	1 wk. Jan.
Cohen, Morris	3 wk. Jan.
Davenport, G	Init. 7/31
Diamond, Max	Init. 12/15/32
Druckman, B	End Jan.
Ehsenkranz, H	2 wk. Aug.
Eisenberg, Sam	End Aug.
Eisman, R	1 wk. Nov.
Elardy, J	2 wk. May '33
Elardy, S	2 wk. May '33
Elwing, John	End Oct.
Engel, L	Init. 7/31
Enright, Ken	1 wk. Oct.
Fair, J	Init. 7/22
Falconeri, Ted	Init. 9/5 $3.50
Falconeri, Joe	2 wk. Oct.
Finkelstein, L	2 wk. March
Feuerstadt, J	3 wk. Jan.
Fire, Sarah	Init. 7/26
Fisher, Dora	1 wk. Oct.
Flores, Jennie	2 wk. Nov.
Fox, Ben	3 wk. Aug.
Freundlich, Morris	Init. 9/7 $1.
Frishcling, Clara	3 wk. Sept.
Fuller, Grace	End March
Gelman, Al	End Aug.
Gibson, Kay	1 wk. Mar.
Ginsberg, Dan	End July
Glazer, Nathan	End Oct.
Gold, Jennie	1 wk. Oct.
Goldberg, Ben	1 wk. Oct.
Goldberg, I	Init. 8/7
Goldstein, Robt	4 wk. Sept
Goldstein, S	End Oct.
Gould, Julius	End July
Green, John	2 wk. Sept
Green, Morris E	Init. 7/19 50¢

Greenberg, Max	Init. 7/29
Grossman, Henry	2 wk. Oct.
Grossman, Sophie	2 wk. Nov.
Herson, A	Init. 7/21
Hertzberg, M	Init. 7/31
Hiester, Mrs	Init. 6/6
Kail, Milton	Init. 7/22
Katzman, Esther	End Dec.
Kawin, B	Init. 1/30 $3
Kesselman, Anna	Init. 7/11
Klapperman, Lena	3 wk. Dec.
Knutsen, Margaret	End Sept.
Korobanik, Jennie	3 wk. Apr.
Krause, Ernest	End Sept.
Kraut, Ida	Init. 7.31
Laman, Dolores	Init. 9/27 $2
Lassner, Irving	End Sept.
Lalantonis, Mary	End Oct.
La Voie, C	Init. 1/22 $1
Lindsay, S	Init. 8/14 50¢
Litman, Phil	3 wk. Sept.
Littman, Ben	3 wk. Feb.
Litsky, Henry	4 wk. Sept.
Lord, Mildred	Init. 9/5
Lotz, Meta	4 wk. Dec.
Lowen, Irving	End Oct.
Marsh, Margaret	2 wk. March
Matisoff, Sam	End Aug.
Max, Sam	Init. 2/23 $1
Mednick, E	Init. 2/33 $1
Meshekow, Chas	1 wk. Oct.
Messenger, Harry	2 wk. Jan.
Meyers, Harry	Init. 8/11 $3
Meyers, Minnie	3 wk. Aug.
Miller, Elsie	End Sept.
Miller, Herbert	Init. 6/29
Miner, Sarah	1 wk. Jan.
Minsberg, Rose	End Jan.
Mintzer, Gussie	Init. 8/11 $3
Malinsky, I	End March
Mollin, Bessie	3 wk. Mar. '33
Newman, L	1 wk. Sept.
Pena, Sara	3 wk. Dec.
Perkinds, M	2 wk. Jan.
Petyus, Alex	3 wk. Sept.
Phillips, Mildred	End Dec.
Pickelner, Al	End Oct.
Polansky, E	2 wk. Jan.
Rabinowitz, M	1 wk. Sept.
Raphael, Jack	End Aug.
Reitman, Jack	End Nov.
Riesen, Mrs. F	1 wk. Feb.
Ringer, Lola	2 wk. Nov.
M. Rittman	End Nov.
Bobin, Mack	2 wk. Oct.
Rojas, Mercy	2 wk. Jan.
Romahn, Chester	1 wk. Oct.
Rosen, Al	End Aug.
Rosen, Esther	3 wk. Oct.
Rosenbloom, B	End Jan.
Rossini, Eva	End Feb.
Rubin, I	End Aug.
Salkin, Hyman	End Aug.

FURRIERS' MEMBERSHIP REPORT, MARCH 20, 1934—Continued

Salkin, Morris	2 wk. Sept.	Stein, Fay	End Dec. '32
Samuels, E	Init. 1/23 $2.	Steinberg, G	1 wk. Jan.
Satt, Mrs	End Feb.	Steinmetz	End Nov.
Schapiro, I	1 wk. Jan.	Stewart, Cora	End Feb.
Schatz, Lena	4 wk. Sept.	Suroff, M	End July
Schlossberg, Hyman	End Feb.	Strahl, Joe	1 wk. Aug.
Schulman, H	End Dec.	Tendrock, N	1 wk. Dec.
Schulman, Mrs. Y	End Jan.	Topez, N	End July
Schusberg, Max	2 wk. Jan.	Vagy, L	1 wk. Nov.
Schwartz, Charlotte	End Oct.	Warren Lillian	2 wk. Feb.
Schwartz, Max	2 wk. Mar. '33	Wasserman, Chas	Init. 9/5 $3.
Schwartz, P	End Oct.	Wasserman, D	Init. 10/17 $4.
Schwartz, Sol	4 wk. Sept.	Weinberg, Sam	3 wk. Nov.
Segel, Gussie	2 wk. Dec.	Weiner, Irving	End Aug.
Seidner, I	2 wk. Nov.	Weinman, M	Init. 8/22 $1.
Seidner, Joe	2 wk. Feb.	Bush, N	
Seigel, Lena	End Nov.	Weinstein, Fanny	4 wk. Mar.
Senker, Al	2 wk. Sept.	Weinstein, J	2 wk. Dec.
Shergei, Jack	End Aug.	Weinthal, C	Init. 8/16 $1.50
Shields, Mrs. T	Init. 9/11 $3.	Weiss, Joe	End Aug.
Shubert, Molly	Init. 7/28.	Whiteman, Bessie	End Sept.
Silver, A	1 wk. Mar.	Windish, M	End Aug.
Silver, Dave	Init. 6/8.	Winter, Geo	3 wk. Jan.
Silverstein, M	Init. 2/6 $2.35.	Witkin, David	Init. 8/25 $2
Simonov, M	2 wk. June '33.	Witkin, Nathan	Init. 9/25 $4
Sketchley, Marie	2 wk. Nov.	Zacharin, Helen	2 wk. Nov.
Socol, M	2 wk. Feb.		

EXHIBIT 10343

LOS ANGELES POLICE DEPARTMENT

Office of In. Bu. Metro. Divn.

FEB. 11, 1935, 12 NOON.

Memo. Re: Fur Strike 635 So. Hill St.
Lt. LANE:

Chief Davis phones and said in view of fact this is a Communist strike, wants PRESSURE put on these pickets 100%, make arrests if at all possible, even such as spitting on sidewalk; if additional men are required to effectively handle same let the Chief know.

The Chief wants a daily report on progress of this strike—CRACK DOWN ON THEM.

F

EXHIBIT 10344

LOS ANGELES, CAL., *July 24, 1933.*

Re: Strike at 719 So. L. A. (In pencil:) room 1012.
L. Rifkin & Sons, Furs.
Officer R. A. WELLPOTT,
   Intelligence Bureau.

SIR: We called on above firm at 8.15 a. m. this date and talked to Mr. Rifkin who said that a group of his employees had made demands on him that he sign up with a Red union. He said he told them he would recognize an American union, but not a bunch of Communists because they were unAmerican. Following his refusal to recognize their union this group of employees called a strike on his plant and large groups of picketeers were on hand this morning. Following are names of employees who made demands and walked out: Joseph Seidner,

Human Drucker, Mercy Rogas, Mrs. Hoffman, Jack Feirstadt, Ruby Eisman, Max Mendelson.

There are six employees who are still working at plant.

We learned from traffic officer on duty in vicinity that earlying this morning there were some 150 picketeers who were blocking entrance to building when radio officers arrived and moved same away from entrance. There were about 30 picketeers around while we were there and we noticed that many of them were the same faces and people who had been picketing in front of 738 So. Broadway (Golden Bros. Millinery Co. strike).

Mr. Rifkin requested a police detail.

Respectfully,

C. J. EVANS.
E. A. GILBREATH.

E:F

EXHIBIT 10345

LOS ANGELES POLICE DEPARTMENT

Officer's Report Concerning Strike at Maurice Ball Furier on 7th St.

Police Division Reporting: Red Squad.

Name of Party_____	Date Occurred_____ Time_____
Res. Address_____	Division of Occurrence_____
Bus. Address_____	Reported to Squad.
Phone_____	Investigated by G45.

DETAILED REPORT

I was downtown Monday and passed Maurice Ball's Furier. There I met Marie Rosen of the I. C. O. R., and Robert Philmore, also of the I. C. O. R. They were the only two I recognized. Officer in charge would not let them talk to me as he made them keep walking in the parade line.

Marie Rosen: 4 ft. 6 in. tall; Weight, 98–104 lbs.; 24 years old; Black hair, straight bob; Black eyes; German Jew.

Robert Philmore: 5 ft. 7 in. tall; Weight, 165 lbs.; 22 years old; Brown wavy hair; Brown eyes; Jew.

Officer's Name: Bill Henderson, Badge G45.
Date of this Report: August 22, 1936.

EXHIBIT 10346

LOS ANGELES POLICE DEPARTMENT

Officer's Report Concerning Chain Phone System of I. W. O.

Police Division Reporting: Red Squad.

Name of Party_____	Date Occurred_____ Time _____
Res. Address_____	Division of Occurrence_____
Bus. Address_____	Reported to Squad.
Phone_____	Investigated by G45.

DETAILED REPORT

The Chain Phone System is used only in case of trouble. In the Venice strike we were all given a number to call. It called the I. L. D. office. We were to ask for Mr. Rogers and say we needed help and tell where we were and they would send help. On the South-East corner of the strike area one Sunday, a fight started and Betima Lenfield and Bod Ponelli called and within fifteen minutes there were two cars loaded with Mexicans there.

Abe Zadow uses it when he has to call his band together. If one of them is in trouble or in Jail, Abe will call Bob Golstaker and Golstaker will call Lilla Allen and so on until everyone in the club has been notified.   After each one calls he leaves right away to go to where the strike or trouble is.

Officer's Name: Bill Henderson, Badge G45.
Date of this Report: August 22, 1936.

J. RESTAURANT AND CULINARY WORKERS

EXHIBIT 10347

[Intra-Departmental Correspondence.   Form 236]

LOS ANGELES POLICE DEPARTMENT

Office of Intelligence Bureau, Metropolitan Divison

MARCH 3rd, 1934.

Re: Strike Situation, Brown Derby Cafe, 1628 No. Vine St.
Capt. WM. F. HYNES,
   Commanding Intelligence Bureau.

SIR: On Thursday, March 1st, 1934, 3 p. m. per your orders, Officers Charles Evans, C. R. Abbott and I went to the Brown Derby Cafe, 1628 No. Vine St. and were informed by Mr. Robert Cobb, manager and president of the Brown Derby, Inc. that at noon two men, a Mr. Brown, business agent of the Cooks local A. F. of L. and a Mr. Van Hook, business agent for the Waiters' Local, A. F. of L., came in and told him to sign a contract with the Culinary Workers' International Alliance.   Mr. Cobb said he informed them he couldn't do that without consulting his other business associates.   He was told by Van Hook that they would give him ten minutes to sign.   Cobb then went to his private office with Mr. Brown to talk the situation over.   Mr. Cobb did not invite Van Hook to his office because of Van Hook's high-handed attitude of threatening to pull the Brown Derby waiters out on strike.   After talking the matter over with Mr. Brown for a period of about 15 minutes, Mr. Cobb said they came out of his office and found that Mr. Van Hook had called all of his waiters out on strike (27 in number).

When we arrived, there were about forty men standing about in groups on the sidewalks near vicinity of the Brown Derby Cafe.   Three detectives from the Hollywood station were there.   Mr. Cobb asked for a police detail, and it was then that I called you and detail was arranged for; Officer Evans and I were assigned till 10:30 p. m. that day.

During the night of March 1st, pickets congregated on the auto parking lots in the vicinity of the Brown Derby and prospective patrons were handed dodgers asking them to patronize other establishments than the Brown Derby Cafe.

Pickets were warned on several occasions not to pass out the dodgers to pedestrians on a public sidewalk.

On March 2nd, 1934, Mr. Wilson, lessee of two parking lots, one north and one south of the Brown Derby Cafe, protested to me that pickets were grouping up in such numbers on his parking lots that some of his patrons were not parking their cars on his lots.   This was said in the presence of business agents of the Union. He requested at that time that police prevent pickets from congregating in groups, sometimes twenty to thirty in number on his parking lots.

After this complaint from Mr. Wilson, pickets were kept from congregating on his property.

On the evening of March 2nd, 1934, the pickets appeared on the sidewalks in the near vicinity of the Brown Derby with an issue of the "Los Angeles Citizen" dated March 2nd, 1934 (copy attached).   This paper carried the headline "Brown Derby waiters refuse to work for 90¢ a day."

At first, when these picketing waiters, who were trying to sell the paper, began shouting "All about the strike at the Brown Derby," I informed these pickets that if they shouted anything about strike at the Brown Derby and not to patronize same, that it was a violation of the picketing ordinance and was so held by the Appellate Court on appeal in the Armentrout case, in which the sale of the "Los Angeles Citizen" was involved in a picketing case at the Rialto Theatre, 8th & Broadway of the city.

I warned those trying to sell the paper that if they persisted in shouting other than what was in the headline, arrests would be made for picketing. For the rest of the evening they were very quiet and were calling in a lower tone of voice only the headline, "Brown Derby waiters refuse to work for 90¢ a day."

Saturday noon, March 3rd, 1934, nine fellows were given "The Los Angeles Citizen" to sell, and were placed near the Brown Derby. They began shouting the headline and especially when people were entering or leaving the Brown Derby.

Again I warned the business agent, Mr. Brown and the man in charge of sale of the paper, that having that number of newsboys all near the Brown Derby was picketing and that they could not use "The Los Angeles Citizen" as a subterfuge to picket any establishment. The "so-called newsboys" were then scattered further up and down the street and only one news vendor continued to shout very loud.

We did not permit news vendors or pickets trying to sell papers to stand in front or cross property line of the Brown Derby establishment.

Friday afternoon and evening, Mr. Buzzell of the local labor Council, A. F. of L. was on the picket line. I was told by pickets that he informed them as to their rights on the picket line, as to how to conduct themselves while selling the "Los Angeles Citizen." He seemed to keep a close watch on all activities of the pickets and officers.

Today, Saturday noon, March 3rd, 1934. Mr. Buzzell was present again, apparently watching the picket line and police officers. On one occasion, when I interferred with a fellow who was writing down auto licenses of patrons of the Brown Derby, Buzzell rushed up to hear the conversation.

Mr. Buzzell, Mr. Ernst, vice-president of the Culinary Workers' International Alliance, and several business agents and secretaries of the union, had a meeting at 2 p. m. this date with Mr. Cobb and several of his business associates. No headway was made at this meeting, so it was reported to me. Another meeting was arranged for next Tuesday.

Mr. Cobb stated he would not sign such a contract with the Union so that he would have no say as to who should work for him or who shouldn't.

Mr. Warren, assistant manager of the Brown Derby, reported to me that some of the bus boys and waitresses had been threatened and warned not to work at the Brown Derby. One bus boy was chased several blocks but pickets were not able to catch him. One boy, employed by the "Derby," was struck in the back and was chased into a corner drug store at Selma and Vine Streets. Because of these unlawful activities on the part of the pickets and it being impossible for two officers to observe both front and rear of place, two officers are kept busy when about fifty pickets are in front and others in rear trying to intimidate those working. It, therefore, became necessary to call for one more additional officer on the day and night watch.

Respectfully,

R. A. WELLPOTT, DL 131.

W:F

EXHIBIT 10348

[Intra-Departmental Correspondence]

LOS ANGELES POLICE DEPARTMENT

Office of In. Bu. Metro. Divn.

JULY 13, 1934.

Re: Strike at Sardi's Restaurant, 6313½ Hollywood Blvd. effective 6 p. m. Wed. July 11–34.

Capt. WM. F. HYNES,
Commanding Intelligence Bureau.

SIR: Pursuant to telephone call from Capt. Hagar, Hollywood Div. to Capt. Justin, Metropolitan Division, yesterday morning, that above mentioned strike had been called, Officer Pfeiffer and I went to Hollywood Station and talked to Capt. Hagar and gave him copies of various city ordinances applicable.

We then proceeded to location of Sardi's Restaurant and talked with one of the partners and manager Eddie Brandstatter, who informed us that two weeks ago the Waiters' Local #17 and the So. Cal. Cooks Asso. Cook's Union Local 468, both affiliated with the American Federation of Labor, had made certain demands, namely increase in wages, shorter working day and split shifts not to cover more than a period of 10 hours, and recognition of the unions and that upon his failure to comply with these demands, about 40 of his employes walked out of his restaurant Wed. July 11 at 6 p. m.

Strikers were replaced by help furnished by the M. & M. and the M. & M. was furnishing two guards day and night. We explained to Mr. Brandstatter the picketing law and what he could expect from the pickets, and just what the police officers could do in regards to the situation.

Starting at 12.15 noon July 12, there were approximately 40 pickets on the line. I talked to J. W. Van Hook, captain of the picket line (who handing me card as representing Waiter's Union Local #17, 110 West 11th St. PR 6207) and explained to him exactly how we expected the pickets to conduct themselves, and explained the various laws such as picketing, blocking the sidewalk, etc.; explained to him that the police were not interested in either side of the difficulties, but were there to see that the law was observed and that we would countenance no violation of any law. Mr. Van Hook promised us his hearty cooperation and said that if we had any complaint re any particular picket to let him know and he would remove them from the picket line.

The pickets remained on the line until 2.30 p. m. at which time they left and said they would be back at 6.30 p. m. Officer Pfeiffer and myself returned at 6.00 p. m. and remained till the pickets left at 8.30 p. m. During this time there were about 50 men and women pickets on the line, some of them dressed in their waiters and cooks' uniforms. Picketing was very peaceful and orderly with the exception of one lady and a young man, who insisted on advising patrons that there was a strike on, or that there was no service in the restaurant, after having been warned this was a violation of the picketing law. At our request Mr. Van Hook withdrew them from the picket line and sent them hone.

I talked with Capt. Hagar of Hollywood Station and told him we had nobody available here to cover this strike regularly and that in my opinion it could be handled by two officers being there from 12 noon to 2.30 p. m. and from 6.00 p. m. till whatever time the pickets left the line at night; that he might later find it necessary to leave one of the officers there throughout the day, and if in the future he needed more help, we would be glad to cooperate as much as possible.

Respectfully,

P. L. PHELPS.
G. A. PFEIFFER.

PLP: F

EXHIBIT 10349

[Intra-Departmental Correspondence]

LOS ANGELES POLICE DEPARTMENT

Office of In. Bu. Metro. Divn.

TUES., AUG. 24, 1937, 12 NOON.

Re: CIO Attempt to Organize Simons Lunch Room.
Memo. for Capt. HYNES.

Mr. Simons of the Simons Lunch rooms, phoned that two or three organizers of the CIO came into his place of business at *712 S. Hill St.* and argued with one of his employees from about 1 a. m. to 4 a. m. this morning—trying to persuade this boy to become an organizer for the CIO. These men are to return tonight for an answer.

Mr. Simons asks that an officer cover because this boy is going to refuse to have anything to do with the proposition and his refusal may result in violence in some form or other. Advised him you would call him after 2.30 p. m. at *TR 6751.*

R. A. WELLPOTT DL 131.

NOTE: 3.45 p. m. Aug. 24—I asked Central Division to have officer be there around midnight.

C. A. SITTS.

K. RETAIL SHOE CLERKS

EXHIBIT 10350

Capt HYNES.   WED., MAY 27/36, 10 a. m.
Mr. Simpson TR 8151 of Store.

Protective Asso. phones he heard a meeting of Union organizers was held on May 21st to plan organizing the Dept. Store employees into unions; advised did not know of same would ask you, so you could inform him

F

EXHIBIT 10351

LOS ANGELES POLICE DEPARTMENT

Office of Intelligence Bureau, Metropolitan Division

MARCH 25, 1937.

Memorandum.
Subject: Strike Called by Shoe Clerks Union.

Pursuant to telephone call this morning, Officer McCullough and myself proceeded to the INNES SHOE STORE, at 642 S. Broadway, TR 8926, where we interviewed the manager, Mr. Proctor, and the owner, Mr. Innes.

Mr. Innes stated that he had heard rumors his store was to be picketed today by the Shoe Clerks Union and had made arrangements through the M. & M. to have two special guards inside the store.

The store employes about sixty people (also there is one store in Hollywood and one in Pasadena) and as far as is known none belong to the union, or are sympathetic to this shoe store strike movement.

The store is open from 9 a. m. to 6 p. m., the employees began arriving about 8.30 a. m. and should be out by 6 15 p. m.

Inasmuch as no pickets have put in appearance yet, we left the telephone number of this office with Mr. Innes and Mr. Proctor, and advised them that in the event any pickets did show up at any time to give us a call, and we would furnish them whatever police protection was necessary, as far as pickets in front of their store was concerned.

Respectfully,
PLP:F   P. L. PHELPS.—
                                                  H. B. McCULLOUGH.

EXHIBIT 10352

[Intra-Departmental Correspondence]

LOS ANGELES POLICE DEPARTMENT

Office of Intelligence Bureau, Metropolitan Divn.

APR. 13, 1938.

Memo. Capt. HYNES.

REQUEST: Police Detail BERLAND'S SHOE STORE, 727 S. Broadway, MI 9769 (Mr. Goldberg).

Per your instructions I went to Mr. Dean Sturgis' office, room 900 Bartlett Bldg. 215 W. 7th St. (Downtown Businessmen's Assn.) and there talked with him and Mr. Goldberg of the BERLAND'S SHOE Co. 727 S. Broadway, MI 9769.

Mr. Goldberg stated that on Thursday evening Apr. 14 he was to meet Union officials (probably of the Retail Clerks Assn AFL) and that he would notify them he would not sign a new contracting, meeting their demands. He said the union has already issued him an ultimatum he must signed by Thursday night. After this meeting, he fears a reprisal for failure to sign a contract—such as stench bombing or window breaking. Therefore, he requests, if possible, police protection on the street *from 9 p. m. Thurs. Apr. 14* until 9 a. m. Fri. Apr. 15th when store opens; and also *from 6 p. m. Fri. Apr 15* until store opens at 9 a. m. Sat. Apr. 16th. Also if a picket line is started at the store Friday morning, Apr. 15th he would like to have officers to cover. As to this request for night detail, the request was only during the EASTER RUSH, ending Saturday night; after that he said he had no worries as to what might happen.

I promised that we would furnish officers for Thursday and Friday nights for the front; also that we would furnish a detail in event of picketing of store on Friday, Apr. 15th. As to protection for his rear entrance in alley and inside the store; advised Mr. Goldberg to procure private guards; which he said they would do.

R. A. WELLPOTT DL 131.

RAW:F

L. NURSES, HOSPITAL AND INSTITUTIONAL WORKERS

EXHIBIT 10353

RADICAL ACTIVITIES

Re: Nurses, Hospital and Institutional Employees Union, Local 19986.

LOS ANGELES, CALIFORNIA, *October 29th, 1936.*

The NURSES, HOSPITAL and INSTITUTIONAL WORKERS' UNION, #19986 held a regular meeting, October 28th at 8 P. M. in the Angelus Hotel, 4th and Spring Streets. There were some 25 members present. The small attendance is accounted for due to the fear many of the members have of being in this organization.

A number of members are employed at HEBREW SHELTER HOME, 325 South Boyle Avenue. LEON B. REICHMANN, Secretary of the Organization and JENNIE DRUTZ, Financial Secretary, were both employed in this Home until recently, when they were discharged for their Union activities. This matter has been taken up with J. W. BUZZELL of the Central Labor Council for the purpose of securing the support of the A. F. of L. in a fight which the Organization is about to launch against the Rest Home. The officers of this Union and Buzzell met with the officials of the Rest Home a few days ago and tried to straighten out the matter. The Institution's representative finally conceded that they would re-hire REICHMANN but absolutely refused to permit Miss DRUTZ to return to work. At this time the Union is agitating amongst its membership to institute a strike against the Home and to surround the place with pickets. It was learned that this Home owns a large hall which is rented out for weddings, banquets, etc., thus affording quite an income to the Home. Members of the Union declare that should this place be picketed, most of the Jewish organizations would refuse to rent it.

Miss FORMAN, a graduate nurse from Mount Sinai Hospital, Cleveland, arrived here from New York about one month ago. She has joined the existing Union but is advocating a separate Union for the Graduate Nurses and is willing to give her spare time to organize it. While she has not as yet received her registration certificate in California, she has applied for same. She is now working in the Wilshire Osteopathic Hospital. She is particularly anxious to organize the Nurses in the Cedar of Lebanon Hospital where she claims Jewish nurses will not be given work. She is also contemplating visiting some of the donors and supporters of this hospital and make complaints to them that "our own girls are not given work in the hospital which you support."

The Union is now getting into shape a list of demands which will be presented to the Jewish Rest Home which include: 8 hour day, 48 hour week, preferential hiring through the Union, minimum $35 a month, 25% increase in pay after 6 months, 14 days sick leave a year with pay, no firing of Union members without sufficient cause and approved by the Union.

EXHIBIT 10354

RADICAL ACTIVITIES

Re: Nurses, Hospital and Institutional Employees Union, Local 19986, A. F. L.

LOS ANGELES, CALIFORNIA, *February 26th, 1936.*

The first meeting of this year of the NURSES, HOSPITAL AND INSTITUTIONAL EMPLOYEES UNION was held Wednesday, February 26th, at Angelus Hotel, 4th and Spring Streets.

There were thirty five members present.

Financial report was read of all the receipts and disbursements since the inception of this Union, 10 months ago.   After all expenses were paid the Union had $97.

Nomination and election of Officers were as follows: Brother Shruck, President; Leon B. Reichmann, Secretary; Jennie Drutz, Financial Secretary; Sister Wise, Educational Committee; Sister Burke and Sister Feider were elected on the Central Committee.

Installation of Officers will be held at the next regular meeting.   Councilman Christenson will be the guest speaker at this meeting.

Arrangements for a dance and social are being made for April 10th to celebrate one year's progress in the Union.

Sophie Feider, pharmacist, spoke for five minutes.   She spoke of the Mine and Maritime Workers.   She stressed how important Unionism is in all walks of life—professional and non-professional life.   She recommended a Mass Meeting be held in the near future to stimulate interest in this new Union.

Sister Feider told writer confidentially of her recent dismissal from the QUEEN OF ANGELS HOSPITAL.   Miss Feider is a very competent pharmacist and held a similar position at the FRENCH HOSPITAL for twelve years.   When she accepted the position at the Queen of Angels Hospital she was guaranteed, verbally, a steady position.   After a few weeks of employment the Sister Superior told her that her services were no longer needed, due to her political affiliations.   They stated that her work was satisfactory but they could not tolerate a person with radical tendencies.   Due to the guarantee that the Sisters gave her she feels that she has a case against the hospital.   Miss Feider at once took it up with the CIVIL LIBERTIES UNION.   Their Attorney McWilliams is handling her case. Joseph Scott retained by the QUEEN OF ANGELS HOSPITAL has offered Miss Feider a settlement of $150.   Due to other professional members in her family she does not want any unfavorable publicity that might reflect upon them, so she may accept the offer.

Miss Feider claims the only way that they could have learned of her activities was through an Intern, now at the Queen of Angeles Hospital who was formerly associated with the French Hospital.   She is positive that he was the informer. The only literature that anyone saw her reading was THE NEW MASSES.

In a former report Miss Feider's name was mentioned as being very active in all radical movements.   Celeste Strack lived with her while attending the University of California, Westwood.   Being a very fine public speaker, Miss Feider has taken an important part in the Saturday Discussion Club which is under the supervision of Eugene LINDER, a well known radical.

Attorney Leo Gallagher is expected to be in Los Angeles for the scheduled meeting at the Epic Hall, Friday night.

EXHIBIT 10355

(Penciled:) oper C. 25 file.

RADICAL ACTIVITIES

Re: Nurses, Hospital and Institutional Employees Union. Local 19986, A. F. of L.

LOS ANGELES, CALIFORNIA, *June 10, 1936.*

An open meeting of the NURSES, HOSPITAL and INSTITUTIONAL EMPLOYEES UNION, LOCAL 19986 was held in the Angelus Hotel, 4th and Spring Streets tonight.

The meeting was called to order at 8 P. M. by the President, John Schalk.

There were about sixty members present.   Due to the late arrival of the principal speaker, C. J. HAGGERTY, Secretary of THE BUILDING TRADES COUNCIL, the Secretary of the Hospital Employees Local, LEON B. REICHMANN spoke for some fifteen minutes on the subject "the necessity of organization".   Reichmann stated that until recent months Los Angeles has not been "union conscious".   He pointed out that during the recent Field Workers strike in this vicinity that the A. F. of L. had been prevailed upon to furnish help and pickets.   He stated that, although the Field Workers did not belong to the A. F. of L., they had turned out to be good Unionists.   The reason that they were not affiliated with the A. F. of L. is that they made such little money—$5 to $7 per week—they could not afford to pay a dollar a month dues required by the International.   While in the past the A. F. of L. would have disregarded the appeal of a nonaffiliated organization, in this case the A. F. of L. well understood that it was necessary to respond in order to hold its self respect. Also that the A. F. of L. probably knew that the Field Workers were more closely associated to the TROTSKYITES then to the Communist Party.

Reichmann stated that the nurses on general duty in ANGELUS HOSPITAL receive the ridiculous wage of $30 per month. He said that after these girls have trained in a technical course for three years to be given such a low wage is a demonstration of the degrading policy of the capitalists and will only serve to radicalize the technical workers along with the unskilled. He said that while the capitalists are trying to save a few dollars and beat down the living conditions of these highly skilled girls for the present they will soon learn that they have been the principal organizers for the radical and union movement.

Reichmann then warned the organization to be conservative and quite in their demands until such time as they have built up a large organization which will give them sufficient strength. He said that in some hospitals hash is doled out to the girls three or four times a week, but if one or two of them complain they would immediately be "fired." While on the other hand if an institution was well organized a demand by a number of employees would be met with good food instead of hash.

Following the above talk C. J. HAGGERTY, Secretary of the Building Trades Council, was introduced.

Haggerty was somewhat conservative and warned the Hospital Employees Union never to be too rash in their action as they must always remember both individually and collectively that they have the lives of many patients in their hands and that regardless of the type of individual patients "a life is a life."

Haggerty stated that he has never been closely associated with Professional workers such as Nurses and did not know much about the organization but that he could assure the Union that it would always receive the whole hearted support of the A. F. of L. throughout the entire country. That every individual in the Union must consider himself or herself an organizer at large and at no time should any member overlook the opportunity to bring in a new member.

He stated that from 1923 to 1929 the Building Trades Craftsmens' wages soared to a peak of $18 per day and that in 1936 it has reached $10 and $12 per day from the depression level of practically zero. He said that wages in some crafts are still going up and that workers in all lines of work are becoming Union conscious, therefore it is up to the many unorganized workers to lose no time in building their organization.

Secretary Reichmann called the writer to one side and asked that she endeavor to organize a meeting of fifty or more Registered nurses to hear a lecture by some prominent doctor on a technical subject. He stated that this doctor could be supplied through his efforts but did not mention the name of the doctor, whom the writer believes may be Doctor Leo BIGELMAN. Reichman then stated that after the doctor had had "his little say" some one from the organization would be there to talk ORGANIZATION to the nurses.

The writer, member of the Executive Board, was notified by Secretary Riechmann, to attend an Executive Board meeting at 2312 East 3rd Street, Tuesday, June 16th for the purpose of working out plans regarding the coming Nurses' Convention which will begin June 21st in Los Angeles.

Reichmann proposed that the writer, with a Committee, arrange with Nurse Matilda Robbins for the latter to speak on ORGANIZATION during this convention.

The Executive Board will also have a discussion regarding the issuance of several thousands leaflets to place in the hands of the visiting nurses.

M. RUBBER WORKERS

EXHIBIT 10356

(In pencil:) "In Feb. 6–34 wants dope re red connections."

(Alleged agitators at Firestone Rubber Co. plant—County, given to Of. C. J. Evans by Capt. Bert Hastings, Sheriff's Office, Thurs. Feb. 1–34)

Ernest Brown	3062 Ardmore Ave., South Gate
Ernest Brown	1505 E 102nd St., Los Angeles
Walter Webster	9304 Madison Ave., South Gate
Louis Sandoval	2615 Pine Place, South Gate

C. A. Penrod_____ 8681 Virginia Ave., South Gate
Walter Neilsen_____ 3312 Tweedy Blvd., South Gate
Davis Boyd
   or
Davis Baillie_____ Lynward, Calif.
Louis Remmerde_____ 9933 San Luis St., South Gate

(These names handed in by Firestone Co. to Sheriff's dept. to investigate.)
(In ink:) "Call Mr. Wheeler. 1:35 PM."

Exhibit 10357

[Intra-departmental correspondence]

Los Angeles Police Department

Office of In. Bu. Metro Divn

Feb. 7, 1934, 9.40 a. m.

Memo.   Re: List Suspected Reds employed in Firestone Co.

Mr. J. A. Meek of Firestone Rubber Co. JEfferson 4241 phones in that he was referred here by Sheriff's office re list turned over him other day for checking as to any definite Communist connections.   Said information came to him sort of second-handed but apparently a reliable source, from someone who was not in company but supposed to have connects with the TUUL; said he would take no action re these men unless something concrete prove of them being Red agitators; as they have been considered to be reliable employes.   Said will call back in couple of days re any information developed.

F

Exhibit 10358

[Intra-Departmental Correspondence]

(In pencil:) "Investigations pending"

Los Angeles Police Department

Office of In. Bu. Metro Divn

Feb. 15–34, 3 p. m.

Capt. Hynes: Mr. Meek of Firestone Rubber Co. JE 4241 phones in again inquiring if anything on list of suspects sent in a few days ago.   Said is very anxious to know of this; says they now have 1,300 employees and management directs him to verify re reports on Reds working within that concern.

Exhibit 10359

4.30 p. m. Apr. 10–34.

Capt. Hynes: Chief Davis phoned in wants you put a check on following tire companies: Goodrich, Goodyear, Firestone, to find out how many Communists are working in those places; wants this information as soon as you get back.

Phelps.

Exhibit 10360

[Intra-Departmental Correspondence]

Los Angeles Police Department

Office of Intelligence Bureau, Metropolitan Division

FRI., FEB. 28, 1936, 3 p. m.

Capt Hynes—Lt. Lane

Memo. Request Red Squad Officer go to BLYTHE, Riverside Co. Cal. to check up one Geo. Roberts, alleged Red strike agitator stopped by L. A. Police Detail there.

Per phone call in from Capt. Horrall of Chief Cross's office Sta. 2549; I phoned him back and he explained as follows:

Mr. Fysh of M & M Tu 6244 had phoned them requesting assistance in checking up on one Geo. Roberts. This subject was questioned by L. A. Officers in Blythe when he came through with an auto with Ohio lic. plates and something suspicious about the plates; when searched he had a gun on him, which it is understood was turned over to Sheriff at Riverside for check on. The car is in Indio. Subject Geo. Roberts was not arrested, but after a check up was released and understood to have come on to Los Angeles, where is now said to be. Mr. Fysh believes subject was a Com. strike agitator in the Goodyear Tire Co. strike back East and may have similar purposes here.

Chief Cross wants a Red Squad officer to go to BLYTHE, contact the L. A. police detail there and confer with them in detail re this case; with a view of learning whether or not there is any definite charge can be placed against said subject. Chief Cross wants this attended to today if possible; call Capt. Horrall back re same.

Exhibit 10361

Los Angeles Police Department

Office of Intelligence Bureau, Metropolitan Division

[Confidential]

MARCH 2, 1936.

Re: Geo. B. Roberts, Organizer United Rubber Workers Union, Hdqrs. Akron, Ohio; and meeting held Sunday March 1st, at F. O. E. Hall, South Gate.

Capt. Wm. F. Hynes,
Commanding Intelligence Bureau.

SIR: Pursuant to your instructions I covered a meeting held by the United Rubber Workers Union, held at the F. O. E. Hall #2082, Independence & States, South Gate, Cal. Sunday March 1st, 10:30 A. M.

This was an organization meeting to establish a local union in Los Angeles of this United Rubber Workers Union of America; an affiliate of the A. F. of L. Mr. George B. Roberts, a national organizer was in charge of the meeting. His local business address is 952 Atlantic Blvd. Los Angeles. There were 17 men present when meeting started, 2 coming in after, making 19 in all. The men present were workers from the Goodyear, Firestone and U. S. local rubber plants. Some of the men explained they had difficulty in locating the hall as it had originally be stated the meeting was to be in Huntington Park—hence the small attendance.

Mr. Roberts opened his talk with greetings from President Green of the A. F. of L.; also from the United Rubber Workers Union in Akron, Ohio, from which city he said he had arrived in L. A. just two days ago.

Roberts spoke in detail of the cause and the progress of the tire workers strike which started Feb. 18th in Akron, Ohio in Goodyear Plant #2 and is still in progress. He read numerous communications from friends and associates there stating they now have a picket line of 10,000 employees; and so far no interference from police. He said several days ago an injunction was granted the Goodyear Rubber Co. against picketing their plant, but so far the police have taken no action.

Roberts strongly denounced company unions as selling out the employees to the bosses and of the bosses using the company unions as stool pigeons. He spoke at length on working conditions in the rubber factories, speed up system and no overtime allowed, longer hours and discrimination against union members. He talked at length on the fact they must organize here because it was very obvious they would have to carry the load caused by the shutdown back East, and that the Eastern unions were looking to Los Angeles for support on their strike.

Mr. Roberts concluded his talk at 12 noon; then held an open forum. Several people in the audience, names not mentioned, talked on organization, working conditions in the various local plants; also talked against the company unions in the various local tire plants.

After this discussion, Mr. Roberts again took the floor and asked all present to sign up; most of those present did so. He pointed out if they failed to organize here the employees would suffer a decrease in wages per hour amounting to about $14 a month, whereas their union dues would only be a dollar a month here.

Roberts then discussed plans for a future meeting to be held within the next ten days or two weeks at a more suitable location and under more definite plans whereby all the workers of the various local plants would be able to attend. Mr. Roberts stated that he would be at his local business address, 952 Atlantic Blvd. Los Angeles to sign up any members present or their friends wishing to join the local union and requested wide publicity amongst the workers be given this address and this new union movement.

Meeting adjourned about 1 p. m.

After the meeting adjourned I talked with Mr. Roberts in person and he informed me that he was official organizer of the United Rubber Workers of America, affiliated with the A. F. of L. and was sent out to the West Coast, with expenses paid by the Union to organize the rubber workers of the various rubber plants in and about Los Angeles. He strongly emphasized that he is an American Union Man and his sole aim in our community was to foster an American Trade Union amongst the local rubber workers under the A. F. of L. and talked very strongly against Communist activities of any kind, and that he would be the first to report to local authorities any attempts of any subversive groups attempting to affiliate with his union.

Mr. Roberts is described as an American about 35 years old, 5' 6'', 140#, slender build, dark complected, small black mustache clear across his mouth, dark eyes. He is a good talker and uses good English; and said he is a former worker on the assembly line in Goodyear Plant #2 Akron, Ohio. He is very neat appearing.

The following is a list of license numbers of cars (and registrations where obtainable) used by men attending this meeting: (all 1936 plates).

6 U 6341 (not on file yet)   8 T 8235 (not on file yet).
8 U 7148   "   "   "
4 T 9802   "   "   "
1 M 8426 (reg. to M. E. Britton, 433 E. 76 St., 1931 Ford vict. coupe).
4 P 4012 (reg. to Leslie Treston, 1871 Lotus St., Pasadena '25 Dodge coach).
2 P 8728 (reg. to Floyd Parroll, 238 N. Freeman, Inglewood, '26 Buick coach).
5 Z 7452 (reg. to Albert Giaconini, U. S. S. Raleigh, San Diego '28 Chev. Coach).

NOTE.—Man who used this car spoke at the meeting stating he had been a union man for 32 years the last 10 of which he worked for Goodyear Rubber Co. he was known by several there. He was an elderly, Italian appearing man, 55–60 years old (this may be his son's car).

Respectfully,

C. A. SITTS, #1394.

S:F

EXHIBIT 10362

JUNE 10, 1937.

DEAR FRANK: Enclosed leaflet distributed at front gate of Goodyear Rubber Co., as shifts changed around 4:00 PM, June 9, 1937.

G–30.

[Attached to above]

GOODYEAR WORKERS.

Lansing, Michigan, Captured by C. I. O. Monday.
Cotton Mill Closed—Why?
Rumored Three Day Week for Rubber Workers.
Reports That C. I. O. Will Organize Army and Navy.
Radio and Press Reports That Lewis Says Steel Workers Will Resort to Arms.
Authorities Order All Pickets Disarmed.
Can the Independents Save the Day? Can We Insure Our Future? Will They Close Our Shop as They Closed the Cotton Mill?
A Meeting of the Goodyear Employees Association Will Be Held Saturday, June 12th, 10:00 AM. at 6202 So. Compton Ave. Come Out and Bring Some One.
Now is the Time for Goodyear Employees to Make an Effort for Themselves. Come Out to Our Meeting and Discuss the Above Reports.
After the Meeting an Election Will Be Held. Members Must Attend.

GOODYEAR EMPLOYEES ASSOCIATION, INC.

N. CENTRAL LABOR BODIES

EXHIBIT 10363

LOS ANGELES POLICE DEPARTMENT
Chief's Office, In. Bu. Metro. Divn.

MON., 5–13–35.

Memo. Lt. LANE.

Dr. Dorn of Hollywood Lutheran Church OL 4411 had contacted Chief's office inquiring re A. Corsenson, 402 S. Mansfield and J. W. Buzzell; phoned him back no cards on these subjects.

He said a friend of his had contact him re indorsing a new RADIO STATION of which these men and following were working for: A. Tornek, R. Lillie, Fred. L. Packard, A. Rosenberg; they have applied to Federation Communications Commission for a station permit; Corsenson is said to be Pres. of Metropolitan Broadcasting Co. and Buzzell a Labor Union man.

Advised him no cards these subjects, but J. W. Buzzell was well-known as Secy. Central Labor Council for years & years; that very unlikely we would have any record on any of them; but understood that Robert Noble and similar groups were trying to get a new FREE SPEECH radio station.

He wants any reliable data we can give him.

Note: No cards on any above men.

F

EXHIBIT 10364

MAY 14, 1935.

REPORT OF UNDERCOVER OPERATIVES

Subject: Robert Noble.

Dr. Dorn, Hollywood Lutheran Church, OL 4411, inquiry regarding A. Corsenson, 402 S. Mansfield, and J. W. Buzzell.

Corsenson, who is president of the Metropolitan Broadcasting Company, has joined with Buzzell, who has been associated with the Labor Council, for a number of years, and the following named men; A. Tornek, R. Lillie, Fred L. Packard, A. Rosenberg, in attempting to start a new broadcast station.

It is reported that Corsenson and Robert Noble are very friendly.   Noble has stated that he is going to help all Unions in Los Angeles Area in their strike efforts and that he is also starting a broadcast station under an amateur permit, to be operating about Wednesday May 15, 1935., and in the event that Will Kindig secures a permit for station it will then be turned over to him and the equipment, which is 500 watt at present will be increased to 5000 watts.

It is believed that this is one movement and these men are all associated together in this enterprise.

Respectfully submitted.

RALPH A. SEARS.

EXHIBIT 10365

RADICAL ACTIVITIES

LOS ANGELES, CALIFORNIA, *May 11th, 1937.*

The regular Monday night meeting of the C. I. O. "Conference" of Southern California was held at 828½ South Broadway, Los Angeles, last night and was opened with BILL BUSICK, Chairman and CHARLES WEST, Secretary.

It had formerly been suggested that this body should be called the C. I. O. Central Council, but it has been definitely decided to call it the L. A. Industrial Council C. I. O.

A telegram was read which was received from the Federated Motion Picture crafts, addressed to Busick, thanking him and the C. I. O. for the wonderful support and cooperation.

DICK COLEMAN reported regarding the Defense Committee and added that tickets are selling very rapidly for the HOMER MARTIN meeting.   Coleman is planning to organize a very large auto caravan to meet MARTIN when he arrives at the airport May 20th, with C. I. O. banners prominently displayed.

It was moved and carried that Busick and West be retained in their present offices until the charter for this organization arrives, after which an election of officers will be held.

A delegate from Mojave Local 272 reported that the workers in his locality are very much Union minded and that they shut down a mine for one day and went 20 miles to organize a new Local.

Busick reported that his organization, the International Ladies' Garment Workers, have three strikes scheduled for this week and he expects to be exceedingly busy.

The Empire Projectionists' delegate stated that in the past two weeks his organization has signed up twenty two new theaters in the C. I. O. Organization.

A Chrysler delegate to this meeting reported that there are but thirty five employees of that plant who have not signed in the C. I. O.

KEN HUNTER, stated that he had received a telegram from JOHN L. LEWIS with the information that he (Lewis) will broadcast over the Columbia network on May 14th at 6:45 P. M.

Delegate GATELY, of Riverside, reported that they are having a great deal of trouble with the A. F. of L. at the Riverside Cement Company and that charges have been filed with Dr. Towne Nylander accusing the A. F. of L. of being a Company Union and that Nylander had forwarded these charges to Washington, D. C.

Bob Roberts reported that he had just returned from a trip to San Francisco and the Bay District and that the Union is progressing very rapidly.   He also said that he had visited TOM MOONEY in San Quentin prison.   Roberts is on the "COMMITTEE TO FREE MOONEY AND BILLINGS" and feels sure that it will not be long before these men are free.

Roberts predicts that within two years the A. F. of L. will be out of existence with the exception perhaps of the building trades.

A motion was made and carried to send as many pickets as possible to aid in the Motion Picture strike.

BOB ROBERTS and Secretary BUZZELL of the Central Labor Council, (A. F. of L.) are to engage in a debate at 6:30 P. M. today at 648 South Broadway, Los Angeles.

Claims are made by the C. I. O. officials that great gains are taking place in the organization of Postal Telegraph, clerks, hotel employees and many other crafts in this locality.

Exhibit 10366

Minutes of the Regular Meeting of the Los Angeles Industrial Union Council, CIO, Held at 833 South Spring St. on Nov. 22, 1937

Chairman: George Roberts   Secretary: C. H. Jordan

Meeting called to order at 8.05 p. m.

ROLL CALL OF OFFICERS

Present.—Geo. Roberts, Chas. West, C. H. Jordan, Wm. Gately, E. Campbell, P. Comorre, I. Lutzky, J. Blumberg, E. Judd.

Absent.—M. Greenseid, M. W. Phelps, H. Hobson, H. Wilson, H. V. Duty (excused), W. D. Cox.

CREDENTIALS

American Radio Telegraphists' Assn #7.—Delegates: C. V. Leiden, A. C. Armstrong, L. R. Burger.   Alternates: W. H. Barrett, R. Surface (new), H. Durmisevich.   Remove: M. G. Mallow, J. C. Lawler, G. Van Ecken.

Inter. Longshoremen's & Warehousemen's Union #1-26.—Delegates: Edward Dinga, R. W. Burroughs.

Inter. Longshoremen's & Warehousemen's Union #1-20.—Alternates: A. H. Day, C. G. Lewis (formerly regular delegate).   Remove: Henry Rickers.

United Automobile Workers #188.—Remove: C. W. Algire, O. Carr, ———— Adams.

United Automobile Workers #215.—Delegate: Bob Robinson (formerly alternate) to replace Sherman Elliott.

United Automobile Workers #510.—Alternate: Rudolph Stoessel (formerly regular).   Remove: Carl Byron.

United Electrical & Radio Workers #1414.—Delegates: Geo. Allen, Sid Busen.   Remove: Al Marra, R. Williams.

United Rubber Workers #43.—Delegates: L. H. Preston, C. W. Dean.   Remove: R. L. Bilskie, M. Norton.

M & S: That the delegates be seated.   C. & S. O.

MINUTES

Regular Council meeting held Nov. 15th minutes accepted as read.

Executive Board minutes of meeting held Nov. 17th read.

M & S: That we take these points up seriatim.   C. & S. O.

(1) Case of dismissal of James Burford, of the Office Workers, by the COMMUNITY CHEST.   Recommendation: that committee from the Council visit the Community Chest, if no answer is received to letter sent by the Office Workers.

Edith Campbell, organizer for the U. O. P. W. A. reported lates developments: Board of Directors of Community Chest to meet tomorrow.   Necessary to write letters, telephone to Chest, protesting this dismissal and demanding reinstatement.   Post cards calling for reinstatement and withholding financial support will be distributed.   Read resolution (attached).

M & S: That we concur in the Executive Board recommendation and adopt the resolution.   C. & S. O.

(2) Proposed amendment referred to Executive Board on unemployment receipts to be accepted as membership for computing delegates to Council.   Recommendation: that we adhere to the constitution as drafted and accepted in regard to this matter.

M & S: That we concur.   C. & S. O.

(3) Resolution drafted by Transport Workers referred to Executive Board calling for setting up central bureau to distribute various services such as picketing, leaflet distribution.   Recommendation: that we non-concur.

M & S: That we accept the recommendation.   C. & S. O.

(4) Recommendation that Douglas local of the U. A. W. A. be instructed either to pay per capita to the Council or withdraw delegates.

M. & S: That we concur.

Discussion: this local also not paying per capita to District Council of the Auto Workers.   Suggestion that the local be asked for an explanation.

M & S: That this be tabled until the next meeting.   C. & S. O.

M & S: That the secretary contact officers of this local, informing them of action taken, & ask for report.   C. & S. O.

(5) Recommendation that locals seeking affiliation to the Council pay 1st month's per capita upon seating delegates—based on number of delegates.
M & S: That we concur. C & S. O.
(6) Recommendation that secretary consider each case of delinquency and write severe letters, where necessary. requesting payments.
M & S: That we concur. C & S. O.
(7) That new delegates cards for 1937 not be distributed to delegates from those locals which are delinquent, and that secretary notify locals to this effect.
M. & S: That we concur. C & S. O.

REPORTS

Legislative Committee.—Will attend City Council meeting at Azusa to attempt to obtain repeal of anti-picketing law.   Trying to arrange meeting with organizer and attorneys for Amalgamated Meat Cutters Union to work jointly on anti-labor injunctions.   RECOMMENDATION: That the Council secretary be instructed to communicate with our congressional representatives urging them to do their utmost to secure passage during this session of Congress of the Ludlow amendment.   This amendment proposes that before war can be declared it must be submitted to the people, except in case of invasion.   Copy of this letter to be sent to all locals urging them to write also.
M & S: That reported be accepted.   C & S. O.
Educational Director.—Classes on Wednesday at Firestone Hall & Friday at Currier Bldg. will begin parliamentary drill this week.   Class will begin tomorrow at the harbor—138 Avalon Blvd. Wilmington, 7.30 p. m.   Two important new pamphlets are obtainable at Brother Heist's office: "THE C. I. O. PROGRAM FOR A BETTER AMERICA," which is John L. Lewis' closing speech to the Atlantic City convention, and "The Company Union Trap."   These are 1¢ each and rates can be had for sets of 100.
M & S: That the Ladies' Auxiliary Committee be discharged.   C & S. O.
Defense Promotion Committee.—Brother Comorre stated he cannot get cooperation.   Chairman suggested all persons interested in this appear at next Executive Board meeting of the Council—Wednesday at 8 p. m.
MOONEY COMMITTEE.—Preparing appeal to Supreme Court.   Program for mass meeting at Philharmonic mapped out.   Delegates to this committee checked up on and agreed to continue.   Hearing Dec. 15th before Senator O'Mahoney, chairman Senate sub-judiciary Committee.   Write letters to him at Senate Bldg. Washington, D. C. asking for favorable & quick investigation.
Question: What action taken on matter of Community Chest—Veterans Service Bureau, which was to be investigated by Boycott Committee.   Secretary informed delegates that Executive Board of the Community Chest was meeting tomorrow and this would be presented, as well as the case of James Burford.
M & S: That we boycott the COMMUNITY CHEST.
Substitute Motion.—That we boycott the Community Chest & prepare a resolution incorporating reasons, including Veterans' Service Bureau, refusal to furnish aid to strikers, the Burford case & other pertinent angles.
M & S: That we defer this for one week.   C & S. O.

COMMUNICATIONS

(1) Resolution presented by Secretary Jordan on the restraining order signed by Judge Reuben Schmidt, served on the Council and the Secretary, as well as a number of other CIO officials, in connection with a strike of the Steel Workers Organizing Committee.   Resolution calls for empowering CIO attorney Al Wirin to act for the Council in this matter.
M & S: That we adopted the resolution.   C & S. O.
(2) Resolution adopted by the Seattle Industrial Labor Union Council (attached) on the case of Harold Pritchett, president of the International Woodworkers of America.
M & S: That we concur.   C & S. O.
(3) Resolution adopted by American Radio Telegraphists' Assn. re the "VARIOPLEX," a machine which eliminates 75% of the staff in a telegraph office, calling for the national office of the A. R. T. A. to take necessary steps to eliminate this machine.
M & S: That we concur.   LOST.

NEW BUSINESS

M & S: That the Executive Board, together with interested parties, prepare an adequate resolution on the "VARIOPLEX", with the suggestion that a special committee be set up by the Department of Labor to investigate the matter and see what can be done for the people being displaced.   C & S. O.

GOOD AND WELFARE

Brother Ramsden, ILWU #1–13 urged attendance at Judge Schmidt's court tomorrow at 10 a. m. where I. L. W. U. case to decide whether incorporation papers can be transferred over to the CIO, will come up.

Brother Gateley, Mine, Mill & Smelter Workers: still holding solid on aqueduct strike up at Banning.   In better condition than ever before.   Work on one end of the tunnel has stopped absolutely because of inability to get competent miners.

M & S: That we adjourn.   C. & S. O.   Adjourned: 10.00 p. m.

BOYCOTT LIST

ALL GOODS MANUFACTURED IN JAPAN, GERMANY AND ITALY
THREE G DISTILLERY
CALIFORNIA CRACKER CO.   (CREAM FLAKE & GOLDEN BROWN)
MRS. LEE'S PIES INC.
ROSENBLUM INC.
KURTGMAN BROS. (KAY BEE SPORTSWEAR CO.)
GENERAL LEATHER GOODS CO.
SANTA FE CIGARS (A. SENSENBRENNER SONS)
CAPEHART AUTOMATIC PHONOGRAPHS
ROGER JESSUP'S DAIRY—LUCERNE DAIRY

NOTE.—"BOYCOTT JAPANESE—ITALIAN—GERMAN MADE GOODS" PLACARDS ARE AVAILABLE AT THE COUNCIL OFFICES.   ALSO HAVE SUPPLY OF "DELIVER ONLY UNION MADE GOODS HERE" CARDS.

Copies of the Constitution of the Council can be obtained by writing sending in your request.   YOPWA #9.

EXHIBIT 10367

[Intra-Departmental Correspondence]

LOS ANGELES POLICE DEPARTMENT

Office of Intelligence Bureau, Metropolitan Division

SEPT. 30, 1937.

Memorandum for Chief DAVIS.

In compliance with your directions of this date, the following is a brief, rough synopsis of the strength of the principal C. I. O. UNIONS in the Los Angeles area:

The COMMITTEE FOR INDUSTRIAL ORGANIZATION, of which John L. Lewis is President, Chas. P. Howard, Secretary, and John Brophy Director, with national office in the Heurich Bldg. 1627 K St. N. W. Washington, D. C. has listed some 23 national affiliated unions as of June 1, 1937 of which some are specifically mentioned below as active in the Los Angeles field.

As to the general strength of the CIO in Los Angeles, it might be said that the Los Angeles Industrial Council, which was recently set up as a central coordinating body for various CIO unions in the Los Angeles area (similar to the Central Labor Council of the A. F. of L.) claims an affiliated membership of 50,000 (this is very exaggerated); it is believed its per capita tax on paying members of from 15,000 to 17,500 is more nearly its real strength, with possibly a leeway of 5,000 more in various other CIO controlled unions.

Principal CIO Unions in Los Angeles area.—(See bottom pg. 2. re AIRCRAFT INDUSTRY)

1. *United Automobile Workers of America.*—This is undoubtedly the strongest CIO union in the Los Angeles area, and is understood to have contracts with the

General Motors plant in Southgate and the Chrysler plant in the East Los Angeles industrial area; hard to estimate its real membership, but possibly 4,000.

2. *International Ladies Garment Workers Union.*—This is very strongly entrenched in Los Angeles and has practically established a closed shop in Los Angeles in the making of ladies dresses, coats, etc., and an estimated membership of about 3,000.

3. *Amalgamated Clothing Workers of America.*—Estimated about 1,500 members, engaged in the making of both men's and women's clothing; especially men's suits.

4. *United Rubber Workers of America.*—Also very active and fairly strongly entrenched in the large rubber plants in and around Los Angeles.

5. *Oil Field, Gas Well & Refiner Workers Union.*—Operates mostly among field and refinery oilworkers and fairly strongly entrenched, especially in the Long Beach fields; said to have signed up Richfield Oil Co. recently. NOTE: This organization while not as yet affiliated with the Los Angeles Industrial Union, has signified it will do so, which would bring in about 4,000 more members.

6. *International Fur Workers Union.*—Believed to have a dominating control in the local fur manufacturing business.

7. *Steel Workers' Organizing Committee.*—Has been active in the Los Angeles area in organizing in various steel plants; no estimate as to strength; but is considerable.

8. *American Newspaper Guild.*—Has been organizing reporters, writers and assistant editors in practically every metropolitan Los Angeles newspaper, except the Times.

Also, there are several other locally set-up CIO unions, such as the Mine, Mill & Smelters Union, which has been conducting a strike against the Metropolitan Water District for the past two months or more at San Jacinto; estimated membership of 1,000 or more.

Also we have the local International Longshoremen's Assn.'s strong local in Los Angeles Harbor, strongly in the CIO with a membership of about 3,000, of which 2,200 has signified their agreement to affiliating with the CIO.

Also the International Longshoremen's Assn. have organized a Warehousemen's Union for warehouse employes and truck drivers and which has practically a complete organization of the wholesale drug companies and considerable strength in the milling and grain business.

Also the CIO unions have shown considerable agitation and potential strength in various other industries, such as:

Dairy Workers Union of America; has conducted a few strikes in this area during the past few months.

United Cracker, Bakery and Confectionary Workers Union; which has been active in conducting a strike against one local cracker manufacturer.

United Trunk & Leather Workers Union; has conducted numerous strikes locally in recent months.

*CIO Aircraft activity.—Mention should be made of the aircraft divisions of the UNITED AUTOMOBILE WORKERS OF AMERICA, which has several locals in Los Angeles area and is at present conducting a strike against the Northrop plant in El Segundo. *Note:* These locals for a time seemed about to capture the entire aircraft industry, but due to failures of its leadership in calling premature and unnecessary strikes has lost considerable strength and prestige among aircraft workers and is now on the wane.

O. MISCELLANEOUS LABOR ORGANIZATIONS

EXHIBIT 10368

LOS ANGELES, CALIF., *Jan. 4th 1928.*

Re: Labor Agitation:

MACHINISTS 311

There were about one hundred and forty members present at the meeting of Local 311 Machinists held at 604 Labor Temple last night. The meetings have been held on Monday night for the past several years but it was decided that the night be changed to Tuesday hereafter and this was the first Tuesday night meeting. The attendance was much better. While several applications for membership were read, only two men were initiated at this meeting, these men were named, *Ed Gayton* and *C. E. Anderson.*

The new officers were installed and the whole meeting was full of pep and it seemed that practically all the members present are thoroughly interested and want to continue the membership drive which Curley Grow is putting on for them.

A letter from the International gave assurance that Grow will be allowed to remain in Los Angeles for six months as his efforts are meeting with success. This communication from the East asked the local members to cooperate with the organizer in this work. Permission was also granted by the International for the membership drive to continue for another six months.

Reports show that the local has expended seventeen hundred dollars since this drive started and that such a good start was shown that it would be considered very foolish to discontinue it now.

Grow made a report stating that the State Highway Commission has written to all their garages in the state saying that a representative of organized labor will call on them soon and advising that these garages line up with the union. Grow assured those present that all the official garages of the State Highway Commission will be organized within the next few months or as soon as they can be reached by the organizers.

Grow told the officers before the meeting that he has enough members lined up in the Baker Iron Works to start a new local if he wanted to. (This would not mean so much as it only takes about ten or twelve members to start a local.) During his report Grow said that he is working with some of the Pipe and Steel workers and hopes to have a surprise for the members in the near future of one big outfit being practically all lined up with the possible exception of some of the old homeguards who are owned body and soul by the bosses.

Poll the President of 311 seems to be a hustler and continually urged all the members to forget their little petty grievances and put all their energy into the organizing campaign and membership drive.

Grow later added that the Auto Mechanics will all be lined up in the Police Department in the very near future. Grow assured the members that he knows what he is talking about in making this statement.

Grow told the Secretary to be very careful and not let any of the names of the members get out of his possession as it has been learned that some of the large employers of Auto Mechanics here are anxious to find out if any of their workers are lined up so they can fire them.

There will probably be a large class up for initiation at the next meeting. Grow claimed that he has a great many signed applications by Auto Mechanics and Machinists both but they were short of funds due to the Christmas season being here but they will all have the money this month.

Exhibit 10369

[Confidential]

LOS ANGELES, CALIF., *Jan. 6th, 1928.*

Re: A. F. of L.

At a meeting (the first this year) of Organizers held at labor temple last night the following information was obtained. This meeting only lasted a little more than an hour and was held for the purpose of getting the organizers and business agents together and to have an understanding so that there can be established a spirit of cooperation. These meetings are to be monthly affairs in the future. The following things came up for short discussion.

a. Reports show that the officers of Electrical Workers 18, Linemen, and Local 83 Insidemen are not working in Harmony. Both Business Agents were present and were urged to come to Labor Temple with the other officers of their respective unions on next Tuesday night at seven o'clock for a conference in the office of the Secretary. There is to be a joint meeting of all the I. B. E. W. officers on that night and it has been reported that local 18 has refused to send representatives or to join in this joint membership drive.

b. A man named Fink or Frink, short light complected Jew was introduced and it was stated that he is going to work among the Laundry Workers and Cleaners and Dyers. This man is evidently from Chicago as he mentioned work done in that City several times.

c. Dale reported that Bosses are trying to get the membership lists of the Machinists union so that the Auto Mechanics who have joined recently can be intimidated and scared into withdrawing from the union or to keep others from joining when union members are discharged.

d. Report made that the Electricians, especially linemen are ready for organizations and that letters are being received from some of the workers asking that organizers be sent on the job. Dale showed a letter from a worker employed by the L. A. Gas, but did not read it.

e. Abe Muir reported that the Movies will be one hundred per cent organized within the next few months, as they are meeting with no opposition and that seventy-five to eighty per cent of all the studio carpenters and Mechanics working on the various studio lots are hired thru union headquarters.

f. Someone in the rear reported that the organizing being carried on among the rubber workers was progressing satisfactorily but that he had nothing definite that he cared to report at this time.

g. Reported that small meetings held at the homes of the creamery and dairy workers are meeting with success and that many have been lined up in this way.

h. It was learned that Dale has asked the Executive Committee of the Central Labor Council for a sum of money each month to be used for some secret purpose which he would not divulge. This matter had been held up and will probably be turned down as they have no power to vote money without knowing what it is for. This was just mentioned and did not enter the discussion at the meeting but was learned after the meeting was over.

i. The Building Trades expect to establish the five day week by April first or shortly after without having to result to a strike. It was reported by Ben Simmons that a great many large contractors are favorable to the five day week.

j. The General Organizing Committee, the Committee of One Hundred, Metal Trades and the Culinary Alliance are all going to be reorganized, new names added and old names dropped.

The rest of the time was taken up in a general discussion of local conditions and prospects for the future from organized labor's point of view.

Exhibit 10370

Los Angeles, California, *February 4th, 1928.*

I. B. E. W. Local No. 18, (Linemen)

The meeting of I. B. E. W. #18, Linemen, held Thursday nite, February 2nd, 1928, at the Labor Temple was attended by approximately seventy-five members.

There were five initiations, the majority of which were reinstatements of old members, The Initiation Fee for Linemen during the organizing campaign has been reduced to $10.00.

International Vice President T. C. Vickers was present, and gave a few remarks, stating that things are moving along very well, and the future outlook was very bright, and that all the members seemed to be putting their shoulder to the wheel. He did not say much as other matters he had to take up would come in the form of communications.

Reed Armstrong, business manager, reported that he and T. C. Vickers, and J. W. Buzzell, had called on Mr. Scaterwood Chief Engineer of the Bureau of Light and Power, seeking a slight increase in wages, and that the Bureau was ready to cooperate with them.

Armstrong stated that they pointed out to the Bureau Officials that the A. F. of L. was the only body in Los Angeles that could furnish men for all trades at any time.

It was the impression of many of the members that the Bureau of Power and Light would grant a slight increase in the wages of the linemen and electricians, and that this would reflect favorable to electricians employed by other public utility corporations, no mention was made of the P. E. the Telephone Company or the Gas Company.

Armstrong further reported that he had placed five men on jobs at the Auto Show at Washington and Hill Street, and would place others this week.

Also reported that he had been in conference with a number of officials of Oil Companies, over hiring and placing Linemen on their jobs, and that they expressed themselves as very favorable, also that the wages and conditions of the Linemen were satisfactory, and would call for men when needed.

Reported that the General Petroleum Company had a building program laid out for the future from Bakersfield south, and that our linemen would secure the jobs.

Reported further that he had sent one man out to a private telephone exchange in the Valley, and that most of his time was spent with the International Organizers on organizational matters.

Communications from International Vice President T. C. Vickers in which he attached photo-static copies of correspondence between himself and Mr. Ballard, Executive Vice President of the Edison Company and head of the Power Distributing Company were read. These letters indicated that Vickers and Ballard had been in conference over wages and conditions in electrical crafts, and that the Power companies had spent many thousands of dollars for lobyists at the various state capitols and National Capitol, and were getting tired of buying the same old dog every year. Ballard's letters signified a willingness that this money should be directed towards a better understanding between capital and labor.

Leon Shook, took the floor following the reading of the communications and stated that since 1921, when the Power trusts succeeded in breaking the majority of unions on the Pacific Coast, that the electrical unions had went through the hardest fight in the history of any organization. He referred to their program of company unions, the black-listing of employees, etc.

It was learned that the City scale for Linemen was around $7.20 per day, and it is proposed to have the City Bureau of Power and light bring the scale to $8.00 or an increase of about 10 percent.

A man from the General Electric, sponsored by the Edison Company, termed as a world traveler, lecturer, and an Electrical Engineer, is to speak Wednesday night, Feb. 29th, 1928, at the Labor Temple Auditorium. He will also show motion pictures of electrical projects and the latest of electrical equipment. All locals have signified by vote their willingness to attend in a body.

EXHIBIT 10371

(Handwritten) Laf 2814   A   79   Aleme   Nadeau
(Handwritten) R. A. Wellpott   YO 9733

8-30-29.

DOMINGUEZ JOB SHELL OIL COMPANY TANKS (NEW CONSTRUCTION) L. A. COUNTY, CONSOLIDATED STEEL CO. JOB, LOCATED AT DOMINGUEZ JUNCTION TANK FARM

Mr. Cleveland in charge of Job.

Detail: Officer F. Hayes—In Charge and officers C. Dixon—1548—DE—2784 Frank Drevlo—1096—MI—2073

Detail must be on job at 7:00 A. M.

Structural Iron Workers (Not employed on Jobs) are attempting to stir up dissension thru intimidation of satisfied employees on the job.

Disperse any persons attempting to picket job or loitering about the job—who have no lawful business around there.

No attempt at picketing, or intimidation of satisfied employees by agitators or organizers should be tolerated.

* Frank Dewar—Sheriff Office Mu-9111—had been notified—we are cooperating with Sheriff's office in this matter.

EXHIBIT 10372

[From 35 NRA/16]

2:35 P. M. SAT. 9-16-33.

Memo for Capt HYNES.

Mr. Hazelberg of Perfection Bakery, 1st and Beaudry. Plant phones in that there is a Union organization meeting scheduled to occur at or around their plant tonight around 6 o'clock. He states organization promoting this is the United Brotherhood of America, of which a Frazer is head; as a precautionary measure against disturbances would like a detail of plainclothes men on hand to prevent any trouble.

Told him would try contact you re detail, says if he is not there ask for Mr. Murdock, MU 1281, who will be familiar with us.

F

(In pencil:) Wellpott & Abbott.

Mon., 9–18–33 9 a.m.

We covered above detail, Sat. from 6.30 pm till 9 pm Sept. 16. There was a company meeting gives a sales talk to assembled drivers and salesmen on a new load of bread the company is putting on the market called the "Sunshine Loaf". Mr. Murdock, sales manager, said they thought that organizers for the "United Brotherhood" might appear and attempt organization; he said the chief agitator for the "United Brotherhood" around their company was an ex-employee, who had been discharged from the company for drinking last month. However, no organizers or agitators appeared at the Perfection Bakery, while we were there whatsoever.

Mr. Murdock also stated the employees of Perfection Bakery were all satisfied with wages and bonus paid and was certain the organizers of the United Brotherhood would make little headway in organizing the Perfection Bakery workers.

A:F

C. R. ABBOTT.
R. A. WELLPOTT.

EXHIBIT 10373

[Intra-Departmental Correspondence.]

LOS ANGELES POLICE DEPARTMENT

Office of In. Bu. Metro. Divn.

JUNE 26, 1934.

Re: Strike call Meeting of Independent Cleaners & Dyers Union, 711 W. 17 St. Mon. night June 25.

Capt. WM. F. HYNES,
Commanding Intelligence Bureau.

SIR: I covered this meeting last night, the meeting being called to order at about 8:30 pm. with an attendance of 250 people, including a large number of known Reds.

Speeches were made by various people pro and con on the question of striking, after which motion was made that strike vote being taken and that a two-third majority would rule.

Secret ballot was taken and counted by five members appointed by the chairman. The result was announced as being 122 in favor of strike, 61 against. After considerable argument on the part of the ones that voted against the strike; the strike was declared in effect as from 6 a. m. Tuesday June 26 and strikers were instructed to report to their various shops at 6 a. m. this morning and see that no one went to work in their plant and then they were to go to the other plants in their district and prevent employees from going to work and get out the ones that were working.

The Union has the town divided into 9 districts, each district having from one to eleven plants in it. At this meeting 29 of the 50 plants in town were represented.

Harry Buchanan was introduced by the Chirman and spoke on behalf of the International Labor Defense and offered on behalf of the ILD to defend the workers during this strike. He also made a short talk regarding the activities of the ILD. It was voted by the strikers to accept the offer of the ILD.

Attorney Grover C. Johnson was then introduced by the Chairman as one of the ILD attorneys, and he made a very inflammatory speech telling the strikers as to what trumped up charges they were likely to be arrested on, and as to how to conduct themselves after arrest, such as not pleading guilty, but pleading not guilty and demanding a jury trial, etc., and stated that no matter what a striker did he was always not guilty and that if he plead guilty then he was a scab.

Various members of the assemblage were instructed to remain for further instructions as to picket duty, etc. At this time I left the meeting (about midnight) came to the office and called Capt. Justin's home, but he was not in. Left word for him to call me.

I then drew up a schedule of the 50 plants affected by the strike and at 2:30 a.m., having not heard from Capt. Justin again called his home but was unable to get him.   The Night Chief having gone home, I phoned the next in command, Capt. of Business Office Morning Watch and advised him of the situation and per his instructions, being still unable to contact Capt. Justin, I phoned the different divisions and advised them of the situation and the localities in their district where they might expect trouble.

Respectfully,

P. L. PHELPS #1527.

P:F

EXHIBIT 10374

[Intra-Departmental Correspondence. Form 235]

LOS ANGELES POLICE DEPARTMENT

Office of Intelligence Bureau, Metropolitan Division

AUG. 8, 1938.

Re: Strike at DURO STEEL Co., 2421 E. 8th St.   TR 35 6

Capt. WM. F. HYNES,
    Commanding Intelligence Bureau.

SIR: Received call at 7:25 a. m. this date that there were about 75 pickets in front of this company; we responded to call and found the employees across the street, with the exception of 12, who were in the picket line—the rest of the pickets had not been previously working for this company.   Shortly after our arrival, men who were across the street (and who are striking employees) left and in a few minutes came back and all went into picket line, making the strike almost 100% effective; only 2 men going inside of company to work.

We talked to the manager, *Mr. Brownstein*, and he stated they didn't know as yet whether the firm would attempt to run in non-union workers or not; that he would have to take it up with Emil Brown, owner of the company; that as yet the management has not come to any decision as to hiring non-union help and continuing to run their business or to recognize the union.   Union involved is UNITED ELECTRICAL RADIO & MACHINE WORKERS LOCAL #1421 CIO Affiliate. We talked to Bob Ontell, a striking employee and he said practically all the company employees had signed up for the union and were on strike for better wages, etc.

Left Officers *F. E. Thomas and O. E. Tompkins* to cover; they will let us know later as to regular police detail.

Respectfully,

L. H. BETTY—W. S. REGUR—C. O. WOOLARD

B:F

EXHIBIT 10375

[Departmental Correspondence. Form 286]

LOS ANGELES POLICE DEPARTMENT

Office of In. Bu. Metro. Divn.

Nov. 9, 1934.

Re: Interference with Drivers & Salesmen of GLOBE BOTTLING WORKS, 721 No. State. St. CA 11151.

Lieut. LUKE M. LANE,
    Commanding Intelligence Bureau.

SIR: Per your instructions, went to Globe Bottling Works, 721 No. State St. at 6.45 a. m. yesterday Nov. 8th and there contacted Mr. Abe Kanner, proprietor & manager of this concern.   Mr. Kanner told us that the day before there were eight automobiles with two to three men in each car parked in near vicinity of the plant and that when one of the company trucks would pull out, one of these cars would follow.   He said that no threats or interference to the drivers had been made by these men, but immediately following delivery these men would contact the customer, present a card stating "Globe Bottling Works Unfair to organized labor," (card attached), and make additional talk along these lines.

I informed Mr. Kanner that according to the activities of the Union as told to us by him, that there was no violation of the City Ordinances or State law, and, therefore, any action of the police department would be limited to investigation.

At about 7.15 a. m. three automobiles arrived at the plant and parked nearby. Mr. Kanner said that these were some of the Union people. We then questioned the occupants of these cars; one car a Buick sedan Lic. 1 P 156, registered to Laurence Dace, 9507 So. Main St.; he being the driver, and accompanied by Louis Jakovick, 1944 Sichel St. and William Krathen, 306 E. 7th St. The informed me that they were members of Local #227, Branch #6, United Brewery Workers, of which John S. Horn was Business Agent of the local. They said they had no intentions of committing any violence, that they would not interfere with drivers, that their activity was limited to presenting one of the unfair cards and stating to the customer that the Globe Bottling Works was unwilling to organize labor.

Another car was a Chevrolet sedan Lic 6 R 7958, with three occupants consisting of Chas. Cobbler, and two other men.

Another car was a Ford roadster, model A, sport coupe, Lic.——— one of the occupants was Isadore Cohn, 1447 E. 21 St.; the driver & owner of car was Fred Beasley Norcom, 6709 Orange Ave. No. Long Beach. These men on Sat. said they work for Bohemian Distribut Co. L. A.

After questioning these men, as the trucks were leaving from the Globe Bottling Works, each one of these three cars followed a truck.

This morning, Nov. 9, 1934 we arrived again at Globe Bottling Works at 6.45 a. m. and at 7.10 a. m. two cars from the Union arrived one being the Chevrolet sedan 6 R 7958, in which there were three men; the other car was a green Hudson sedan Lic. 8 N 597, occupied by three men, registered owner and driver was Ed Swanz, 1406 S. Flower St. who was driver of this car this morning, and his two companions were Isadore Cohn & Fred B Norcom, mentioned above.

Shortly after questioning these men in the Hudson automobile, Mr. John S. Horn, Business Agent of Local #227 United Brewery Workers, arrived at the plant and came to our car and asked us if we were from the department, and introduced himself, and stated that they were not going to violate any law or interfere with the drivers, that there would absolutely be no rough stuff. He further stated that he had gone to the City Hall and had received advice as to the legality of their tactics, and that they were lawful.

Shortly after the conversation with Mr. Horn, one of the drivers came to us and stated that they, the drivers of the Globe Bottling Works, did not want any part of the Union. He said they were very well satisfied under the existing conditions that prevail, that their time was practically their own, and that they did not have to account for every hour they were out on the route, and that they were making more money than the Union scale. He said they would be cutting off their own noses to spite their face to join that Union. There was no one out on strike at this place or anyone at the plant that is asking any assistance from this Union to organize them.

From our investigation, we find that there is no specific violation of any city ordinance or state law and that the police cannot act in this matter. However, it is my opinion that the Union is using high pressure methods to force the Globe Bottling Works and its employees to organize with the Union—this being done by the Union instituting an attempted boycott of this firm's products, by distribution of the above mentioned cards and having Union members give the firm's customers a follow-up talk.

Respectfully,

R. A. WELLPOTT DL 131
T. E. RYAN #994.

W:F
Encl.

Exhibit 10376

[Intra-Departmental Correspondence]

Los Angeles Police Department

Office of In. Bu. Metro. Divn. 7/25/35

Memo. Re: Demands & Resolution send Bank America by Carpenters & Joiners of America Local 1976, 2630 Brooklyn Ave.

Mr. Christensen, spec. agent Bank America phones above sent them a resolution of protest with certain demands re hiring the right kind of people, etc. Signed by Max Karp. as business rep. and Fergan as record secy.

Advised him this was probably an AFL local but that the New Com. policy of abandoning their old TUUL unions and working within regular unions had made some progress in some unions and caused certain "left wing" motions, etc. sometimes to be put over. Said had no cards above men.

He may call with letter to show us what they are doing.

F

Exhibit 10377

[Intra-Departmental Correspondence]

Los Angeles Police Department

Office of _____

MARCH 18TH, 1937

Capt. HYNES: Officer Stevens of the vice squad called and said he had a friend by the name of J. B. Gearhart, who is a building contractor, and who belongs to Carpenters Union Local #320.

Mr. Gearhart informed Officer Stevens that there are about six communist agitators among the members, who keep agitating trouble, especially among the Japanese members. There is one agitator in particular, whose name is Peter Schecter, 8460 San Juan Ave., South Gate, Phone # Jefferson 1030, who seems to be the ring leader. This Schecter, is said to teach a communist school in the vicinity of Third and Hill. He is said to teach every night in the week, except Sundays; and Tuesday nights, in particular. Mr. Gearhart, according to Officer Stevens, desires to know if this man Schecter has a Police record.

If he has such record, it would help in ousting the party from the organization, and thus save a lot of trouble. Officer Stevens wants to know if the man Schecter has a prior police record, and said he would call tomorrow about four P. M.

(Typed) TETER #1539.

Exhibit 10378

[From: 5-Strike Detail file]
[Intra-Departmental Correspondence]

Los Angeles Police Department

Office of In. Bu. Metro. Divn

WED., SEPT. 6–37.

REQUEST FOR POLICE DETAIL RALPHS GROCERY STORE (NEW STORE OPENING) 4821 LANKERSHIM BLVD. FOR SAT. OCT 9TH, 1937 9 A. M. TO 7

Mr. Hildebrand of the Ralph Grocery Co. TR 8721 phones and request police detail of 2 or 3 uniform officers for opening of their new market as above Saturday morning Oct. 9th, 1937; asks police detail; be there around 9 a. m. or little before; probably will have to remain all day; expects labor troubles.

Capt. WM. F. HYNES.

H:F

ASSIGNED: Officers Uhlick and Ashton
(In pencil:) Report back 2 p. m. no pickets

EXHIBIT 10379

[Intra-Departmental Correspondence]

LOS ANGELES POLICE DEPARTMENT

Office of Intelligence Bureau, Metropolitan Division

JANUARY 23, 1934.

Re: Meeting of Motion Picture Employees Asso. held at 5402 Hollywood Blvd. 8 pm. Monday, Jan 22, 1934.

Capt. WM. F. HYNES,
   Commanding Intelligence Bureau.

SIR: Per your instructions, we attended above meeting, which was held in a hall in the Hollywood Conservatory of Music.

There were about 48 people present. One of the main speakers was Helmar Bergman. This fellow is a very able speaker, positive and convincing. He understands his subject and spoke in particular on the necessity for an industrial union among the motion picture employes, going to some length. He brought up repeatedly regarding the A. F. of L. criticising it and the International Brotherhood of Electrical Workers and the methods they employed in conducting the last strike; that the A. F. of L. in conjunction with the studioes broke the strike, pointing out that through the loss of the strike it was necessary to organize an industrial union and that all crafts in the industry should be included.

After speaking along that line, he asked if anyone had any questions he would do his best to answer and if he couldn't, perhaps someone else could take the floor and answer. Most of the questions put to him he came back with an answer in a hurry.

One fellow got up and criticized some of the remarks that he wasn't stating true facts to the people gathered there; they got into a controversy and he had the fellow sit down (this man was a member of Local 37, International Brotherhood of Electrical Workers). Then a fellow named Blicks (evidently an official in the electrical union) spoke at some length and questioned Bergman as to the advisability of an organization of this character, mentioning re the trouble back in Washington, D. C. of the union being before them back there. Bergman made quick answer to questions by Blicks, saying that the present unions were controlled by misleaders and that a bureaucracy existed, and that they were not truly representatives of the rank and 'file, that the industrial union would be absolutely controlled by the worker himself from the rank and file, not by some high salaried union official.

The gist of the whole thing, as he went on, is that this was a *motion picture employes association* which was merely used as an open forum in discussing the problems that come up as to workers in the motion picture industry and leading up to the formation of a *Motion Picture Workers Industrial Union.* He went into a lot of explanation regarding that.

He was asked from the floor by a man if this industrial union, as he termed it, had any connection with the industrial unions that caused the strike in Imperial Valley and the milk strike here and he said absolutely not, that it was not affiliated with any, that it was a separate organization.

After that he introduced this fellow Wolf. Wolf made a little talk and one could tell the difference between the two. He was not as able as Bergman. He explained as to what the Motion Picture Workers Industrial Union was, stating it already had drawn up a Constitution and by-laws with dues at 25¢ a month, no initiation fee, and that the by-laws required that no official receive more than $15.00 a week salary. He said he would be glad to sign up anybody in the union.

Then a man asked what was behind this union, what was its basis, that if it stood alone what chance would it have, that there were already two or three unions existing. Wolf made a part answer but steered away from talk re affiliation; answering some other questions foreign to that part. Another man said that a union could not function on such dues.

Then some other questions were asked as to this industrial union and Wolf said he would read a part of the Constitution and that would clarify it, so he started to read the preamble, that membership was open to all regardless of race, creed, color or political affiliation, that the purpose of the union was to build a militant united front industrial union, that it supported federal unemployment insurance, etc. (regular Communist subsidiary statements). No mention was made of affiliation, only in this way that it was interested with other organizations in the class struggle, that where other workers are in the class struggle they will support them.

In the audience they had "plants," several men, and they would get up and make some little talk, making it sound good. One fellow got up and said that he was a white collar man, a writer and reader in a studio, said that he is a member of a Writers Guild in the Motion Picture industry (he seemed to be a "plant") this fellow said he was a writer, had written some scenarios. He told about the last strike, how he would have liked to have gone out with them, that he was sympathetic, and then he said he was a worker even if a writer and that if they could get all the people into one industrial union they can call a general strike and then they can win.

Right after this white collar man, a man got up and said he was a laborer in the motion picture industry and spoke of how he was working alongside of prop men and other crafts in the motion picture industry and how they were being paid half the wages of craftsmen; yet, he said he thought it was a preparation that in the event of a strike this laboring class he belonged to could take the place of the craftsmen, and he thought it was very necessary to organize this industrial union so that they would have a united front in all crafts in one union so a general strike could be called in case of either of the crafts had a grievance.

Another thing mentioned by Wolf was that anybody who signed up would have his name protected, so that the studios would not know about them being member of this industrial union, so anyone who was working in the studios would not have to fear losing their jobs.

They asked if any more meetings of the association of motion picture employes were to be held, and a motion was made, seconded and carried to meet every *Monday night;* a collection was taken up for hall rent and they gathered $4.16. It was noticed there was no rush to sign up. They had cards there for applications, which set forth place for name, address, studio, what union, etc. Seven or eight of these were passed out by Wolf in the aisle. There was no literature passed out; only a few papers on the speakers' table.

Next Monday will be sort of an open forum to discuss the "company union within the industry and the conditions of the workers within the union."

Some of the audience took the speakers to task and made quite an issue. One man after he had inquired re taking everybody into this Motion Picture Workers Industrial Union, and they said they would take in all motion picture employes, and when he asked them if they were going to take in the scabs, that was answered they would take in everybody; then this fellow said *"Count me out!"* Then a "plant" got up and said that two months ago he had heard it mentioned re taking in all the people into the union including the scabs and in that way they could educate them.

Exhibit 10380

Los Angeles Police Department
Intelligence Bureau

FEB. 7–35.
Detail

11.30 p. m., WEDNESDAY, FEB. 7–35.

Empire Theatrical Craftsmen's Union, Fraternal Brotherhood Hall, 8th and Figueroa.

Officers Wellpott & Pfeiffer. (2).

By Direction:

WM. F. HYNES,
H:F   *Acting Capt. Dets. LAPD COMDG. IN. BU.*

Memo for CAPT. HYNES.   Feb. 8–1933.

Covered above mentioned meeting last night in LeGrand Fraternal Brotherhood Hall, 8th Place & Figueroa, meeting being called to order by Mr. Crasher, Chairman, at 12 o'clock. We did not go in the hall where meeting was but stayed out in entrance of lodge rooms where meeting was being held so as to be able to observe any suspected activity of members of the Motion Picture Projectionists' Local Union #150.

About 12:30 a. m. observed a Ford four door sedan drive by on 8th Place and this car passed about four times (when first observe it only had two men in it.) At about 1 a. m. this car again was passing building and had four men in it. We stopped the car and I questioned occupants and found that the driver was E. W. Apperson, Bus. Mgr. of Motion Picture Projectionists Local #150; with him were 3 other projectionist, members of Local #150, named Peter Slater, C. T. Savage and Paul Mahoney. Apperson had picked Slater & Mahoney up at 8th and Broadway just previous to driving by.

On Questioning these men they stated their object in observing this place so closely was to ascertain whether any members of Local #150 were attending this meeting of the Empire Theatrical Craftsmen's Union. They denied they had any intent of committing any rough stuff. We shook each one down individually and searched the car, but there were no weapons or any other paraphanalia that might be used. Told them their actions seemed rather suspicious and thought it would be best for them not to show around there any more this morining. They left and were not seen anymore. License # of Apperson's car was 9X6457, Ford, black, four-door sedan. Model 1930.

EXHIBIT 10381

[Reverse side of Memo for Capt. Hynes: Feb. 8, 1933]

At 3 a. m. some 15 men left the meeting to go home, but meeting was still in progress. Not thinking it necessary for us to remain longer we left at 3 a. m. Would estimate there were between 60 and 70 people present.

Respectfully,

RAW:F

R. A. WELLPOTT.
G. A. PFEIFFER.

EXHIBIT 10382

[Copy]

O'KEEFE & MERRITT CO.

MANUFACTURERS OF GAS APPLIANCES & ELECTRIC REFRIGERATORS
3700 East Olympic Blvd.

LOS ANGELES, CAL., *October 21, 1936.*

Honorable Chief of Police JAMES E. DAVIS,
City Hall, Los Angeles, Calif.

DEAR SIR: As you probably know, about a month ago, a lot of pressure was put on our employes by a few local agitators and a labor agitator from San Francisco, which might have developed into a serious problem if it were not for the fact that you gave us such excellent co-operation.

We wish to express our appreciation to the Police Department and to commend in particular Lieut. Rudolph Wellpott, who was put in charge of the detail. We feel that the firm and tactful manner in which he handled the situation was a credit to the Department and his ability in matters of this kind makes him a real asset to Southern California.

Again thank you, we are
Very truly yours,

O'KEEFE & MERRITT Co.
(sgd) D. P. O'KEEFE.

DPO:R

NOTE.—Sent over from Chief's Office Oct 23–36 to Capt. Justin, Commanding, Metropolitan Divn. Copied and returned Capt. Justin Oct. 26/36.

Exhibit 10383

[Intra-Departmental Correspondence]

LOS ANGELES POLICE DEPARTMENT

Office of In. Bu. Metro. Divn.

WED., JULY 14–37.

ASSIGNMENT OF OFFICERS: ARMORED TRUNK CO. 1806 S. MAIN ST. PR 8461 8 A. M.—
3 P—5 P

NOTE.—8. a. m. Mr. Knell, mgr. this co. member M&M phones picket line beginning to form; states union is Leather Goods, Luggage & Trunk Union, of CIO; states no one out has 8 employes; hours 8 a—5 p; asks p. c. officer mornings and evenings.

Officer K. L. Teter responded.

NOTE.—8.35 a. m. Teter phoned back 8 pickets there; are orderly; they will cover this spot *7.30 a—9 a and 3 p—5 p;*

F

Exhibit 10384

CALIFORNIA CRACKER CO.

3840 So. Broadway Place

LOS ANGELES, CALIFORNIA, *Sept. 10, 1937.*

CHIEF DAVIS,
Los Angeles Police Dept., Los Angeles, Calif.

DEAR CHIEF DAVIS: I wish to thank you for the fine cooperation we received during our recent labor trouble with the CIO. It is gratifying to know that we completely won, if such a thing were possible, and the pickets withdrew recently of their own accord. This was without any concessions on our part whatever.

I think a large amount of this credit is due to Mr. PAUL L. PHELPS #1527 and his very able assistant, Mr. M. T. GEBHART, No. 1204, and their other assistant who was only with us a short time, Mr. C. J. CARTER. Through their humane and intelligent manner of handling this strike, they were able to prevent any serious trouble of any nature, as a matter of fact, we had no arrests during the entire period, which to me seems to be a very remarkable job.

Assuring you and your department of my grateful appreciation, I remain

Yours very truly,

CALIFORNIA CRACKER COMPANY,
By D. B. LEWIS, *President.*

DBL:FS

Copy of this letter sent over for READING by Paul L. Phelps from CHIEF'S OFFICE on Sept. 16, 1937; copy returned to Chief's office, Margaret Connor, On Oct. 6–37.

F

Exhibit 10385

[Intra-Departmental Correspondence]

LOS ANGELES POLICE DEPARTMENT

Office of Intelligence Bureau, Metropolitan Division

[Via Teletype]

AUGUST 20th, 1937.

C. F. REYBURN,
Sheriff, Riverside County, Riverside, California.

Re our telephone conversation this date, be advised that Mr. M. R. Murchison of California Hardware Company First and Alameda Street informs that Earl B. Hinkle General Merchandize Store, Banning—Purchased thirty dozen (30) baseball bats on Wednesday noon August 18th which were picked up by Hinkle's own delivery truck and were paid for in currency.   Purchaser very well dressed informed that they were forming a soft ball league—But bought no balls.

JAMES E. DAVIS, *Chief of Police.*

Information.from Capt. Wm. F. Hynes, Intelligence Bureau.   MU–4891.

EXHIBIT 10386

[Intra-Departmental Correspondence]

LOS ANGELES POLICE DEPARTMENT

Office of In. Bu. Metro. Divn.

AUG. 21–37 SAT. 9 a.

Re: Purchase 30 doz. ball bats presumably for using of strikers against METRO WATER DIST. Banning district.

Memo Capt. HYNES.

Mr. Kinsey of hdq office Metro Water District, 3rd & Broadway phones in connection with above, these bats were purchased from Calif. Hardware Co. 1st & Alameda last Wed. and party buying same gave name of Louis Henkle; it appears Sheriff Rayburn interrogated and released Mr. Henkle from connection; Mr. Henkle is due at Purchasing Agent office this morning for interview with officials of Water Dist. as he is incensed at use of his name.   Mr. Kensey thot you might want to sit in at talk this morning for Sheriff's Office Riverside; office 5th floor, 3rd & Bdwy. P. A. Mr. Joseph.

F

EXHIBIT 10387

[Intra-Departmental correspondence]

LOS ANGELES POLICE DEPARTMENT

Office of Intelligence Bureau, Metropolitan Division

[Confidential]

SEPT. 21ST, 1937.

Re: Withdrawal Detail Officers from SANITARY MATTRESS Co., 1548 Industrial St.

Memo Capt. HYNES.

Beg to inform you this morning received a phone call from Officer Slauson that when he went into the office of the Sanitary Mattress Co. to use the telephone, Mr. Blum, an owner of the company, asked Officer Slauson "Who they were?" meaning Slauson and Gourley.   Slauson informed him they were police officers detailed at this location because of the strike.   Blum then asked him: "Who sent you?"   Officer Slauson told him: "My office has detailed me down here."   Blum replied to Slauson that they hadn't asked for any officers there; and didn't see why they should be there.

Instead of using the telephone at the office, Slauson went across the street to an ice company and phones reporting the above.   I then phoned Mr. Iske, who had requested a police detail there yesterday morning, and informed him of Mr. Blum's attitude.   Mr. Iske told me to pull the detail off and let them go to Hell; that that Jew would be in to see him pretty quick and he would burn him up. Iske said the reason he had requested police detail was simply to try to help them out in their present difficulty.

Detail was withdrawn 9.45 a. m. this date.

W. F.   R. A. WELLPOTT   DL 131.

Exhibit 10388

[Intra-Departmental Correspondence]

Los Angeles Police Department
Office of In. Bu. Metro. Divn.

WED., OCT. 20–37, 3.20 p. m.

Memo. Re Expected Labor Trouble Ellis-Klatscher Co. (wholesale variety merchandise, notions) 740 S. L. A. St., TR 6461.

Mr. Klatscher of above company phones he has 100 employees, mostly warehouse, is to have conference with representatives of Longshoreman-Warehouse Union of CIO 4 p. m. this date re signing a contract; expects may be a strike call afterwards.

Business open 8.30 to 5.30 p.

This concern has no trucks; all deliveries by United Parcel Co.

Advised him if strike develops and picket line formed and he needs police help to phone us.

F

Exhibit 10389

[Strictly Confidential]

Los Angeles, Calif., *Nove. 22, 1937.*

Memo. for Chief DAVIS.

The following information relative to a meeting of the *American Newspaper Guild*, held at Hollywood Plaza Hotel, 8 P. M. Friday, November 19, 1937, received from confidential and reliable sources:

The most important event of this meeting was a report by *Urcel Daniel* of the speeches made by Chief Davis before women's clubs. According to her, the talks consist of a lot of "baloney" about the CIO, the CP, etc., followed by a warning that all newspapers in Los Angeles except the Times are now Guild dominated and, therefore, their news is unreliable.

Slim Connelly of the Herald, Charles Daggett, Industrial Unionist, Tom O'Connor, Daily News, and others talked over several plans of action, including a resolution to be published in the Industrial Unionist and else (this was lost). It was finally decided to organize a large committee to call on Mayor Shaw and to arrange with him to have Chief Davis present when the committee called. About thirty were nominated, and the Guild's executive board was ordered to select the most "respectable" members of the Guild—Ted LeBerthon was favored for the job because he is such a reactionary red baiter himself. The line the committee was instructed to take was to make it an issue between the Guild and the Chief, and not to take up any kindred subjects. "Let it be understood that, so far as the Guild is concerned, Chief Davis is going to lay off" was the way Connelly expressed it.

Exhibit 10390

Los Angeles Police Department
Intelligence Bureau

JULY 6, 1938.

Capt. W. F. HYNES.

DEAR SIR: The following is a list of the Striking Employees at Taylor Milling Corporation, 1520 San Fernando Rd., Los Angeles:

Luttrell, J. N., 3009 Future P. L., Los Angeles   x.
Luttrell, H. L., 3215½ Isabel Dr., Los Angeles   x.
Hobbs, Allison, 525 Bridewell St., Los Angeles   x.
Hobbs, Jake, 3425 Loosmore St., Los Angeles   x.
Maddox, J. A., 3018½ Asbury St., Los Angeles.
Heagey, C. F., 1215 Crystal St., Los Angeles.
Wood, A. J., 1213 Crystal St., Los Angeles.
Boggio, Jim, 3133 Chaucer St., Los Angeles.

Culp, Harold, 3439½ Alice St., Los Angeles   x.
Alvarado, Moses B., 1005 E. 7th St., Los Angeles   x.
Simpson, Guy, 2932½ Asbury St., Los Angeles.
Packer Geo. D., 12125 Kagel Canyon, San Fernando, Cal.
Phillips, James, 3012 Asbury St., Los Angeles.
Foster, S. Fred, 3311 Division, Los Angeles.
Culp, L., 641 Cypress Ave., Los Angeles.
Estrella, Luis, 3444 Michigan St., Los Angeles.
Heller, Elmer, 3016 Asbury St., Los Angeles.
Gower, James Alva, 3374 Division, Los Angeles.
Douglas, Arthur, 1945 Isabel.
Penberthy, Phillip, 2828 Future St., Los Angeles.
Bell, H. S., 226 N. Olive St., Los Angeles.
Gibbs, Earl, 738 Towne Ave., Los Angeles.
Davis, Mike, 943 E. 111 Dr.
Fuller, Earl A., 2659 Carleton Ave., Los Angeles.
Carreon, U. L., 1448 Cypress, Los Angeles.
Martinetto, C. R., 2818 Elm St., Los Angeles.
Lopez, Vincent, 2662 Loosmore, Los Angeles.
Weatherford, Dewey, 303 So. Ave., 57, Los Angeles   x.

C. J. EVANS.

EXHIBIT 10391

NA-MAC PRODUCTS CORPORATION

1027 North Seward St.

HOLLYWOOD, CALIF., *May 13, 1938.*

Mr. JAMES E. DAVIS,
    Chief of Police, City Hall, Los Angeles, Calif.

DEAR CHIEF DAVIS: I surely wish to thank you, on behalf of our Company, for the aid you and your police Department rendered us during the striking condition, which was finally called off on May 11, 1938.

Finally, after seven weeks of picketing, the strike was called off and the men have returned to work.   One of the head executives of the Union came from the East, and inasmuch as he could find no apparent reason for this strike, ordered the men back to work.

During the past few weeks, your men were here on time, regularly, and did not leave their post of duty until after the "picketers" had left for the day, and only due to their efforts, no damage was inflicted by the pickets to anyone, nor to any part of the factory.

Again, we wish to thank you, and we want you to know it is indeed gratifying to know we have such an organization, under your guidance, to serve the City of Los Angeles.
    Sincerely,

NA-MAC PRODUCTS CORP.
By WILLIAM NASSOUR, (signed)
William Nassour, *President.*

WN: HK

4. MISCELLANEOUS DOCUMENTS RELATING TO UNION ORGANIZATION AND STRIKES OF AGRICULTURAL LABOR

EXHIBIT 10392

LOS ANGELES, CALIF., *June 7, 1933.*

Re: Strike in Celery Fields, Venice-Sawtelle Divisions.
Capt. WM. F. HYNES,
    Commanding Intelligence Bureau.

SIR: Per phone call from Sgt. Griffin of Venice Div. this morning that trouble was being had in celery fields in that vicinity, caused by agitators amongst the Mexican field workers, we went out to Venice Division and there talked with Sgt. Griffin, who said that early this morning some 150 Mexicans were along the roads by these fields and that some of them had gone in to agitate among Filipinos who had taken Mexican field workers' places in harvesting celery.

Sgt. Griffin also told us that yesterday the Mexican Consul was out there, advising and directing the Mexican field workers who had gone out on strike. Strikers said they were being paid 15¢ an hour and they wanted higher pay.

This morning Sgt. Griffin and two other officers dispersed a number of Mexicans loitering about the fields; later they were seen going to 4065 Ocean Park Ave., where a meeting was scheduled to be held about 10 a.m.

We went to 4065 Ocean Park Ave. and there found sixty or seventy Mexicans gathered, and in the midst of their group were two white fellows and a Jewish woman. We listened to their conversation and gathered therefrom that these three were Communist organizers. They appeared very nervous after our arrival and asked the group through an interpreter if their families were in need of food and milk, which they promised to bring them this afternoon.

As the three were leaving, I stopped them at their car, which was a Buick sedan, License #3 R 9037, registered to Harry Goldstein, 150 Raymond Ave., Ocean Park. I questioned the man who seemed to be the leader of the three, and he told me his name was AL BRENNAN, that he had been residing in Los Angeles during the past year, had formerly lived in Stockton, Cal.; this man was 28 years old, tall and slender, light complected, apparently an American; other man was 21 years of age, Jewish, gave his name as MORRIS LOUIS, residing in Ocean Park, came from Frisco three weeks ago; girl gave her name as ADELE BARTH, about 25 years old, Jewish; she had numerous pimples on her face and her eyes had been blacked—some discoloration still left, (may have been received in San Diego riot May 30). On checking her driver's license we found her name as ETHEL SHAPIRO (?) address 2731 E. 48th St. Los Angeles. She said a friend of her's, who runs a grocery store, loaned car to her for them to use.

All three of these subjects denied any connection with the Communist Party or any of its subsidiaries, but we found when girl showed her driver's license that she had a membership card in the I. L. D. In side pocket of car we found a bundle of calendar folders of meeting dates for Youth Branches of I. W. O. for March and April, 1933. From Brennan, we took a one sheet bulletin titled "BOLE-TIN PRO HUELGA, dated Venice Cal. 5 de Junio 1933 (printed in Spanish). and a handbill put out by "Action & Strike Committee of "Cannery & Agricultural Workers Ind. Union."

After questioning these three subjects, I informed them that we knew that their purpose in being among these field workers was not to lend aid and food as they had stated to this group, but that they really were there to create dissension and unrest among them. I warned them to stay away, owing to their affiliation with the Communist Subsidiary organization—Agricultural Workers Ind. Union.

I then went to the group of Mexicans assembled there in meeting and informed them that these three people were Communist agitators. I asked if they wanted to be led or influenced by any such organization and they immediately answered they did not and were not aware that the Communists were taking part in the strike movement. I spoke to them regarding a raise in pay, saying they must also take in consideration that the grower himself was receiving very little for his product and therefore was unable to pay a very high scale of wages; told them that if their Consul was advising and directing them, I was sure they would not get into any trouble, but if they were Communist led and directed, it might lead to trouble for them, such as deportation, etc. Told them that as long as they were peaceful and not resorting to any violence or violation of any law that they would have no trouble with the police. They handed us a number of Spanish Bulletins (dated 5 June 1933) distributed by Armando Flores.

Some of these men said they would have nothing to do with these three sub-jects, such as taking food, from them or advice.

We then went to West Los Angeles Division and there spoke to the Lieutenant on Day Watch and he informed us there was no further trouble reported in that division, and that the handbills that Officer Wallace phoned us about yesterday, were "Boletins Pro-Huelga, 5 Junio 1933" (similar to copy taken from Brennan, mentioned above).

We then went down to the lettuce fields in West L. A. Div. where trouble among the field workers had occurred in the past few days, and there found that white people (elderly) were harvesting celery. Was told that these people were from the Unemployed Coop. Relief Asso. Unit #69; they were not having any trouble in the fields at this time.

Respectfully,

R. A. WELLPOTT—RYAN—PFEIFFER—BAZAR.

RAW:F
Encls.

Exhibit 10393

[Intra-Departmental Correspondence. Form 235]

Los Angeles Police Department

Office of Intelligence Bureau, Metropolitan Division

Oct. 14, 1933.

Detail

Meeting of Cannery & Agricultural Workers Industrial Union. 14804 Calvert St. (just outside of Van Nuys) Officers Wellpott, Chas. Evans, Sam Evans.

Sat., Oct. 14–33, 7 p. m.

(Note: Capt. Haak of Valley Division requested detail of men to cover meeting of the Cannery & Agricultural Workers Ind. Union at the above stated address, for which circulars have been distributed throughout the Valley among the Mexican population, urging them to bring their families and declare for organization of the agricultural workers.

This is, no doubt, a Communist organization, affiliated with the TUUL.)

By Direction:

Wm. F. Hynes,
Acting Capt. Dets. LAPD Comdg.

H:F

Exhibit 10394

Los Angeles Police Department

Office of In. Bu. Metro Div

Jan. 6–34, 11.07 a. m.

Confidential Memo.

Mr. Fysh TU 6244 of M. & M. phones in that they are establishing Employment Office (connection supplying milkers Dairy Strike) at rooms 284–5 Rosslyn Hotel, 5th & Main; expect bus with men to come there with men from 12 noon to 3 pm today; requests officer be detailed to cover (uniform).

Asks Officer see Mr. Perkins, mgr. room 284 at 11.45 am re.

Says bus will come in alley on 5th between Main & Spring in alley, coming west on 5th.

f

Copy Capt Horrall

Exhibit 10395

Capt. Hynes: The License Number of my Sedan is 6–D–1899. Please see that I am not picked up when I take these strikers and leaders around. It is a Diana, Gray Sedan. 8. year 1926.

I am reporting at the headquarters, 546 So Los Angeles Street at Ten this morning to take the leaders around.

Something was said about expecting trouble in Belvedere so this may be where I'll be going as Summers wants to go there. I am not sure of this however.

If you think there is any chance of getting some work in this line I'll accept that secretaryship.

G–60

My back dues and other expenses last night were $1.55. I'll also have to have expenses for my car if I am to continue.

Exhibit 10396

[Intra-Departmental Correspondence]

LOS ANGELES POLICE DEPARTMENT

Office of In. Bu. Metro Div.

JAN. 6–34, 10:40 a. m.

Confidential Memo. Capt. HYNES.

Opr. 50 phones asks you lay off car LIC 6 D 1899 which is a gray DIANA sedan; says his (your) men haling leaders around in that at 10 o'clock.

Says ILD attorney instructed them to keep in pairs so can't be picked up for loitering, unlawful assembling or any of those things and if just two together on conspiracy.

Says of course they had report last night re putting up money.

Says at beginning they are going to have verbal picketing; they claim about 45 to 48 dairies affected at noon; cars are being dispatched to all those places. First two days not going to do any rough stuff.

Has data for you re meeting last night's conference, can reach at home.

Exhibit 10397

LOS ANGELES, CALIFORNIA, *January 6th, 1934.*

SMWIU: As instructed Agent covered the Executive Committee meeting of the Steel Metal Workers Industrial Union, Section of the TUUL. This meeting was held at 546 South Los Angeles, last night.

Lillian Goodman, Comrade Norton, (This man is an old TUUL members and is still a member of Local 311, Machinists, A. F. of L. under his right name which is Andy Neuman) Ed Burk, Comrade Plath, Comrade E. Nelson, Shapiro, There were others there connected with the Milkers. Kope was around there and came into the SMWIU meeting then went back to his own bunch which was holding a round table conference, but not as a business meeting. Most of these were strangers to Agent as were two of the Comrades in the Metal Workers group.

Nelson was chairman for the evening, as the regular chairman could not attend as he is in the hospital. This is comrade True who is in a bad way, having some of his fingers amputated.

This being the first meeting of the new year officers were elected for the coming six months term. They did not elect the Secretary as a motion was made to put this over for two weeks until the next meeting when they expect a larger crowd. Only one man was nominated for the secretaryship to replace Norton, who can not handle the job any longer as he has ten other obligations, he said. The man nominated was Comrade Burk.

Nelson was elected Chairman. Plath elected Literature Agent. Shapiro was elected to the Executive Board.

A discussion regarding the General Cable Corporation. It was reported by Nelson that this corporation is building a very large plant in L. A. and will furnish the cable for the power transmission for Boulder Dam. Moved and carried, directing every member to procure all information possible regarding this corporation and to try and get jobs in the shops.

Committee elected, composed of Nelson, Shapiro and Burk to report in full at the next meeting regarding the chances of getting jobs, or what jobs are to be open in that factory. This committee is also obligated to bring in a comprehensive report regarding the pay and hours in the steel and metal industry in and around Los Angeles.

Nelson proposed that members should secure jobs in this plant in order to be on the ground, in order to organize the workers when operations start.

A mass meeting of all steel and metal workers will be held in February, date and place to be announced later. The information they wanted is for the Agitprop Committee.

Applications were given out and those present were urged to get out and organize. Application blanks enclosed.

Agent talked with the Milk Drivers group and picked up the following information which may be of interest.

1—Every effort is to be made to keep the strikers from getting into trouble at the beginning of the Milk Strike which will take place at noon today.

Kope claims that they must be peaceful the first day or two in order to get the public sympathy.   Lillian Goodman said that if this strike is not won quickly there will be plenty of trouble.   She thinks that the employers will pull plenty of rough stuff in order to get the people to think the strikers are doing it.

Kope claims that the paid stools of the employers' group will try and start fights etc. but that all strikers must keep cool and take a lot at the start.

It was reported that the Producers have already started importing professional strikebreakers and have put up a large fund for this purpose.

ILD Attorneys have carefully looked up the law on picketing, loitering, unlawful assembly etc and it was reported that if but two persons are together the police or the Sheriff forces can not arrest them for any of the following.   Loitering, as two persons are allowed to stop and converse, Unlawful assembly, Loitering or conspiracy.

At the beginning only verbal picketing will be resorted to.   There is to be no manhandling of scabs the first two days.

It was estimated that between forty-five and forty-eight dairies will be effected by the strike.   None of these were named.

Cars are being dispatched this morning in an effort to sign up the workers for the zero hour.   It was also reported that comrades in San Bernardino and Kern Counties are going out also.

They expect similar reports from Ventura County.

Leaflets urging workers to stay away from here and not come to scab have been sent as far as Texas and to the States of Oregon and Washington.

G–60

Exhibit 10398

C. E. Myers, *Covina*.

Attendance—Meeting re Milk Strike—Jan. 10, 1934

H. D. Snider—Ice Cream Council of So. Calif., 514 E. 8th St.
R. A. Soty—Golden State Co., Ltd., 1120 Towne Ave.
Earl Maharg—C. M. P. A.
H. S. Hazeltine—American Fruit Growers, Bendix Bldg.
T. M. Erwin—Calif. Poppy Dairies, Rush & Central Ave.
L. M. Hurt—County Livestock Dept.
M. B. Rounds—Agric. Extension Service, 524 No. Spring.
A. A. Hopkins—Sheriff's Office, Hall of Justice.
B. R. Holloway—Holly Hatchery, 15248 Sherman Way, Van Nuys.
Srev Moore—Editor California Dairyman, 949 Maple Ave., L. A.
E. W. Biscailuz—Sheriff.
Frank Pellissier.
J. A. McNaughton—Agr. Union Stock Yards.
A. Schleicher.
D. W. Jessup—Roger Jessup Farm, 315 N. San Fernando Rd.
Guernsey Frazer—Frazer-Evans-American Legion, 705 Bixby Ave.
James O. Cook—Cal. Fruit Growers Exchange.
Dr. Geo. P. Clements.
T. E. Day—Golden State Co., 1120 Towne Ave.
R. C. Perkins.
Rowland Dunsmore—Van Nuys.
Roy K. Cole—Whittier.
Merritt H. Adamson.
James E. Davis—Chief L. A. Police, City Hall.
F. A. Stewart—Anderson-Clayton Co., 534 Cotton Exchange Bldg.
Arthur E. Clark—L. A. Milk Industry Board, C. of C. Bdg.
C. B. Moore—Western Growers Protection Assn.
Homer A. Harris—Asstd. Produce Dealers & Brokers of L. A.
W. J. Kuhrt—L. A. Milk Industry Board, 520 C. of C. Bdg.
C. L. Smith—Safeway Stores, 1925 E. Vernon.
A. I. Stewart—Safeway Stores, 1925 E. Vernon.
W. R. Wood—California Cultivator, 317 Central Ave.
Geo. B. Hodgkins—Calavo Growers of Calif., 4803 Everett.

H. E. Whitney—American Fruit Growers, Inc.
Wm. McCowan.
H. J. Ryan.
John R. Quinn—Chairman Board of Supervisors.
F. R. Carter—Arden Farms, Inc., El Monte.
Lorette King—Sec. So. Calif. Restaurant Assn.
A. T. Schaber—Schaber Cafeteria Co., 620 So. Broadway.
M. H. Kimball—Asst. Farm Adviser, Univ. of Calif. 524 No. Spring.
Wm. Francis Ireland—Asstd. Bakers of So. Calif., 325 Coulter Bdg.   MU. 5925.
Robt. F. Callender—So. Calif. Bakers Bureau, 554 C. of C. Bdg.
K. Mukaeda—Central Japanese Assn. of So. Calif., 312 E. 1st St.
H. W. Postlethwaite—Riverside.
H. D. Newcomb—Institute of Am. Meat Packers, 562 I. W. Hellman Bdg.
H. W. Amelung—P. C. A., 1513 Mirasol.
J. M. Friedlander—Calif. Fish Trades Industry, 914 Bankers Bdg.
Gen. W. P. Story.
J. W. Glasgow—Santa Fe Ry., 560 So. Main St.
W. S. Rosecrans.
Sidney Hoedemaker—Pig'n Whistle, 945 Venice Blvd.
Wm. H. Stabler—Western Dairy Products Co.
A. W. Christie—Cal. Walnut Grs.
Con Cowan—Cal. Walnut Grs.
C. E. Reifsteck—Secy. So. Calif. Milk Dealers Assn.
H. H. Bushwell—California Milk News, 514 E. 8th St.
Mrs. John S. Thayer—L. A. Dist., Calif. Fed. Womens Clubs.
A. L. Chandler—M. O. D.
S. M. White—So. Calif. Retail Grocers, 110 W. 11th St.

Exhibit 10399

[From: 11—Radical Organizations files]

[Intra-Departmental Correspondence]

Los Angeles Police Department

Office of In. Bu. Metro Div.

JAN. 12, 1934, 1.40 p. m.

Confidential Capt. HYNES.

B phones:

"Letter going to be sent out to all labor organizations today inviting them to a United Front meeting Wed. 8 p. m.—place not definitely decided—probably Music Arts if they can get it, trying to get hall now. They are trying to get in all organizations they can, especially any from A. F. of L. they can for support, cooperation and boycott.

"Here's been the fly-in-the-ointment, the public that wants to help in the boycott don't know who by the leaflets with all the leading dairies listed, this is causing confusion, so they made a decision. Had a fraction meeting and decided to concentrate against Jessup, Adohr and L. A. Products. Here's the joker, they are going to try to get the public to swing over to Borden and Arden. Borden is going to be approached to try to line Borden up to buy their milk from the producers who have settled with the Union. Arden is not to be approached at all, but going to leave it alone. In that way, they figure the boycott will be more effective against Adohr and Jessup.

Supposed to be a meeting of milk drivers this afternoon at 4 o'clock, there will be a committee come down, Baylin will go in with them.

The Jessup affair is going to be played up and make a big political issue at the coming elections, going to point out that Jessup's signature means no more than his word in a political campaign.

Committee of 3 came from A. F. of L. meat packers today, are very much interested in the strike going on and trying to work out a program with Meyer (Baylin) where they can pull the meat packers out again.

"I have been appointed to take a Committee up to the Police Commission or City Council (this afternoon) to apply for a permit for Tuesday. We are trying to get a permit, of course they are going to parade anyhow. Here is basic route:

At 2 o'clock they will leave the Plaza, after having had a meeting at Plaza, Tuesday, at 2 they leave Plaza, go south on Main to 1st, west on 1st to Broadway, south on Broadway to 9th, east on 9th to Main, north on Main to 7th, east on 7th to Wall, to 741 Wall St. for a big mass meeting.

"Going to make this application in about 15 minutes, the application will point out that this parade is to be orderly, two abreast, to solicit public sympathy; permit in the name of the Food Workers Union.

"Business Agent, I am giving to understand, of the Bread Drivers has approached Baylin offering to cooperate the two groups in their coming strike.

"You know what happened yesterday—they are pretty suspicious. Last night's Times came out and said the Party had a fight amongst itself; there wasn't supposed to be anybody know this but the Section Committee. Rose interpreted this that somebody inside the section meeting gave it out.

EXHIBIT 10400

[From: 11—Rad. Org. file]

[Intra-Departmental Correspondence]

LOS ANGELES POLICE DEPARTMENT

Office of Intelligence Bu. Metro. Div.

MON., JAN. 22, 1934, 3.50 p. m.

Confidential.

E phones as follows:

Things pretty quiet. Going to be a meeting at 6 o'clock of Central Strike Committee, meeting in back room; may be a meeting of all milkers tonight; this is to be decided by Gen. Strike Com. This meeting is re re-organizing the Gen. Strike Com.

Says "Steves hasn't been around very much, is due in 6 o'clock he laid out all day figured they were looking for him. He is dressed in a brown suit, wearing a brown cap.

Opr. accompanied a protest committee to Board of Supervisors this morning. Hanoff is back in town.

Opr. has to attend a meeting at 7 o'clock tonight of organizers. Hanoff said something re taking opr. off of the milk strike because not much going on; will report on this later.

Says general opinion seems to be most of fellows are going back to work, not many hanging around because pretty well scared.

Opr. further says they don't say a great deal about the arrests several asked him what they were going to do with "Denver;" told them didn't know. They are pretty badly demoralized. Opr. don't know what it (strike) is resting on apparently some of them seem to be having a good time out of it.

Opr. asked to check up on those causing trouble and behind same; also check up on one Dan Harden (active down below); asked to check up mostly on those behind the "rough stuff."

Re: Max Shoen he is still in San Bernardino.

H:F

EXHIBIT 10401

[Copy]

LOS ANGELES, *Saturday, January 27, 1934.*

Informant Reports:

Following instruction to make suitable arrangements with Supervisor Verne Smith of the Agricultural Workers League, informant was invited to escort Smith to visit the Agricultural Industrial Unions at Oxnard, Ventura, Santa Paula and Santa Barbara, as Smith is a stranger in this section.

On account of police activities at Oxnard, the Supervisor met the Agricultural organizers at the International Labor Defense Offices at 844 "A" Street, the present of Smith in Oxnard being unknown to the membership, which includes many hundred Mexican, also other nationalities of agricultural workers, and several Japanese families.

The organizers in Ventura and Santa Barbara counties are Mexicans, and the informant was of great assistance to Smith as the latter did not understand the Spanish language, and informant interpreted for him when necessary, which Smith said he appreciated.

The active organizers who are very influential among the agricultural workers in both counties are: Bartolomeo Sales, Flores Miguel and Juan Madrid. These men operate between Oxnard, Santa Paula and Santa Barbara, and appear to be doing very effective work among the Mexican element in their organizing.

Supervisor Smith examined the membership roll calls and advised the above organizers that while membership is good (about 112 members in the two counties), they must even do more work, as the workers are so numerous and it is to the workers benefit to join the National Agricultural Workers Industrial League, which is the first large Radical Union in the United States, Supervisor Smith gave the organizers a bundle of leaflets written in Spanish, inviting the agricultural workers to meet the organizers and to form Ranch and Farm Committees, also to spread the word around to other camps or ranches, inviting the workers to the two weekly meetings taking place at Oxnard, Ventura, Santa Paula and Santa Barbara.

While the informant was alone with Supervisor Smith, I was told, Smith informed him that the Chairman of the Executive Committee of San Francisco had told him during a conversation they had recently, that what the Agricultural Workers League Officials at San Francisco wish is to oust Frank H. Buck, a ranch owner of Vacaville, California, the Chief of Police and a Gospel Minister there, for their activities against the organizers of the Agricultural Workers League in that town.

Smith said he is not acquainted with that town, and made inquiries of the informant how far Vacaville was from San Francisco, but stated that from what he has heard from the Chairman of the Executive Committee, the Workers at Vacaville must have had rough treatment at the hands of the above mentioned men, and they are pretty angry with these men and have promised to even their score with them.

Smith mentioned the head of the American Legion at Visalia, as being the next in line for a "good lesson" at the hands of the Agricultural Workers of the District for the false arrest of Pat Chambers during the cotton pickers strike.

Smith mentioned that things were getting "pretty hot" at San Jose, and the organizers for the Agricultural Workers League at #81 Post Street, have been informed by reliable persons in sympathy with the Communist Movement, that Sheriff Emig and the officials of the American Legion had planned to "get those reds," referring to the organizers in San Jose, by "framing them" for their activities in organizing the agricultural workers, also for the activities of the Civic Liberties Union in the San Jose lynching which occurred a short time back. The Civic Liberties Union thru A. L. Virin, however discredited the San Jose authorities, for their interest in the two men lynched for the kidnapping and murder of the Hart boy.

Smith told the information that he immediately understood this as soon as he received the report from the San Jose organizers; that the best thing to do was to remove any obstacle from San Jose concerning the activities of the Agricultural Workers League at #81 Post Street, San Jose, to 429 "J" Street, Sacramento, "right near the Governor," so there would be more chance to receive some protection if needed. The informant said he thought, however, judging from what Smith told him, that the Officials of Trade Union Unity League at San Jose became uneasy, and invited the Supervisor to have them moved to Sacramento, or some other place.

Smith mentioned the intensive work which will be started as soon as possible in Kern County. The informant remarked that he thought the strike in Kern County was settled, however, Smith replied "settled hell, it has not started as yet, for the way those officers treated the strikers and the murder of those poor workers, you call it settled?"

Smith read from a memorandum he had in his pocket, concerning labor conditions in Kern County, Madeira County, Kings County, and many others which could not be remembered in detail, but which stated that the National Farmers League, another branch of the Agricultural Workers League, wish to get away from a gang of "Jew crooks," whom Smith named as the "Lux Company," who operate in several counties of Northern California.

He stated that before the State of California is finished, there will be many farmers and farm worker rebellions; that the period of the peonage is over, and the agricultural workers, no matter whether they are white or black, American or Mexican, must receive a decent living wage, as well as sanitary conditions in camps, or where they have to work.

Smith told of the trouble at Pescadero, Calif., basing his information on the report he received from Organizer Spaulding, who has reported to him that the fight against the land owners started when the organizers of the Agricultural Workers Industrial League at Pescadero formed a union of this league with an initiative membership of about 100 members.

The organizers at once started to formulate a code of their own, and decided that the Filipino and the Mexicans should receive 25 cents instead of 20 cents an hour for picking on the field. That the pay day should be every week, and the Agricultural Workers Industrial Union should be immediately recognized by the land owners, and since the strike, the union now demands that all the arrested leaders of the strike be immediately released.

The list of those arrested as trouble makers, as turned over by Smith to the Office of the local International Labor Defense, is composed of the following: Eric Kaufman, Juan Sampson, Ettore Castillo, Alfonso Valdo and Carl Small.

Spaulding, in his report informs the Supervisor that land company owner of over 16,000 acres of land in the Pescadero district is the "Shoreland Properties Incorporated," and that the trouble started when an Agent for this Company, named Moore, who is also a Constable, arrested many of the workers who were on strike; and that he (Spaulding) would not bet "one single cooper" on the life of this Agent Moore, as the Filipinos and the Mexican workers are very angry with him. Spaulding also said he would not like to be in Moore's shoes for all the money in the United States.

33–C
1–29

Exhibit 10402

[Intra-Departmental Correspondence]

LOS ANGELES POLICE DEPARTMENT

Office of In. Bu. Metro. Divn.

THURS., MAY 7, 1936.

MEMO. Reports sent WALTER GARRISON of Asso. Farmers, LODI, Calif. Copy Memo on Rose Chernin, April 9, 1936. Copy Minutes Co. County PWUU For May 3, 1936 (#9). Copy Report top fraction PWUU, May 3, 1936 (#9)

Exhibit 10403

[Intra-Departmental Correspondence]

LOS ANGELES POLICE DEPARTMENT

Office of In. Bu. Metro. Divn.

TUES., JULY 21–36.

Re: Communist Activity in Milkers.
Memo. Capt. HYNES.

Mr. Art Clark of Associated Farmers, 442 Cham. Com. Bldg. care office bldg. PR 3431; phones in re following subjects: James ZALOUDEK, now living #1515 Pioneer Blvd. Artesia, Milkers Club, active; E. C. "Denver" Fowler; V. E. Adair, Secy. Milkers Club.

Advised re Fowler active in Milkers strike '34 and re arrest by Sheriff's Office. Advised no cards on Adair and James Zaloudek; but if wanted would make further inquiries.

He said re Steve Somers & "Denver" Fowler understands they had a split-up recently in the Milkers Club, part going with one and part with the other; said recently held meetings rm. 219 Stimson Bldg.; that at present Zaloudek was most active in the movement. He is making an investigation of.

F

EXHIBIT 10404

AUGUST 12, 1936.

DEAR CAPTAIN HYNES: Beginning with a conference in the offices of the Regional Labor Board in the Federal Building in September 10, 1935 when he said: "If the Mexicans workers of Los Angeles County are not organized now, I'll see that they are before winter is over."

Ricardo Hill, Mexican Consul in Los Angeles in charge of the affairs of the Mexican government in Southern California, has been continually engaged in urging his countrymen to join the Federation of Mexican Agricultural Workers Unions.

In this effort his remarks have not been addressed to Aliens but to American citizens as well. Throughout the winter Consul Hill, accompanied first by William Velarde and later by Lillian Monroe, appeared before meetings of Mexicans in Los Angeles, Venice, El Monte, Jimtown near Whittier, and other Mexican colonies were farm laborers live and repeatedly urged their becoming members of the union. Indeed in Orange County citrus strike Lucas Lucio, vice consul under Hill, has been a union organizer for months. Without the support of the Mexican consuls office Velarde's union would never have attempted the costly vegetable and citrus strikes of the past few weeks. The first thing Mexicans told me when I asked them if they wanted to strike was; "No, but the Mexican government is going to back us up."

To support this we have had the spectacle of Consul Hill inviting Mexican labor union officials to Los Angeles from Mexico City and on June 4, in the Unitarian Church, these "friendly visitors from the republic to the south" openly urged Mexicans to join the local union headed by Velarde and aid the strike. They promised support from Mexico in the way of finances. Alessandro Carrillo, Alfanso Madariaga, of the Mexico City Federayion of Workers and Eduardo Innes, secretary general of the powerful Oil Worker's Union, were the leaders here and the Western Worker of June 11th devoted considerable space to the meeting. Chief Davis and the Red squad were attacked for their work in keeping peace in the Venice celery strike at this session which of course was attended by Consul Hill.

From the beginning of this year's farm strikes Associated Farmers of Los Angeles and Orange County have insisted that if Hill withdrew his support from the union there would be no trouble and in the end of the citrus strike we were treated to the astounding picture of Hill claiming he was "settling" labor troubles which he had a powerful part in starting. Agricultural employers of both counties are determined that the consul overstepped his position and feel that in the interests of harmony between themselves and Mexican workers, Hill should be replaced.

Sincerely yours,

ARTHUR CLARK,
Executive Secretary, Associated Farmers of Los Angeles.

EXHIBIT 10405

(In pencil:) Send to Capt. Hynes.

ASSOCIATED FARMERS OF CALIFORNIA, INCORPORATED

1301 Hobart Building, 582 Market Street

SAN FRANCISCO, CALIFORNIA, *Sept. 14, 1936.*

Mr. JAMES DAVIS,
Chief of Police, Los Angeles, Calif.

DEAR CHIEF DAVIS: We are enclosing for your information copy of a letter just received from the Department of State, Washington, D. C. It makes it positive that Lucas Lucio is not a Mexican vice-consul and "is not in any way connected with the Mexican Consulate at Los Angeles or elsewhere."

Furthering our protest against the activities of Mexican Consul Ricardo Hill we are taking the privilege of sending a copy of your report to the Secretary of State.

Sincerely yours,

ASSOCIATED FARMERS OF CALIFORNIA,
By FRED GOODCELL.

EXHIBIT 10406

ASSOCIATED FARMERS OF ORANGE COUNTY, INC.

Phone 455

PLACENTIA, CALIFORNIA, *November 2, 1937.*

Capt. WILLIAM F. HINES,
  Intelligence Service, Los Angeles Police Dept.,
          Los Angeles, Calif.

DEAR CAPTAIN HINES: Mr. Strathman and the writer was in your office this morning and your Mr. Folsom asked about a certain issue of the Open Forum. We want to say that we have all the issues of the Open Forum from June 1934 to date.   We would be glad at any time to let you use any of these issues.

Miss Kyte, our office secretary, informs me that you have in your possession a considerable portion of our file on Ricardo Hill, former Mexican Consul in this area.   Possibly you have forgotten that you have such information and, of course, we wish to retain it intact, so we would appreciate your mailing same to us if and when you are through with it.

Thanking you for your cooperation and assistance, we wish to assure you that records of this office are at your service at any time you may desire same.

Yours very truly,

(Signed) GEO. A. GRAHAM,
                          Secretary.

gg/ck

EXHIBIT 10407

1.15.2   Nov. 4, 1937.

Mr. GEORGE A. GRAHAMS,
  Secretary, Associated Farmers of Orange County,
              Placentia, Calif.

DEAR MR. GRAHAM: Reference is had to your letter of Nov. 2nd, 1937 concerning the return of certain correspondence regarding Ricardo Hill former Mexican Consul in this area, and which was loaned to the undersigned.

1 am returning herewith the following:

Letter from Ricardo G. Hill to Mr. Strathman, Secy. Placentia Chamber of Commerce, dated July 7, 1936;

Letter from Senator Hiram Johnson, U. S. Senate to Mr. S. H. Strathman, dated July 11, 1936;

Notice to Orange Growers of Orange County from Ricardo G. Hill, Mexican Consul, dated June 6, 1936;

File copy of letter S. H. Strathman to Ricardo G. Hill, June 25, 1936;

Clippings from Santa Ana Register, Sat. Oct 12, 1935 titled "Mexican Consul urges 2,500 citrus pickers not to strike on wage question";

File copy of letter from Orange Growers of Orange County to Ricardo G. Hill, Consul of Mexico, Los Angeles, June 9–1936;

Copy of a letter from Cordell Hull (Secretary of State) to Honorable Hiram W. Johnson, U. S. Senate, July 8, 1936;

Memo. of "Information for the Division of Mexican Affairs, Dept. of State relative to the activities of Mexican Consul officials in labor unionizing & labor strikes in So. Cal."

Newspaper clipping titled "Mexico Tells Consuls to ban political work" (postmarked from Mexico City, March 28 (1936)

It is trusted that the enclosed covers all the correspondence you referred to, for which please acknowledge receipt.

Very truly yours,

WILLIAM F. HYNES,
    Capt. of Detectives, L. A. P. D.,
      Commanding Intelligence Bureau.

H:F
Encls. as listed above.

Exhibit 10408

Los Angeles Police Department
Office of In. Bu. Metro. Divn.

7-12-35.

Memo.

At 1st & Central, Japanese Temple, 7.30 pm tonight, a meeting sponsored by 3 Japanese radical organizations, the Cal. Japanese Workers Asso., a Japanese Gardeners Asso. & the Japanese Farmer Laborers of So. Cal. sponsor Kanju Kato, a militant labor leader recently arrived from Japan.

From Mr. Mittwer.

F

Exhibit 10409

Confidential Memo.   MONDAY, Oct. 11, 1937.
OPR G-75 reports.

Today at 10 a. m. attended meeting at State Labor Commission's office in room 410 State Bldg., which meeting was presided over by Mr. Thomas Barker, Deputy Director, Dept. of Industrial Relations, State of California.

This meeting was for the purpose of bring a complete understanding and agreement made last year by the vegetable produce employers and the Mexican agricultural workers' organization known as the C. U. C. O. M. (Confederated Union of Agricultural and Mexican Laborers), which union's business address is 128 N. Main St. Los Angeles.

Mr. Barker's position in the case was as an intermediary to hear and transmit from both parties to one another whatever grievances they might have. He was voted this position since no other party convenient and just could be brought forth by either of the two parties; this agreement is only in effect for the remainder of this year.

For a better understanding of the Mexican organization, he asked the cooperation of the Mexican Consulate only to the extent of furnishing a member in the capacity of interpreter and the local Mexican Consulate assigned Mr. Patricio Osio as such.

The agreement reached today, that is to stand firm and was accepted by both parties is:

That the field inspector of the CUCOM upon showing his credentials to any of the Japanese employers, may speak to any of the Mexican laborers so long as he does not cause any agitation and does not take up too much of their time.

It was further agreed that the Japanese employers will pay Mexican labor a minimum of 35¢ per hour, not only to the union worker, but any other individual who may be employed by the Japanese in an agricultural capacity. Heretofore, the CUCOM claims that the Japanese were bluffing by not putting to work members of this organization, saying that they could employ anyone else and pay cheaper wages, which also, according to the agreement which was strictly specified by Mr. Barker to both parties today and then agreed upon.

It any time there is not enough work whereby a laborer can obtain a full eight hour day's work the Japanese will fill the balance of the day by paying the 35¢ an hour minimum.

I had a special secret conference with Mr. Barker only and he explained that he finds the Mexican laborer a great lover or his wife and children and that upon the calling of a strike by a small number of individuals, by intimidation of the rest of the workers—members of the family and in general disrupt their homes if they go to work they are able to effect strikes; as the Mexican laborer having the safety and welfare of his family in view does not attend work and not having any representation to speak for him, the Mexican laborer is thus generally understood as going out on strike.

A. IMPERIAL VALLEY LETTUCE PACKERS STRIKE, 1934

EXHIBIT 10410

11 IMPERIAL VALLEY, *February 11, 1933.*

Strictly Confidential.

Mr. ELMER HEALD,
    District Attorney, Imperial County, El Centro, Calif.

DEAR ELMER: As you no doubt are aware by this time, the Communist party is again attempting to start a campaign of agitation in Imperial Valley concentrating particularly at this time on the Agricultural Workers in an endeavor to organize them into the Agricultural Workers Industrial Union (AWIU) of Southern California a communist subsidiary and branch of the Trade Union Unity League, which in turn is the American section of the Red International of Labor Unions, affiliated with the Communist International of Russia.

The Communist Party leaders from the district to the L. A. Section are desirous of forming at least 3 branches of the Agricultural Workers Industrial Union in the Valley towns; at the same time utilizing the AWIU in order to establish several units of the Communist Party in Imperial Valley, which will eventually lead to the formation of other Communist subsidiary and auxiliary organizations, such as the "International Labor Defense," "Unemployed Council," and "Friends of the Soviet Union" etc. in the principal valley cities.

Pat Chambers a well-known communist agitator, formerly of Los Angeles, who also has been active in San Bernardino, San Diego and for that matter throughout the state, has been placed in charge of the organizational work in the valley by the Los Angeles Section Communist leaders and has been in El Centro and vicinity for the past several days, going under the assumed name of John Williams and receiving mail in the form of propaganda circulars sent to him from Los Angeles under the later name, General Delivery, El Centro.

So that you will have no difficulty in making him, I am enclosing his photograph. It is more than likely he is being assisted by one or two other communists; however, if you will place a tail on him at the Post Office you will more than likely learn all of his contacts and hideout.

If it is your desire to stop this agitation and organizational work at its inception, would suggest you don't delay getting him out of the valley too long as he is of the persistent and agressive type, a typical soap-box orator and active at all times.

For your information, a little over two years ago, Chambers was sent by the Communist party to San Diego where he organized an Unemployed Council and assisted in the formation of Communist Party units and other subsidiary and auxiliary organizations, later being sent to San Bernardino, accomplishing somewhat similar results. His communist activities while in Los Angeles caused him to be arrested on numerous occasions for participation in numerous communist demonstrations, riots, disorders and other unlawful activities.

I am also enclosing two sets of mimeographed circulars, one in English and the other in Spanish which are being circulated in the Valley by Chambers in connection with attempts to organize agricultural workers.

Sincerely yours,

WM. F. HYNES,
Acting Capt. of Detectives LAPD,
Commanding Intelligence Bureau.

WFH:F
Encls.

EXHIBIT 10411

Chambers of
V. N. THOMPSON, *Judge*

THE SUPERIOR COURT
County of Imperial

EL CENTRO, CALIFORNIA, *Feb. 15, 1933.*

Capt. WM. F. HYNES,
    Intelligence Bureau, Los Angeles Police Department,
        Los Angeles, Calif.

MY DEAR CAPTAIN: Copy of your letter of February 11th, written to Elmer Heald, containing information about late developments in connection with communist activities in Imperial Valley was duly received.

A conference with the Sheriff and chiefs of police is being held, for the purpose of meeting the proposed activities and taking care of Mr. Pat Chambers in the proper way.

Thank you very much for this information, Captain.

I noticed in the paper a week or two ago where another attempt to dislodge yourself and all of the "Red" squad is being made,—this time in the name of "economy."   If we can be of any assistance to you in the matter, we are ready to "go to bat" for you.

With very kind regards, I remain

Respectfully yours,

V. N. THOMPSON.

EXHIBIT 10412

[Postal Telegraph]

SAN DIEGO, CALIFORNIA, *January 13, 1934.*

A. N. JACK,
    Care Jack Bros. & McBurney, Brawley, California:

I am authorized by Mr. Frank C. MacDonald State labor commissioner to tender to the employers and employees in the Imperial Valley lettuce and vegetable industry the good offices of the representatives of the division of labor statistics and law enforcement of the department of industrial relations of this State to act as mediators and conciliators in an effort to bring about a peaceful settlement of the farm labor strike in your county.

STANLEY M. GUE,
Deputy Labor Commissioner.

EXHIBIT 10413

[Postal Telegraph]

JANUARY 13, 1934, DAY LETTER 230 p. m.

STANLEY M. GUE,
    Deputy Labor Commissioner, 604 California Theatre Building,
    San Diego, California:

I am sure the employers in Imperial Valley appreciate the offer of the good offices of the representatives of your division   Stop   Mister John R Lester in my office making same offer when your telegram arrived   Stop   Many employers like myself are quite sure there is no real strike of our employees in progress   Stop   Through meetings held past few months representatives of employers and employees have agreed from time to time upon wage scales for various classes of work our employees have been well satisfied   Stop   The heads of the Mexican Workers Association notified representatives of the employers several times within past three weeks that radical agitators were in valley fomenting trouble   Stop   Our employees have been desirous of continuing work all this past week they have been driven from fields by threats of violence to themselves their families and their homes   Stop   Apparently there are fewer agitators in the valley today the laborers feel more secure in working in fields and are returning from the brush river beds and ditch banks and going to work   Stop . If you can arrange keep agitators from this district there will be no trouble   Stop   Our own employees are not asking for higher wages they realize we are selling products below cost of production   Stop   Outside people only were recommending and asking for higher wages

(typed)   ALVIN N. JACK.

EXHIBIT 10414

[Postal Telegraph]

JAN. 18, 1934.

Hon. JAMES ROLPH, JR.,
    Governor of State of California, Sacramento, Calif.

The members of this organization wish to compliment you on the efficient manner in which your State highway patrol handled the situation in Imperial

Valley this past week and especially commend the work of Captain Frank Oswalt Stop   If it had not been for the splendid cooperation of your men with our local county and city officers we no doubt would have had serious trouble   Stop   We are now facing an even more serious situation and your assistance in this emergency is of great importance to this valley for the preservation of life and property   Stop Would appreciate your advice as to what action we may expect

Same wire to E. Raymond Cato, chief state highway patrol.

WESTERN GROWERS PROTECTIVE ASSOCIATION.
GEORGE SWINK, *President.*

EXHIBIT 10415

[Western Union]

BRAWLEY CALIF, 1.18.34.

E. RAYMOND CATO,
    Chief, California Highway Patrol,
        Sacramento, California.

Representing our respective members we tender our sincere thanks and appreciation for the assistance furnished in maintaining law and order in this community and surrounding territory   Stop   Under Captain Oswalt your fine body of efficient patrolmen cooperating with our police and sheriff averted what might have resulted in disaster   Stop   Agitators and trouble seekers already here are laying plans for revival of strife and disorder on a greater scale and we therefore petition your continued aid and assistance to the end that we might live in peace and enjoy the comfort of security.

Signed:

BRAWLEY CHAMBER OF COMMERCE.
BRAWLEY ROTARY CLUB
BRAWLEY KIWANIS CLUB
AMERICAN LEGION POST, No. 60.

EXHIBIT 10416

[Western Union]

BRAWLEY, CALIF, 1.18.34.

E. RAYMOND CATO,
    Chief, California Highway Patrol,
        Sacramento, California.

We the undersigned landowners growers and shippers of the Imperial Valley tender our thanks and appreciation for the assistance furnished in maintaining law and order in Brawley and surrounding community Stop   Under Captain Oswalt your most capable patrolmen cooperating with our police department and sheriff department averted what might have been a very disastrous outbreak upon our good citizens   Stop   This is not a strike of field workers but instead appears to be a winter resort for communistic and radical agitators   Stop   This element being reinforced daily through outside sources and are now laying plans for a revival of disorder on a larger scale and we ask your continued aid and assistance to the end that we might live in peace.

Signed:

A. ARENA & COMPANY.
AMERICAN FRUIT GROWERS INC.
PEPERS BATLEY COMPANY.
JACK BROS. & McBURNEY CO.
FARMERS PRODUCE COMPANY.
BEST MONGER COMPANY.
SEARS BROS. & COMPANY.
THE S. A. GERRARD CO.
WESTERN FRUIT GROWERS INC.
PRODUCERS & DISTRIBUTORS INC.
MILLER CUMMINGS COMPANY.
GEORGE A DAHL COMPANY.
A. S. GARGUILO COMPANY.
RICHAMAN & SAMUELS COMPANY.
STRIEBY & WHIPPLE COMPANY.

EXHIBIT 10417

[Western Union]

BRAWLEY, CALIF., 1.18.34.

E. RAYMOND CATO,
   Chief, California State Highway Patrol,
               Sacramento, California.

Assembled in special meeting we the board of trustees of city of Brawley convey our grateful appreciation for the assistance you furnished during our troublesome period we also commend Captain Oswalt for his valiant service and wholehearted cooperation with our Chief of Police Cromer and sheriffs department Stop Your patrolmen and all men of the highest type and character and hold your respect and admiration we congratulate you in their selection Stop Situation at this hour is tense and we are authoritatively informed that an outbreak of greater seriousness is assured shortly and under the circumstances expect further assistance when Captain Oswalt deems it necessary.

(Signed) THE BRAWLEY CITY COUNCIL,
          R. L. BAKER, *Mayor, City of Brawley.*

EXHIBIT 10418

JAN. 21, 1934., 9:15 P. M.

GEORGE L. CAMPBELL,
      Sheriff, El Centro, Calif.

Kindly have Alvin N. Jack of Brawley teletype or wire me immediately statement setting forth nature of agreement as to hours wages and working conditions entered into by growers and Imperial Valley Mexican Workers Assn. and names of leaders of that organization prior to calling of strike by Communist Cannery and Agricultural Workers Industrial Union. Also advise date of meeting in Brawley which resulted in riot, and date of meeting of Mexicans held in Mexicali at which plans were discussed for raids on ranches and attacking jail in El Centro.

JAMES H. DAVIS, *Chief of Police.*
WM. F. HYNES, *Capt. Intelligence Bureau.*

EXHIBIT 10419

LOS ANGELES POLICE DEPARTMENT
Office of In. Bu. Metro Div'n

Name: Capt. HYNES.   JAN. 22, 1934.

Following message phoned in from Bus. Of. Det. Bu. Brawley, Cal. Jan 22–34 9 a. m.

"JAMES E. DAVIS,
        Chief of Police:

Answering teletype sent through Sheriff's office, El Centro, agreement with workers provided for wages $2, 9 hour day or 22½¢ hour with minimum 5 hours per day if called to field, with further understanding no strikes be instigated and no additional pay expected unless living is increased materially over those prevailing last October or else marketing of our winter crops shows a profit. Above scale applied for lower classes of work. Irrigators, teamsters, etc. generally paid more money. Lucio O'jeda, President and Jose Sierio Secy. Mexican Workers, which were set aside by Cannery & Agricultural Workers Ind. Union late in December. O'Jeda notified me last Friday his organization broken up, would not be restored. There now is no Mexican workers' organization functioning other than that led by Communists. Meetings in Brawley and we understand also in Mexicali were held and are being held almost continuously night and day therefore impossible to give you exact date asked for

ALVIN N. JACK."

NOTE: Mc. of. picked up original message to take to you Met. Veh. Dept.

EXHIBIT 10420

[Western Union]

MGAAA LONG SD12 165 DL—   BRAWLEY, CALIF., *Jan. 22, 1934* 900A.

JAMES E. DAVIS, *Chief of Police:*

Answering teletype sent through sheriff's office El Centro agreement with workers provided for wage two dollars nine hour day or twenty two half cents hour with minimum five hours per day if called to field with further understanding no strikes be instigated and no additional pay expected unless living expenses increased materially over those prevailing last October or unless marketing of our winter crops showed a profit   Stop   Above scale applied for lower classes of work   Stop   Irrigators teamsters etc generally paid more money   Stop   Lucio OJeda President Jose Sierro Secretary Mexican Workers Association which was set aside by cannery and agricultural workers industrial union late in December Stop   OJeda notified me last Friday his organization broken up would not be restored   Stop

There now is no Mexican workers organization functioning other than that led by communists   Stop   Meeting in Brawley and we understand also in Mexicali were held and are being held almost continuously night and day therefore impossible give you exact dates asked for.

ALVIN N. JACK.

Received Detective Bureau:
JAN. 22, 1934.
By T. H. POST, 10 A. M.
(Handwritten) Capt. Hynes.

EXHIBIT 10421

[Teletype Message to LAPD]

1–23–34.

POLICE DEPT. LOS ANGELES:

Re your No. 2 this date; They had a gathering at Brawley tonight.   Everything passed off quietly.   Mr. Wrrin, their main speaker was kidnapped from the planters hotel in Brawley.   He was taken out the other side of Calipatria and released.   He walked back into Calipatria and is now on the way to El Centro in company with a Deputy Sheriff.

GEO. L. CAMPBELL,
Sheriff Ect. Cp PIS AcK NM.

ACK LOF CLB HM.
CAPT. HYNES,
Intelligence Bureau.

EXHIBIT 10422

LOS ANGELES POLICE DEPARTMENT

Office of In. Bu. Metro. Div.

JAN. 23, 1934, 11:30 A. M.

Memo.

Phone call from BRAWLEY, Chief Cromer and Alvin Jacks in which later read a copy of restraining order served on Sheriff and Chief of Police to prevent interference with a meeting in Brawley tonight, order reads:

"It is therefore ordered that defendants George Campbell, (Chief) Cromer and each of them appear before Fed. Court Judge Kerrigan 29th day of Jan. at San Diego as to why it shouldn't be made permanent.

"It is further ordered the defendants Geo. Campbell, Lon Cromer and all persons acting under their order or in cooperation with the defendants be and they are hereby enjoined and restrained from preventing or interfering with the holding of a meeting Jan. 23, 1934 between the hours of 7:30 P. M. and 11 P. M. at the premises at 10th and   St., Brawley, prevent members of the American Civil Liberties Union or the general public from entering said premises between said hours.   Provided, however, this order shall not prevent and shall not be deemed to prevent the defendants or other persons acting under orders or in cooperation with said defendants from attending said meeting or taking notes of proceedings held and speakers names at said meeting and from arresting any person who shall violate any law of the United States or State of California."

Said this petition brought by Clinton J. Taft for and on behalf of the members of the American Civil Liberties Union against Sheriff Geo. Campbell and Lon Cromer and as to 10 John Does.

Said they had a city ordinance preventing meetings unless permit was secured, and further this organization had made no such application for a permit.

Suggestion made that representative City Attorney go with official certified copy said ordinance and lay this before Federal Judge in San Diego.

EXHIBIT 10423

LOS ANGELES POLICE DEPARTMENT

Office of In. Bu. Metro Div'n

JAN. 23, 1934, 2:45 P. M.

Confidential
Memo.

Further phone call from Jacks at Brawley to effect a wire sent Governor Rolph signed A. L. Wirin and Helen B. Marsden, reading:

"Local officials, vigilantes and other lawless elements in Imperial Valley threaten to violate Federal injunction protecting civil liberties Union tonight at Brawley. Heretofore your highway patrol has been taking orders from Capt. Hynes, notorious Los Angeles Red baiter and law violator. We ask you personally order Cato to protect meeting, uphold the Constitution and avert bloodshed."

Says also a wire in from Asso. Press San Diego to Brawley News re this.

Say also a wire sent by Civil Liberties Union to U. S. Marshal, San Diego:

"Authorities Imperial Valley have suspended U. S. Constitution and turned it into a scrap of paper. Vigilantes now threaten violence bloodshed in defiance of Federal Judge Kerrigan's order protecting meeting. We request you send representatives to Brawley arrest those in violation workers constitutional rights."

Further said Co. Attorney Heald is on his way over to Brawley, that a meeting of representative citizens is to be held this afternoon; said Mexicon Consul was advising his nationals to stay away from this meeting.

H:F

EXHIBIT 10424

[Copied from the Los Angeles Times, January 24, 1934]

MAN SEIZED IN STRIKE—"KIDNAPING" LAID TO VIGILANTES—BRAWLEY AFFAIR ATTRIBUTED TO LAWYER'S ACTIVITIES FOR LETTUCE PICKERS—MOVE FOLLOWS INJUNCTION BALKING INTERFERENCE WITH GATHERING

BRAWLEY, Jan. 23 (UP).—A. L. Wirin, American Civil Liberties Union attorney, who was kidnaped by a band of thirty vigilantes this evening, telephoned the local headquarters of the union that he had been dropped off in the desert eighteen miles from here by his abductors.

Earlier, reports that three others had been taken with Wirin were denied by Marshal George Wright, who said he spoke to Mr. and Mrs. Grover Johnson of San Bernardino and David Sokol of Los Angeles, after the asserted abduction took place.

Wirin declared he had not been harmed.

BRAWLEY, Jan. 23 (UP).—Three men and a woman were "kidnaped" tonight assertedly by a citizens' vigilante committee which objected to their efforts in behalf of striking lettuce workers here in Imperial Valley.

The three men, all attorneys, and the woman were taken from a hotel here tonight and placed in several automobiles which drove off. Those assertedly kidnaped are A. L. Wirin, attorney for the American Civil Liberties Union; Mr. and Mrs. Grover Johnson of San Bernardino and David Sokol, Los Angeles attorney.

FOLLOWS INJUNCTION

The kidnaping followed issuance of an injunction earlier today by Federal Judge Kerrigan restraining Sheriff Campbell of Imperial county and Police Chief Cromer from interfering with a "free speech" meeting tonight.

This evening, as the group was preparing to leave for the meeting of strikers, the band of men descended on them and after a brief minor struggle drove off with the four.

The incident was witnessed by a score or more in the Planters Hotel, but no attempt was made to aid them against the determined citizens' committee.

POLICE PROMISE HUNT

Immediately after the vigilantes had left with their prisoners Miss Helen Martin, San Diego, reported the kidnaping to police, who said they would attempt to find the quartet.

Wirin and Johnson both had engaged in verbal and legal battles with the growers in behalf of the strikers. Johnson had been cited for contempt of court several days ago when he failed to appear at a hearing in a local court. Wirin protested all legal rights of the strikers had been violated.

LEGION RIOT SQUADS ORDERED OUT IN STRIKE

BRAWLEY, Jan. 23.—Riot squads composed of war veterans from Calexico, El Centro, Imperial and Brawley gathered here this evening in response to an emergency call from Capt. Charles Delp, commander of the American Legion post in El Centro, to aid city and county officers to prevent disorder in connection with a mass meeting called by the American Civil Liberties Union.

According to A. L. Wirin, attorney and spokesman for the union, the meeting was to be held as a protest against methods used by county officers in quelling the recent strike of lettuce field workers.

Police Chief Cromer of Brawley and Sheriff Campbell refused permission for the meeting to be held. They were overruled when attorneys obtained an injunction from United States District Judge Kerrigan.

A call for the aid of the veterans' riot squad was sent out this afternoon when information reached the Sheriff's office that a group of radicals from San Diego was coming to Imperial Valley to speak at the meeting.

A crowd of 400 persons, mostly Mexicans, crowded into the East Side Hall, where the meeting was scheduled to be held, and finally dispersed after being addressed by Chester Williams and Oaten Beverly, representatives of the Interchurch Fellowship League of Los Angeles.

EXHIBIT 10425

MARCH 23, 1934.

Dear Members and Prospective Members:

Many have joined our Association, many more should. Our membership now includes shook companies, paper companies, railroads, banks, alfalfa growers, citrus growers, asparagus growers, professional men and merchants in addition to melon and vegetable growers and shippers.

You, perhaps, are beginning to realize from newspaper articles, from the speeches you heard at the Mass Meeting at the fair grounds today and from personal conversations, the menace facing our industry in the Imperial Valley.

Much work is to be done combating this evil if we hope to continue the growing and shipping of all kinds of produce from the Imperial Valley. As an illustration of the activities of our communist antagonists we quote extracts from pamphlets they are getting out today. These from two calling for a meeting to be held in Calexico, California, at 3:00 pm, Sunday, March 25th, 321 Second Street.

AGRICULTURAL WORKERS MASS MEETING

Come to this meeting to hear discussions on wages for the coming melon season and what we can do to make them higher. A report will be made on the three prisoners from the lettuce strike who were sentenced to 6 months in jail. They are Emma Cutler, Dorothy Ray and Stanley Hancock. The meeting will be under the auspices of the American Civil Liberties Union with the assistance of the Cannery & Agricultural Workers Industrial Union. Further discussion will be about the Mexican Consul, Joaquin Terrazas, and the fake union he is building. The only Union that fights for higher wages and better conditions and against deportations is the Cannery & Agricultural Workers Industrial Union.

ATTENTION: AGRICULTURAL WORKERS OF IMPERIAL VALLEY! ATTENTION!

It was the ILD (INTERNATIONAL LABOR DEFENSE), the fighting, mass defense organization of the working class, that furnished LEGAL AID to the arrested strikers of the Lettuce and Pea Pickers strikes. It was the ILD that gave AID AND RELIEF to the families of the arrested strikers.

NOW, because the workers of Imperial Valley have learned that only through organization into a militant union like the CANNERY & AGRICULTURAL WORKERS INDUSTRIAL UNION, can they ever win living wages and BETTER WORKING CONDITIONS, and because they are joining the C & AWIU in greater numbers, the bosses and growers and rich ranchers of Imperial Valley, through *their mouthpiece*, the *traitor Mexican Consul Terrazas*, are *threatening to deport* all Mexican workers who join the C & AWIU.

THE INTERNATIONAL LABOR DEFENSE FIGHTS DEPORTATIONS!

The only way for the workers of Imperial Valley to crush out the growers and rich ranchers' vicious use of deportations against workers who are organizing to better their conditions, is *greater organization!* ORGANIZE the *unorganized workers* into the C & AWIU—organize branches of the International Labor Defense (ILD)—organize defense committees of the ILD *in each camp*, in *each field, in each shed*. When workers are being *threatened with deportation*, organize mass demonstrations of workers to protest against deportation, JOIN THE ILD and *get others to join*. Only through *mass organization* can we find the *strength* to *smash* the *deportation terror* of the *growers and bosses*.

WHAT TO DO WHEN ARRESTED!

If the police arrest you, *give them only your name*, do not give them any other information about yourself or about other workers, *because they will use this information against you and against your fellow workers*. Get in touch immediately with the DEFENSE COMMITTEE IN YOUR CAMP, FIELD, OR SHED—or get in touch directly with the ILD. Never plead guilty when arrested for strike activity, union activity or ILD activity. Always plead not guilty—a worker is never guilty in the bosses court! *Always demand a jury trial!*

The ILD defends all class war and political prisoners!

Please let us have your membership subscription.

Yours very truly,

IMPERIAL VALLEY GROWERS & SHIPPERS
PROTECTIVE ASSOCIATION,

(Stamped) A. N. JACK, President

EXHIBIT 10426

[State-Wide Teletype Systems]

Regular   X   Date 4–9–34
Emergency   Time 5:15 PM
                                                     LOP NO:

To: RODNEY CLARKE,
      Undersheriff Imperial Valley,
                  El Centro, Calif.

Notify A. W. Jack, Brawley, that Captain William Hynes will be in San Diego tonight and tomorrow and will arrive Brawley late Tuesday night or early Wednesday morning.

JAMES E. DAVIS, *Chief of Police.*

Detail Handling: Intelligence—Capt. WM. F. HYNES.

EXHIBIT 10427

IMPERIAL VALLEY GROWERS & SHIPPERS PROTECTIVE ASS'N
BRAWLEY, CALIFORNIA, *April 27, 1934.*

To All Growers & Shippers in the Imperial Valley.

GENTLEMEN: We regret to inform you that the American Civil Liberties Union groups in Los Angeles and San Diego have elected to come to the Imperial Valley, Saturday, April 28th, on what they term a good will tour.

In my opinion no tour of the Imperial Valley by members of the American Civil Liberties Union could by any stretch of the imagination be called a good will tour.

The purpose of this communication is to give you solemn warning that trouble can be anticipated the next five or six days. In fact we have information from reliable sources which leads us to believe our loyal workers will be attacked between May 2nd and May 5th and in our opinion this so called good will tour is for the purpose of sowing the seed of discontent and preparing the ground for the more militant agitators who will follow.

Yours very truly,

IMPERIAL VALLEY GROWERS & SHIPPERS
PROTECTIVE ASSOCIATION,
By: (Signed in ink) A. N. JACK, *President.*

ANJ is

EXHIBIT 10428

[Confidential]

MAY 6, 1934.

Last Saturday, May 5th, a group of Los Angeles and outside people made a trip to the Valley and to Brawley. In the party, using several cars, were: Dr. Alexander Erwin; Clinton J. Taft, director of the American Civil Liberties Union; Anthony Pratt of the Municipal League of Los Angeles; Professor Voorhees of Pomona College; James Carter, an attorney, 1023 Rowan Bldg.; R. F. Sparks, W. F. Stevens; R. C. Gartz, son of Mrs. Kate Crane Gartz—noted for her contributions to the Communist Party and ACLU; Helen McCarron, secretary to the Director of the Young People's Work of the So. Cal. Methodist Episcopal Conference; Monroe Sweetland, national secretary of the Students League for Industrial Democracy—left Socialist, and several other students.

Dr. A. Erwin and a group, including attorney James Carter and several women, were driven to the Valley by R. C. Gartz in his Dusenberg straight 8, License 3 T 8334, while another group left in a green Chevrolet, License 9 A 3240; others left in other cars whose license numbers were not obtained. It was learned that R. F. Sparks' car, with others, had broken down outside of Pomona, and that he was later transported to the Valley in car driven by Professor Voorhees of Pomona College.

The trip was scheduled as a "Goodwill Tour," and though much was expected in the way of conferences, the group got nowhere.

Various Red publications, including the "Open Forum," will blast Glassford in their next issues for, as they say, doublecrossing them on this trip. They claim that Glassford faithfully promised them that he would furnish an escort for them at the Immigration Station, and that he absolutely failed to keep his word. When the group arrived in Brawley they went to the Dunlak Hotel. They were met by about thirty vigilantes who had been informed by the hotel clerk that the group were enroute to Brawley and would gather at the Dunlak Hotel.

Clinton Taft got in touch with the Planters Hotel and made arrangements to meet Glassford there. The entire group then marched over to the Planters Hotel, but Glassford did not show up. It was reported by several of the local workers who are members of the Cannery Workers Industrial Union that the vigilantes had brought pressure to bear on Glassford and had stopped him from sending the escort and also from meeting with these busybodies at all.

Following his instructions, Agent contacted some of the leaders in the CWIU and learned that they are planning a strike in the Valley among the melon workers at the height of the picking season. They say that this time they will show the vigilantes a thing or two about terrorism. Some of the comrades who were supposed to be in Brawley were attending a conference up north, as Agent learned in San Diego on his return trip.

Agent learned that the workers, led by the Communists, are forming a counter-attack organization to fight the vigilantes on the same ground and with the same tactics as are used against the workers. There is a great amount of hatred being instilled into the workers by the leaders of the CWIU and Communists, and Agent believes that anything is apt to happen when the melons are ripe. They will be careful, however, so they say, and no Communist leader will issue instructions to the workers to break the laws. Neither will any Communist be allowed to break any serious law. Of course, they will pay no attention to local ordinances as they do not believe that they amount to much.

Agent was informed that all meetings having to do with action in the Imperial Valley will hereafter be held either in San Diego or in Los Angeles. This information was picked up by Agent after arriving in Los Angeles.

Chester Williams was asked not to make the trip into the Valley Saturday, but to stand by in Los Angeles and direct activities and keep tab on things here. He was in constant communication with the ACLU bunch in San Diego, and he got wires and phone calls from the members of the caravan at frequent intervals.

Williams intends to go into the Valley again this week sometime. He thinks that it will be possible to organize a real invasion into the territory—one so large that the vigilantes will not dare to do anything to them. In the meantime, the Communists are to organize their side of things and so further swell the ranks of outsiders going into the Valley for an "investigation" or "conference." THIS IS CONFIDENTIAL and was divulged only this afternoon by Williams himself. Williams has been in communication with Lawrence Ross, local head of the Communist Party here, on this matter.

---

5. RELATIONS OF INTELLIGENCE BUREAU WITH VARIOUS EMPLOYER ASSOCIATIONS AND CORPORATIONS

A. ASSOCIATED APPAREL MANUFACTURERS

EXHIBIT 10429

LOS ANGELES, *Sept 1–33* 11 a. m.

Memo. Re Labor Troubles among members associated apparel mfgrs.

Mr. Rhodes, secretary of above asso. phones in says he would like advice and cooperation this Bureau in handling any labor troubles, strikes, etc. that are likely to occur from time to time now and in near future with Unions; says the most disturbing factor is what he termed the "left wing" or Needle Trades Workers Ind. Union.

Wants to come down and talk with you; his phone TR 1034, 117 W. 9th St.

Says it seems funny, but the Inter. Lady Garment Wkrs Union now have their quarters and sign out just across from his place.

Says he has 130 members in his asso. manufacturers of womens dresses, coats, uniforms, etc.

Mentioned re Lettie Lee, Inc. as one, told him we were sending man down re this.

F

(In Pencil:) "phoned will contact Tues. he is closed Sat. and Mon."

EXHIBIT 10430

[Intra-Departmental Correspondence]

LOS ANGELES POLICE DEPARTMENT
Office of Metro Div. In. Bu

OCT. 10–33, 5.30 p. m.

Confidential.
Memo. Re Strike Plans.

Mr. Booth of Associated Apparel Asso. phones in he was delivered an unsolicited report from the Pinkerton people today that an executive member of Communist Party attended a secret meeting of all organizers of the Needle Trades Workers Ind. Union at 755 So Main where they said that *starting tomorrow* all Los Angeles dressmakers, men and women are to form pickets, members of CP mingling with the strikers to see that no nonunion workers take the place of the strikers, all pickets to report tomorrow morning.

F

EXHIBIT 10431

[Intra-Departmental Correspondence]

LOS ANGELES POLICE DEPARTMENT
Office of In. Bu. Metro Div

DEC. 4, 1933, 1 p. m.

Memo. Request Detail 834 and 850 So. Broadway.

Mr. Booth of Associated Apparel Mfgrs. Asso. phones in says some picketing expected this afternoon both above locations, refers to complaint of Mona Lisa Shop, 203–850 So. Bdwy, (this is same location as Lowe Bros. Shop).

NOTE: Sam Evans will cover, 3 pm as well as 3 men from Vag Squad.

F

B. CALIFORNIA WALNUT GROWERS ASSOCIATION

EXHIBIT 10432

[Intra-Departmental Correspondence]

LOS ANGELES POLICE DEPARTMENT
Office of Intelligence Bureau, Metropolitan Division

OCT. 9, 1935.

Capt. WM. F. HYNES,
    Commanding Intelligence Bureau.

Re: Labor Trouble at CAL. WALNUT GROWERS ASSO. 1745 and 2180 E. 7th St.

SIR: Per instructions Officer Irvine and myself called at 1745 E. 7th St. (7th & Mill Sts.), and interview Mr. Cowan, production mgr. & assistant sales mgr., who stated that amongst the approximately 500 girls employed by the association in their two sorting plants, they had about 50 or 60 agitators and trouble-makers and that on Saturday, Sept. 28 they (the Association) had laid off the entire plant with instructions to come back to work Monday, Sept. 30th; and that Saturday Oct 5th they again laid off all the help and were now sending out cards telling workers to come back to work, but neglecting the 50 or 60 agitators amongst them.

The plant at 2180 E. 7th St. resumed operations this morning with half a crew, consisting of new help, and Friday, Oct. 11th the old help will also report to work at this plant. Tomorrow, Thursday morning, Oct. 10th the plant at 1745 E. 7th St. will resume operations with half a crew consisting of new help and Sat. Oct. 12th the old help will also report to work at this plant.

So far there has been no trouble and there were no pickets at the plant at 2180 E. 7th St.; however there was a window broken by a rock at this plant, but it is our belief that this was an accident. Neither was there any trouble or picketing at 1745 E. 7th St.

Working hours at the plants are 7.30 a. m. to 11.30 a. m.; 12 noon to 4 p. m., with recess at 10 a. m. and 2 p. m.

I left Bureau's phone no. at both plants and informed them we might possibly have a police detail for a few days, but if we did not and they had any further trouble to let us know and we would cover.

Respectfully,

P. L. PHELPS #1527.

P:F

C. INDUSTRIAL ASSOCIATION OF SAN FRANCISCO

EXHIBIT 10433

[Interdepartment Correspondence. 30 Legal]

LOS ANGELES POLICE DEPARTMENT

Chief's Office

To: Captain Warren Justin, Metropolitan Div Date Sept. 25, 1934.
From: J. Finlinson, Acting Chief.
Subject: Copies of letters from Paul Eliel (Industrial Ass'n of S. F.) re: American Civil Liberties Union and alleged activities of police in southern California.

SIR: The attached copies of reports are forwarded for your attention.
JF:O

[Copy]

[Attached to above memorandum]

INDUSTRIAL ASSOCIATION OF SAN FRANCISCO

Alexander Building

SAN FRANCISCO, CALIFORNIA, *September 17, 1934.*

Hon. JAMES E. DAVIS,
    Chief of Police, City of Los Angeles, Los Angeles, California.

DEAR CHIEF DAVIS: We are attaching hereto, for your confidential information, extract from private report which has been made to us in connection with investigation to be conducted by the American Civil Liberties Union relative to certain alleged activities of the Police Department in Southern California.

Very truly yours,

INDUSTRIAL ASSOCIATION OF SAN FRANCISCO,
By PAUL ELIEL.

PE:B
Enc.

At San Francisco late this evening the board members met for the usual Saturday business meeting, and it was learned that the first discussion was the report from the American Civil Liberties Union of Los Angeles, which is connected with the Communist Party, as far as the defense of so called political prisoners is concerned. The report is regarding several marine strikers who were beaten up by the Police at Wilmington during the marine strike.   The names appearing in this report are the names of Communist members who are either marine workers or longshoremen of the San Pedro-Wilmington district who making cases against the Police Department of Los Angeles, also against the Policemen who did the beating; and now the Union is trying to connect the Industrial Association, the Chamber of Commerce and the Shipowners of that district, as being the instigators of the beating of these men:

James Lacy beaten up by Hache and Cole.
Carl Carlson, Longshoreman beaten up by Officer badge No. 828.
Duncan McDugal beaten up by Officer Cole.
Henry Jensen beaten up by the Police Red squad captain.
Ricardo Ramos beaten up by the same two officers Hache and Cole.

Archie Crawford beaten up by Red Squad Officers name of officers unknown.
Joe Johannenson beaten up by Cole and other officers.
Joe Figueroa beaten up by four red squad men names unknown.
Dudley Crawford, beaten up by strikebreakers, names unknown.
Harry Rice, Nathan Citron, B. Deer and Harold Taylor slugged by vigilantes.
The cases of those men is being investigated by the American Civil Liberties Union because the vigilantes, it is said, were in the employ of the Ship Owners.
Herman Pauls, sailor arrested and beaten up by Officer Thompson.
Arthur Jenkins beaten while enroute to the Wilmington Police Station.
This case is also being investigated on account of the identity of the patrol car's number.
Ruel Stanford, beaten up by red squad officers, names unknown.
All of the men who were beaten up were released without being booked at the Police Station and no charges were made against them.   The American Civil Liberties Union, the International Labor Defense, the National Committee for the Defense of Political Prisoners, the Committee for the Defense of Public Rights, and the entire membership of the I. L. A. are working together in order to bring to trial every case, either individually or collectively, against the Police Department, individual officers and others involved.   The list is not complete and other names will be reported as soon as obtained.

EXHIBIT 10434

11 S. F.

INDUSTRIAL ASSOCIATION OF SAN FRANCISCO
Alexander Building

SAN FRANCISCO, CALIF., *December 5, 1935.*

Hon. JAMES E. DAVIS,
   Chief of Police, Los Angeles, Calif.

DEAR CHIEF DAVIS: Kindly accept our thanks for the information contained in your letter of December 2d, No. 1.15.2, with respect to John B. Pelletier.   This will enable us to trace the alleged naturalization and we will be glad to advise you if anything of an interesting nature develops.
   Yours very truly,

INDUSTRIAL ASSOCIATION OF SAN FRANCISCO,
   (Signed)   ALBERT E. BOYNTON, *Managing Director.*

AEB:JE

"FOR SOUND INDUSTRIAL RELATIONS"

EXHIBIT 10435

INDUSTRIAL ASSOCIATION OF SAN FRANCISCO
Alexander Building

SAN FRANCISCO, CALIF., *December 7, 1935.*

Hon. JAMES E. DAVIS,
   Chief of Police, Los Angeles, Calif.

DEAR CHIEF DAVIS: Thinking that perhaps the attached file of copies of letters and telegrams forwarded to Superior Judge Harris of San Francisco in connection with the Louise Todd case may be of interest to you, we are transmitting them for your information.
   Yours very truly,

INDUSTRIAL ASSOCIATION OF SAN FRANCISCO,
   (Signed)   ALBERT E. BOYNTON, *Managing Director.*

AEB:JE
(Enc.)

(In pencil:) Get address and place of employment of each who signed telegram. Give this to Chief in a report.

MARGARET.

EXHIBIT 10436

35 Ind. Asso.   S. F.

INDUSTRIAL ASSOCIATION OF SAN FRANCISCO
Alexander Building

SAN FRANCISCO, CALIF.,
December 30, 1935.

Hon. JAMES E. DAVIS,
  Chief of Police, Los Angeles, Calif.

DEAR CHIEF DAVIS: Acknowledging your letter of December 26th, Reference No. 1.15.2, we thank you very much for the information which you have forwarded to us concerning William Schneiderman.

Yours very truly,

INDUSTRIAL ASSOCIATION OF SAN FRANCISCO,
(sgd) ALBERT E. BOYNTON, *Managing Director.*

AEB:JE
Jan. 2 '36

"FOR SOUND INDUSTRIAL RELATIONS"

EXHIBIT 10437

]Note: Copy for files of Chief's Office red letter 6271-83]

35 Inc. Assn.

1.15.2   DECEMBER 24, 1937.

Mr. ALBERT E. BOYTON,
  President, Industrial Association of San Francisco,
            Alexander Bldg., San Francisco, Calif.

SIR: Reference is had to your letter of Dec. 8, 1937, inquiring as to record and background of one A. F. SCHINDLER, organizer for the C. I. O. in the Oil Workers Field.

Please be advised we have no record of this subject as having been active in Los Angeles.

Very truly yours,

JAMES E. DAVIS,
Chief of Police.
By: WILLIAM F. HYNES,
Capt. of Detectives, LAPD,
Commanding Intelligence Bureau.

H: F

D. INDUSTRIAL ASSOCIATION OF THE EAST BAY, GEORGE W. BARKER, EMPLOYEE,

EXHIBIT 10438

BILL: Will much appreciate anything you have on the subject of LOUIS ROSEN, of the TWOC, who has an office at 1210½ West Washington Blvd. He has been organizing the bag industry in LA (according to my dope) and now is barging in on some others. If it can be established that he is sour a crimp can be put in a lot of things.

FEB. 24, 1938.

Memo Capt. HYNES.

This date we went to 1210½ W. Washington Blvd., which is the location of a C. I. O. Union hall, 2nd floor, for Warehousemen; we asked for Mr. LOUIS ROSEN, but were advised by man there Rosen was not in; but was in the office between 7 am and 9 a. daily; Mr. Rosen is an organizer for this Union and can be reached by phoning Richmond 0268, office phone.

C. W. WOOLARD—JOHN FLAHERTY.

EXHIBIT 10439

LOS ANGELES POLICE DEPARTMENT

Office of Intelligence Bureau, Metropolitan Divn.

FEB. 28, 1938.

Confidential.

Memo. for Mr. G. W. BARKER, Room 1003 Finance Center Bldg., Oakland, Calif.

DEAR MR. BARKER: Reference is had to your recent note to Captain Hynes (who is on special days off) in which you inquire as to one LOUIS ROSEN and we have confirmed that he is connected with the Longshoremen & Warehousemen's Union of the C. I. O., located on 2nd floor at 1210½ West Washington Blvd. this city; and is apparently an organizer among the warehousemen.

This subject may be Louis Schneiderman, alias Lou Sherman, et al, the well-known Communist of So. California; when Capt. Hynes returns to duty will ask him if he can confirm this.

Yours truly,

FRANK H. FOLSOM, steno. for Capt. HYNES.

(Written in pencil:) Not the same man.

(See attached copy of 3x5 paper)

E. MERCHANTS AND MANUFACTURERS ASSOCIATION

EXHIBIT 10440

LOS ANGELES POLICE DEPARTMENT

Office of In. Bu. Metro. Div.

JAN. 6–34, 11.07 a. m.

Confidential Memo.

Mr Fysh TU 6244 of M&M phones in that they are establishing Employment Office (connection supplying milkers Dairy Strike) at rooms 284–5 Rosslyn Hotel, 5th & Main; expect bus with men to come there with men from 12 noon to 3 pm today; requests officer be detailed to cover (uniform).

Asks Officer see Mr. Perkins, mgr. room 284 at 11.45 am re.

Says bus will come in alley on 5th between Main & Spring in alley, coming west on 5th.

f

Copy Capt Horrall.

EXHIBIT 10441

LOS ANGELES POLICE DEPARTMENT

Office of In. Bu. Metro Div

5.30 p. m., JAN. 6–34.

Request: Relief Officer M&M Hdqrs Rooslyn Hotel 5th & Main.

Mr. Fysh of M&M phones from their present hdars. rem. 284 private wire MI7751 that Officer Sperry has been on duty there from 11 am; asks if another officer can be sent down to cover this spot till midnight.

Also would like this spot covered all day tomorrow, as expect it will be more "hot" than today.

F

Copy Capt Horrall (in pencil) "covered."

EXHIBIT 10442

[Intra-Departmental Correspondence]

LOS ANGELES POLICE DEPARTMENT

Office of In. Bu. Metro Div

JAN. 16, 1934.

Memo.   Request for Data per attached form on 1934 strikes by M&M ASSO.

Mr. Fysh of M & M came in and asked for any data to meet attached form re strikes in Los Angeles running into 1934; supplied him some data re Seronow Furniture Mfg. Co., which terminated Jan 3–34 (that is picketing terminated);

Also re L. Rifkin & Co. 719 So. L. A., strike starting early Dec '33 and still on (called by Furriers Dept NTWIU)

Also re Kertzman Bros & Co. 604 E. 8th St. starting early Dec '33 called by Amalgamated Clothiers Union.

Said if any more occur would appreciate being informed.

F

(Attached to above memorandum)

LABOR STRIKES IN LOS ANGELES DURING YEAR 1934

Name of Concern:
Address:
Nature of Business:
Strike Called—Date:
Strike Called off—date:
Name of Union Calling strike:
Name of Organizers and Business Agents:
Number of Persons Employed:
Number of Persons participating in strike:
Number of Persons Not striking, but out of work account strike:
Cause of strike and nature of demands presented:
Present Wage Scale:
Total Amount of Wages Lost by Employees Striking:
Remarks:

EXHIBIT 10443

LOS ANGELES STEAMSHIP COMPANY

Los Angeles Harbor, Wilmington, California

MARCH 20, 1934.

MERCHANTS & MANUFACTURERS ASS'N.
  1008 I. N. Van Nuys Bldg., Los Angeles, Calif.

(Attn. Mr. F. R. Fysh.)

GENTLEMEN: This is to request that you be good enough to serve on a committee, with Capt. William F. Hynes of the Los Angeles Police Department and Mr. E. Nichols of the Marine Service Bureau, to secure and furnish to the Steamship Operators at Los Angeles Harbor such special police officers as they may require to protect their employees and property in case of a Longshoremen's strike is called next Friday, the 23rd.

Please signify your willingness to serve on such Committee to Captain Robert Hill, Chairman, Special Committee, Marine Service Bureau, 258 W. 7th St., San Pedro, Calif.

Yours very truly,

J. B. BANNING Jr.,
for Special Committee, Marine Service Bureau.

JJB:LF
cc: Capt. R. Hill
  Capt. William F. Hynes
  Mr. E. Nichols.

EXHIBIT 10444

[Intra-Departmental Correspondence]

LOS ANGELES POLICE DEPARTMENT

Office of In. Bu. Metro Divn

1–21–36   4.15 p. m.

Memo. Lt. Lane.

Mr. Fysh of M&M phones in truck of California Wholesale Grocery Co. will be in San Pedro district at 9.30 tomorrow morning and will have the following stops.

9.30 a. m. 402 Beacon, then 507 Front, 109 E. 5 St., 609 Beacon, 641 Beacon, 103 W. 6, 522 Beacon, 123 W. 6, 210 W. 6, 617 Centre, 1110 So. Pacific, 1210 So. Pacific, 1507 S. Grand, 1201 S. Gaffey, 701 S. Pacific, 528 S. Pacific.

(In pencil:) "Avalon School, Wilmington, Nite Hound, Analicene Blvd, Wilmington"

States driver of this truck was intimidated down there yesterday. Wants police protection for above.

F

EXHIBIT 10445

[Intra-Departmental Correspondence]

LOS ANGELES POLICE DEPARTMENT

Office of Intelligence Bureau, Metropolitan Division

FRI., FEB. 28, 1936, 3 p. m.

Capt. HYNES—Lt. LANE.

Memo. Request Red Squad Officer go to Blythe, Riverside Co. Cal. to check up one Geo. Roberts, alleged Red strike agitator stopped by L. A. Police Detail there.

Per phone call in from Capt. Horrall of Chief Gross's office Sta. 2549: I phoned him back and he explained as follows:

Mr. FYSH of M&M Tu 6244 had phoned them requesting assistance in checking up on one Geo. Roberts. This subject was questioned by L. A. Officers in Blythe when he came through with an auto with Ohio lic. plates and something suspicious about the plates; when searched he had a gun on him, which it is understood was turned over to Sheriff at Riverside for check on. The car is in Indio. Subject Geo. Roberts was not arrested, but after a check up was released and understood to have come on to Los Angeles, where is now said to be. Mr. Fysh believe subject was a Com. strike agitator in the Goodyear Tire Co. strike back East and may have similar purposes here.

Chief Cross wants a Red Squad officer to go to Blythe, contact the L. A. police detail there and confer with them in detail re this case; with a view to learning whether or not there is any definite charge can be placed against said subject. Chief Cross wants this attended to today if possible; call Capt. Horrall back re same.

EXHIBIT 10446

LOS ANGELES POLICE DEPARTMENT

Office of Intelligence Bureau, Metropolitan Division

MARCH 13, 1936.

Memorandum for Chief DAVIS.

With reference to your request for such data as we have regarding FRANK KRASNESKY of the Butcher's Union, please be advised subject is Organizer and Secretary for the Amalgamated Meat Cutters Union Local #551 of San Pedro and vicinity. He resides at 1503½ Weymouth Ave. San Pedro, phone San Pedro 1278–R. He is also said to be a member of the Central Labor Council of San Pedro. He has been in charge of picket line at Smith's Market, 529 S. Pacific Ave. San Pedro for the Butcher's union.

Subject is described as a man 48–50 years old, dark hair, streaked with gray, about 5'9'' dark eyes, about 170# apparently Polish; drives an old sedan; wears a moustache.

Officers who have covered labor difficulties at Smith's Market 529 S. Pacific Ave. and the Savings Center Meat Market, 627 S. Pacific Ave. San Pedro, state subject has cooperated fairly well with them in their duty of maintaining law and order.

So far as known, Mr. Krasnesky has no Red tendencies, but is simply considered as a regular union organizer under the American Federation of Labor.

There is no record on subject in our Bureau of Records & Identification.

Respectfully,

WILLIAM F. HYNES,
Acting Capt. of Detectives, LAPD,
Commanding Intelligence Bureau.

H:F

EXHIBIT 10447

POLICE DEPARTMENT,
City of Detroit, March 17, 1936.

Mr. JAMES E. DAVIS,
Chief of Police, Los Angeles, Calif.
(Att: Lieut. Luke M. Lane)

DEAR SIR: Replying to your letter of Mar. 11th, I wish to advise you that Frank Krasnasky is not known to my officers working on labor conditions, and his name does not appear in the other records of this Department.

Yours truly,

HENRY PIEL,
Chief of Detectives.

(Penciled note:) Inf. wanted by Fred Fysh, M. & M. Assn., Tu 6244.   Phones by Lane, March 24–1936.

EXHIBIT 10448

[Intra-Departmental Correspondence]

[(In ink:) "hours 7:15–8:30 a 11:30 a–2:30 4:15–5 p."]

LOS ANGELES POLICE DEPARTMENT

Office of Intelligence Bureau, Metropolitan Division

WED., *Sept 15, 1937.*

Request for Officers:

BEVERLY KNITTING MILLS, 5TH FLOOR, 1240 S. MAIN ST. RI 6396

Mr. Onthank special agent of M&M phones he has been requested to arrange for police protection above firm today;

Asks officers be there 4 p to 5 p today;

Tomorrow 7.45 a–8.45 a and again 4 p to 5 p

[(In ink:) "3.45 pm PL Phelps, EW Ford."]

States this is rather large knitting mfgr. firm about 75 employees, Mr. GRIFFIN mgr, that last night employes had a vote whether or not to go on strike and turned it down; however, that Bill Busick of ILG. W. U.   CIO said there was a strike there right now; and that this morning union organizers induced employes to go down to Union Hall where they were talked to, resulting in no one showing for work, all are now out and mgr. decided to close production until NEXT MONDAY; when he will issue a call for his employes to return.

[(In ink:) "Becktel Mfg. Co. Pr8465"]

However on 6th floor same bldg. is another firm works with Beverly, making sweaters, etc. for them; there employes are working now and it is feared union picket line may intimidate them into quiting work also; hence request for immediate detail TWO UNIFORM OFFICERS TODAY & TOMORROW.

Advised Mr. Onthank if not possible to cover would have Lt. Wellpott phone him by 3.00 at M&M TU 6244.

F

EXHIBIT 10449

[Intra-Departmental Correspondence]

LOS ANGELES POLICE DEPARTMENT

Office of in. bu. metro. divn

FRI., OCT 22, 1937.

Memo Assignment of Officers: Jones Knitting Mills, 1013 W. Santa Barbara, PA 3115.

About 10 a. m. this date Mr. Onthank spec. agent of M&M phoned there was a picket line at above location, about 35 men, supposedly members of CIO under direction of Wm. Busick, an organizer for ILGWU pickets were there at 7:30 A. and later taken away to a meeting, and they returned at 10 a. m.

Mgr. of plant Mr. Ellis Jones.

ASSIGNED: Officers L. P. Walter & W. C. Hayes.

EXHIBIT 10450

[Intra-Departmental Correspondence]

LOS ANGELES POLICE DEPARTMENT

Office of In. Bu. Metro. Divn.

WED., JULY 14–37.

Assignment of Officers: Armored Trunk Co., 1806 S. Main St., Pr 8461 8 a. m.— 3 p–5 p.

NOTE: 8 a. m. Mr. Knell, mgr. this co. member M. & M. phones picket line beginning to form; states union is Leather Goods, Luggage & Trunk Union, of CIO; states no one out has 8 employees; hours 8 a–5 p; asks p. c. officer mornings and evenings.

Officer K. L. Teter responded.

NOTE: 8.35 a. m. Teter phoned back 8 pickets there; are orderly; they will cover this spot *7.30 a–9 a and 3 p–5 p:*

F

F. PACIFIC-AMERICAN TANKSHIP ASSOCIATION

EXHIBIT 10451

PACIFIC AMERICAN TANKSHIP ASSOCIATION

304 Severance Bldg.

[Personnel Office]

LOS ANGELES, CALIF., *April 7th, 1936.*

LIEUT. LUKE LANE,
    Red Squad, L. A. Police Dept., City Hall, Los Angeles, Calif.

DEAR LIEUT. LANE: At Mr. Groundwater's suggestion I am sending you a copy of report which came to our hands which may be of interest to you.

Sincerely yours,

WM. C. BALL, *Shipping Master.*

EXHIBIT 10452

[Copy]

MARCH 20, 1936.

A. X. REPORT 3–20–36

Maritime Federation at the Beach cities has planned headquarters for "rank and file" communications to be kept at 246 West 14th St. San Pedro. This address is the Workers Center of the San Pedro District. A. H. Peterson in charge of the San Pedro branch of the International Labor Defense will do all the correspondence work for the Council of the Maritime Federation. There is a group of rough necks who are designated as a flying squadron for that district. Their names are:

(Leo Rudolph; Ray McElroy; Arthur Jolley; Bernard Lynn; John Hollam; Max Olshansky; Claude S. Brooks; Earl Strickland; and Raymond Dyer.)

The instruction to this group is that they will cover every maritime workers' meeting.

It is reported that *Charles McLaughlin*, section organizer for Orange County, has been assigned, starting at once, to the organization work with two other sub-organizers, *Jack Blumberg* and *Frank Dupree* to work among the cannery workers in Southern California.

Robert Lloyd, member of the Teamsters Union, has been sent to San Pedro by the Party to organize a union as known as the Brotherhood of Teamsters, Chauffeurs and Stablemen. Same headquarters as the Vegetable Oil Workers Union, San Pedro.

G. Retail Merchants Credit Association

Exhibit 10453

[Intra-Departmental Correspondence]

Los Angeles Police Department

Office of _____

(In pencil) Nov. 19–37.

James C. Sheppard
J. A. Gross.

Dear Captain Hynes: Please get me everything you can "on" James C. Sheppard, Atty of Mathes and Sheppard in the Rowan Bldg. He is under "J. A." Gross of the Retail Merchant's Credit Assn. of L. A.

These men are in absolutely the *key* position to act or prevent any constructive action being taken by any of the department stores, and I do not know how much else. They are very definitely "in the know"—all the right answers and laughs at the right places. They certainly know what is going on and what it is all about.

I got to Gross some months ago and did not feel SURE of him. I would like his whole business record, affiliations. Whether he was OK in the Secret Service etc. Race, religion. etc. Where he was educated. some of his friends if possible.

Same with Sheppard. I wish you yourself could make contact with both of them. I would like to have your reaction.

When you need a good laugh sometime we will tell you about Mrs. Ochs' Inglewood meeting.

I have been giving much thought to the possible wisdom of women doing anything that would help. Something does seem to me possible, that would not be just silly or else an obstruction to your work. Any *"chance"* seems worth thinking about and discussing. As I see it the only possible way would be through pooling what we *all* have and working out each strategy with a group who truly understand.

H. Store Protective Association

Exhibit 10454

Wed. May 27/36   10 a. m.

Capt Hynes.
Mr. Simpson TR 8151 of Store.

Protective Asso. phones he heard a meeting of Union organizers wa held on May 21st to plan organizing the Dept. Store employees into unions; advised did not know of same would ask you, so you could inform him.

F

I. WATERFRONT EMPLOYERS ASSOCIATION OF SOUTHERN CALIFORNIA

EXHIBIT 10455

WATERFRONT EMPLOYERS ASSOCIATION OF SOUTHERN CALIFORNIA

SAN PEDRO, CALIFORNIA, *September 28, 1936.*

To Members:

The following information may be of benefit to you in planning your operations in the event of the interruption in our normal working conditions by reason of a tie-up on October 1st.

It will be optional with each operator to bring his ship or ships into the dock or to leave them at anchor.

If the ships are brought to the dock or allowed to remain at the dock, each individual operator will be expected to arrange for such watchmen and fire protection as they deem necessary. If you wish additional watchmen for use aboard ship or on your piers it is our recommendation that you contact Mr. Bodel at Michigan 8741, Los Angeles. The cost of such watchman service must be paid for by the operater for the service.

In the event ships at anchor should require the services of caretakers they can be secured by calling our Association. The Association will deliver such caretakers and watchmen as you may wish to the particular vessel which you may designate. After that has been done it will be necessary for each individual operator to see that these men are taken care of, protected and fed. It has been suggested that in order to care for a vessel, provisions should be made for not less than ten men exclusive of guards; three in the deck department, three engineers, three fireman, and one cook. The vessel owner or agent must supervise the caretaking of their own ships by means of their own individual port organization.

It is expected that many ships will be fully provisioned upon arrival at anchorage but that others may require supplies. In the event the firm or firms with whom you have heretofore dealt are unable to make delivery of such miscellaneous supplies as may be needed aboard vessels at anchor, by contacting the Association you can secure information as to how such delivery can be effected.

At the present moment it would appear desirable to exert every effort in an endeavor to have a minimum amount of undelivered cargo on the piers on October 1st as it is quite possible that we will be unable to affect deliveries after that date without disturbance. If there should be any change in this situation you will be advised.

Steps should be immediately taken to clean all premises as much as possible from rubbish and debris in order to minimize the danger from fire.

The Police Department has informed us that they will establish a suitable harbor district headquarters through which the assignment of special or additional police patrolmen will be handled, and as soon as this has been accomplished we will advise you whom to contact. Until that time, in the event of any disturbance requiring the services of the Police Department, you will contact them through the already established channels.

Very truly yours,

E. NICHOLS, *Secretary-Treasurer.*

J. MISCELLANEOUS COMPANIES

EXHIBIT 10456

[Western Union]

1936 Sep 13 PM 11 44.

PRA 140 39 NL—TDPR Vancouver Wash 13
Lieut. Rudy WILLPOTT—
   Care Red Squad, Los Angeles Police Dept. LosA—

Understand A B Reser assistant business agent Fish Cannery Workers Union is organizing in Monterey is supposed to have police record in Los Angeles. Please check and wire me record in detail collect care Cal Pack Vancouver Washington. Kindest regards—

OTIS R BOHN.

(In ink:) "no answer"

EXHIBIT 10457

(In pencil:) "Send to Capt Hynes"

[Western Union]

COLLECT   1936 SEPTEMBER 16.

(In pencil:) "AA 3–19–"

OTIS R. BOHN,
        Care of California Packing Corporation,
                            Vancouver, Wash.:

No record A B Reser have had other inquiries re this subjects activities in and around San Pedro.

JAS. E. DAVIS, *Chief Police.*

"Capt Hynes
Intelligence   }Crossed out.
AJS 9:50 A M"

(Stamped:) "F. R. Parsons"

EXHIBIT 10458

[Intra-Departmental Correspondence]

LOS ANGELES POLICE DEPARTMENT
Office of In. Bu. Metro. Divn.

OCT. 16, 1937.

Memorandum.

Assignment of Officers: Gilfillan Bros. Inc., 1815 Venice Blvd. EX 1291, for 8 a. m. Tues. Oct. 19, 1937.

Mr. Peter Heiser, sales mgr. above co. requests two p. c. officers to be at their premises in connection with a demonstration by members of the C. I. O., to swing over employes of their concern to a C. I. O. union.

ASSIGNED I. M. Deaton, I. B.
            L. P. Walter, I. B.

D:F

EXHIBIT 10459

[Copy]

HOLLYWOOD-MAXWELL CO.

6773 Hollywood Blvd. Hollywood, California

Telephone Hollywood 2254

SEPT. 14, 1937.

Mr. JAMES E. DAVIS,
        Chief of Police,
                Los Angeles, California.

DEAR SIR: This letter is being written to you in order to express our deep appreciation of the services rendered by Officers E. A. Gilbreath and Tom Crowley in connection with the recent strike of the employees at this plant.

The officers were at all times eminently fair and courteous to everyone, but were sincere and efficient in the performance of their duties and prevented entirely any untoward disturbance which more than likely would have occurred if not so judiciously and efficiently handled.

We wish to congratulate you for having such men as these on your force.

Yours very truly,

HOLLYWOOD-MAXWELL CO.,
By (sgd)   Dr. J. R. BOWEN.

NOTE: Another letter from same Co. had been sent addressed to Chief Davis on Sept. 8, 1937, which stated:

"During a recent strike in our production department two men from the Red Squad rendered excellent service to us.   We wish to express our appreciation of the help given by Mr. E. A. GILBREATH and Mr. TOM CROWLEY."

Signed—HOLLYWOOD-MAXWELL CO.,
By   Dr. J. R. BOWEN, President.

These letters sent over for READING by officers concerned from CHIEF'S OFFICE on Sept. 16–37; originals returned to Chief's Office.   Margaret Connor on Oct 6–37.

F

EXHIBIT 10460

[Intra-Departmental Correspondence]

LOS ANGELES POLICE DEPARTMENT
Office of In. Bu. Metro. Divn.

MAY 6, 1937   5 p m.

Request 8 uniform officers L. A. Ice Co. 679 Mesa St. tomorrow May 7

Memo. Capt. HYNES.

Capt. Cappo of M. G. M. studios phones in that company is shooting more pictures at this spot tomorrow from 8:30 a. m. to about 4 p. m.   Would like 8 uniform officers to keep the peace.

Asks you to call him back RE 0211, STA 380.

NOTE: This is same spot Jackson & Merchants covered this afternoon.

F

(In pencil:)
C. J. Evans.
Nelson.
Allison.
Dimon.
Varver.

EXHIBIT 10461

NA-MAC PRODUCTS CORPORATION
1027 North Seward St.

HOLLYWOOD, CALIF., May 13, 1938.

Mr. JAMES E. DAVIS,
   Chief of Police, City Hall, Los Angeles, Calif.

DEAR CHIEF DAVIS: I surely wish to thank you, on behalf of our Company, for the aid you and your police Department rendered us during the striking condition, which was finally called off on May 11, 1938.

Finally, after seven weeks of picketing, the strike was called off and the men have returned to work.   One of the head executives of the Union came from the East, and inasmuch as he could find no apparent reason for this strike, ordered the men back to work.

During the past few weeks, your men were here on time, regularly, and did not leave their post of duty until after the "picketers" had left for the day, and only due to their efforts, no damage was inflicted by the pickets to anyone, nor to any part of the factory.

Again, we wish to thank you, and we want you to know it is indeed gratifying to know we have such an organization, under your guidance, to serve the City of Los Angeles.

Sincerely,

NA-MAC PRODUCTS CORP.,
By WILLIAM NASSOUR, (signed)
WILLIAM NASSOUR, President.

WN: HK

Exhibit 10462

[Copy]

O'Keef & Merritt Co.

Manufacturers of Gas Appliances & Electric Refrigerators

3700 East Olympic Blvd.

Los Angeles, Cal., *October 21, 1936.*

Honorable Chief of Police James E. Davis,
City Hall, Los Angeles, Calif.

Dear Sir: As you probably know, about a month ago, a lot of pressure was put on our employees by a few local agitators and a labor agitator from San Francisco, which might have developed into a serious problem if it were not for the fact that you gave us such excellent co-operation.

We wish to express our appreciation to the Police Department and to commend in particular Lieut. Rudolph Wellpott, who was put in charge of the detail. We feel that the firm and tactful manner in which he handled the situation was a credit to the Department and his ability in matters of this kind makes him a real asset to Southern California.

Again thank you, we are
Very truly yours,

O'Keef & Merritt Co.
(sgd)   D. P. O'Keefe.

DPO:R

Note: Sent over from Chief's Office Oct 23–36 to Capt. Justin, Commanding, Metropolitan Divn.   Copied and returned Capt. Justin Oct 26/36.

Exhibit 10463

Los Angeles Police Department

Office of In. Bu. Metro. Divn.

Sept. 13, 1935.

Confidential.

Mr. Johnston of Standard Oil comes in and states he learns confidentially:

"It was learned that at the Board meeting held at 68 Haigh St., a communication was received from the Nat. Cen. Com. commenting on the work being done by the old Ex. Com. of the Marine Workers Industrial Union, which is now in Los Angeles, headed by *Hayes Jones*, in which Harold Baxter is a member. The communication does not mention if the party is coming to S. F. right away, or will later come. However, that every communication intended for them is to be sent to *Joe Simon* 430 S. Palos Verde in San Pedro, California."

F

Exhibit 10464

[Intra-Departmental Correspondence]

Los Angeles Police Department

Office of Intelligence Bureau, Metropolitan Division

May 11, 1937.

Re: Expected Strike Call on Arden Farms Co. Distributing Plants, 8 p.m. Wed May 12–37.

Memorandum: Capt. Hynes.

Chief Davis called and sent over to this office Mr. Fred W. Whitaker, executive secy. Dairy Industries, Inc. PR 0129, 417 Chamber of Commerce Bldg. residence phone CR 7631. The Chief is extremely anxious to assist this party in his difficulties; he stated that he had received so much help and cooperation from this party during the recent election and for us not overlook returning full cooperation.

Mr. Whitaker stated that Mr. Dail of the Chauffeurs & Truck Drivers Union Local #208 has served notice it is going to call a strike against the Arden Farms Co. on May 12, Wednesday night, 8 p.m.   The two distributing plants that he is concerned with are located at 1918 W. Slauson Ave.; the Arden Dairy Farms Co. Mr. Garrett, night manager; the other is at 103 S. Hamel Dr. or Road; Mr. Ferguson, night manager.   These plants are in operation 24 hours per day and will necessitate a 24 hour police detail.

Mr. Whitaker stated that he had been in touch with the M & M Assn. and is arranging for a number of guards from the Bodell Detective Agency and if necessary, they will place a guard on each delivery truck that delivers the milk to the homes.

(103 S. Hamel Drive or Road may possibly be in Beverly Hills; Mr. Whitaker is to call me back re this.)

At each plant there are two gates to cover—the entrance and exit gates.

He does not know at this time whether he wants officers assigned at 8 p.m. tomorrow night, or to have them here on reserve so they may be called by phone in case of picket line starting.   However, he will gather more information and will call me tomorrow and discuss the situation further.

LUKE M. LANE.

LL:F

POLICE IN AMERICA

An Arno Press/New York Times Collection

The American Institute of Law and Criminology.
Journal of the American Institute of Law and Criminology:
Selected Articles. Chicago, 1910–1929.

The Boston Police Strike: Two Reports. Boston, 1919–1920.

Boston Police Debates: Selected Arguments. Boston,
1863–1869.

Chamber of Commerce of the State of New York.
**Papers and Proceedings of Committee on the Police Problem,
City of New York.** New York, 1905.

Chicago Police Investigations: Three Reports. Illinois,
1898–1912.

Control of the Baltimore Police: Collected Reports.
Baltimore, 1860–1866.

Crime and Law Enforcement in the District of Columbia:
Report and Hearings. Washington, D. C., 1952.

Crime in the District of Columbia: Reports and Hearings.
Washington, D. C., 1935.

Flinn, John J. and John E. Wilkie.
History of the Chicago Police. Chicago, 1887.

Hamilton, Mary E.
The Policewoman. New York, 1924.

Harrison, Leonard Vance.
Police Administration in Boston. Cambridge, Mass., 1934.

International Association of Chiefs of Police.
Police Unions. Washington, D. C., 1944.

The Joint Special Committee.
**Reports of the Special Committee Appointed to Investigate
the Official Conduct of the Members of the Board of Police
Commissioners.** Boston, 1882.

Justice in Jackson, Mississippi: U.S. Civil Rights
Commission Hearings. Washington, D. C., 1965.

McAdoo, William.
Guarding a Great City. New York, 1906.

Mayo, Katherine.
Justice to All. New York, 1917.

Missouri Joint Committee of the General Assembly.
**Report of the Joint Committee of the General Assembly
Appointed to Investigate the Police Department of the
City of St. Louis.** St. Louis, Missouri, 1868.

National Commission on Law Observance and Enforcement.
Report on the Police. Washington, D. C., 1931.

National Prison Association.
**Proceedings of the Annual Congress of the National Prison
Association of the United States: Selected Articles.**
1874–1902.

New York City Common Council.
**Report of the Special Committee of the New York City
Board of Aldermen on the New York City Police Department.**
New York, 1844.

National Police Convention.
Official Proceedings of the National Prison Convention.
St. Louis, 1871.

Pennsylvania Federation of Labor.
The American Cossack. Washington, D. C., 1915.

Police and the Blacks: U.S. Civil Rights Commission
Hearings. 1960–1966.

Police in New York City: An Investigation. New York,
1912–1931.

The President's Commission on Law Enforcement and
Administration of Justice.
Task Force Report: The Police. Washington, D. C., 1967.

Sellin, Thorsten, editor.
The Police and the Crime Problem. Philadelphia, 1929.

Smith, Bruce, editor.
New Goals in Police Management. Philadelphia, 1954.

Sprogle, Howard O.
The Philadelphia Police, Past and Present. Philadelphia,
1887.

U.S. Committee on Education and Labor.
The Chicago Memorial Day Incident: Hearings and Report.
Washington, D. C., 1937.

U.S. Committee on Education and Labor.
**Documents Relating to Intelligence Bureau or Red Squad of
Los Angeles Police Department.** Washington, D. C., 1940.

U.S. Committee on Education and Labor.
Private Police Systems. Washington, D. C., 1939.

Urban Police: Selected Surveys. 1926–1946.

Women's Suffrage and the Police: Three Senate Documents.
Washington, D. C., 1913.

Woods, Arthur.
Crime Prevention. Princeton, New Jersey, 1918.

Woods, Arthur.
Policeman and Public. New Haven, Conn., 1919.

AMERICAN POLICE SUPPLEMENT

International Association of Chiefs of Police.
**Proceedings of the Annual Conventions of the International
Association of Chiefs of Police.** 1893–1930. 5 vols.

New York State Senate.
**Report and Proceedings of the Senate Committee Appointed
to Investigate the Police Department of the City of
New York.** (Lexow Committee Report). New York, 1895.
6 vols.

THE POLICE IN GREAT BRITAIN

Committee on Police Conditions of Service.
Report of the Committee on Police Conditions of Service.
London, 1949.

Committee on the Police Service.
Minutes of Evidence and Report: England, Wales, Scotland.
London, 1919–1920.

Royal Commission on Police Powers and Procedures.
**Report of the Royal Commission on Police Powers and
Procedure.** London, 1929.

Select Committee on Police.
**Report of Select Committee on Police with the Minutes of
Evidence.** London, 1853.

Royal Commission Upon the Duties of the Metropolitan
Police.
**Minutes of Evidence Taken Before the Royal Commission
Upon the Duties of the Metropolitan Police Together With
Appendices and Index.** London, 1908.

Committee on Police.
**Report from the Select Committee on Police of the
Metropolis.** London, 1828.